Testing the Spirits

Exposing Dark Sayings and Embracing the Light of Jesus

Sabin Geyman

WestBow
PRESS
A DIVISION OF THOMAS NELSON

Copyright © 2012 Sabin Geyman

All rights reserved. No part of this book may be used or reproduced by any means, graphic, electronic, or mechanical, including photocopying, recording, taping or by any information storage retrieval system without the written permission of the publisher except in the case of brief quotations embodied in critical articles and reviews.

Scripture taken from the HOLY BIBLE, NEW INTERNATIONAL VERSION ®. Copyright © 1973, 1978, 1984 by International Bible Society. Used by permission of Zondervan

Scripture taken from the NEW AMERICAN STANDARD BIBLE ®, Copyright © 1960, 1962, 1963, 1968, 1971, 1972, 1973, 1975, 1977, 1995 by The Lockman Foundation. Used by permission.

Bible quotations taken from the King James Version of the Bible.
Copyright © 1989 by World Bible Publishers.

Front cover: Before the Fall, lions ate grass; after the Fall, they ate other animals. Therefore, in the long sweep of history, they represent strength in peace as well as destructive power. Judah is described as a lion's whelp (Gen. 49:9), but little lions grow into big lions—lions that can defend their own and defeat their enemies (Revelation 19 and 20). The Lion of Judah will destroy His enemies in righteousness. On the dark side, the devil walks around like a roaring lion in search of people to devour (1 Peter 5:8).

Back cover: The Lord God of Israel is the one who can send lightning (Job 38:35), and accompanying the ark of His testament in the temple of God are lightning, thunder, an earthquake, and hail (Rev. 11:19). Lightning is even likened to the coming of the Son of Man, who will come in the clouds with power and great glory, sending His angels to gather up His elect from the four winds (Matt. 24:27, 30–31).

WestBow Press books may be ordered through booksellers or by contacting:

WestBow Press
A Division of Thomas Nelson
1663 Liberty Drive
Bloomington, IN 47403
www.westbowpress.com
1-(866) 928-1240

Because of the dynamic nature of the Internet, any web addresses or links contained in this book may have changed since publication and may no longer be valid. The views expressed in this work are solely those of the author and do not necessarily reflect the views of the publisher, and the publisher hereby disclaims any responsibility for them.

All images © iStockphoto.com.
Any people depicted in stock imagery provided by iStockphoto are models, and such images are being used for illustrative purposes only.

ISBN: 978-1-4497-4498-4 (sc)
ISBN: 978-1-4497-4497-7 (e)

Library of Congress Control Number: 2012911978

Printed in the United States of America

WestBow Press rev. date: 08/29/2012

Contents

Preface: Contending for the Faith ix

Introduction: The Importance Of Discernment xv

1. Arguing for Absolute Truth 1
2. Debunking the Hoax of Evolution 13
3. America's Social Decline 60
4. Exposing the Conceits of the New Age 100
5. Psychological Self-Absorption 162
6. The Unholy Pride of Unitarianism 188
7. Toward a Global False Religion 203
8. Toward a Global Antichrist Government 225
9. Receiving Jesus, Guarding One's Heart, and Keeping
   One Eye on Israel 252

Afterword: How To Spot A Mortal Enemy 273

Postscript: Failed Diversity Policies 283

Appendix: Anatomy Of Appeasement 293

Acknowledgements 303

Endnotes 305

This book is dedicated to all people of goodwill who love Jesus' truth and light and eschew evil. May we encourage each other even as the world darkens around us.

"For God so loved the world, that he gave his only begotten Son, that whosoever believeth in him should not perish, but have everlasting life. ... [B]ut he that believeth not is condemned already, because he hath not believed in the name of the only begotten Son of God" (John 3:16, 18b KJV).

"Mr. Worldly Wiseman is an alien, and Mr. Legality is a cheat; and for his son Civility, notwithstanding his simpering looks, he is but a hypocrite and cannot help thee. Believe me, there is nothing in all this noise that thou hast heard of these sottish men, but a design to beguile thee of thy salvation."
— *The Pilgrim's Progress*

"For the time will come when they will not endure sound doctrine; but *wanting* to have their ears tickled, they will accumulate for themselves teachers in accordance to their own desires, and will turn away their ears from the truth and will turn aside to myths. But you, be sober in all things, endure hardship, do the work of an evangelist, fulfill your ministry"
(2 Tim. 4:3–5 NASB).

"[W]e are no longer to be children, tossed here and there by waves and carried about by every wind of doctrine, by the trickery of men, by craftiness in deceitful scheming"
(Eph. 4:14 NASB).

"This know also, that in the last days perilous times shall come. For men shall be lovers of their own selves, covetous boasters, proud blasphemers, disobedient to parents, unthankful, unholy, without natural affection, trucebreakers, false accusers, incontinent, fierce, despisers of those that are good, traitors, heady, highminded, lovers of pleasures more than lovers of God; having a form of godliness, but denying the power thereof: from such turn away. For of this sort are they which creep into houses, and lead captive silly women laden with sins, led away with divers lusts, ever learning, and never able to come to the knowledge of the truth"
(2 Tim. 3:1–7 KJV).

"Know this first of all, that in the last days mockers will come with *their* mocking, following after their own lusts, and saying, 'Where is the promise of His coming? For *ever* since the fathers fell asleep, all continues just as it was from the beginning of creation.' For when they maintain this, it escapes their notice that by the word of God *the* heavens existed long ago and *the* earth was formed out of water and by water, through which the world at that time was destroyed, being flooded with water. But by His word the present heavens and earth are being reserved for fire, kept for the day of judgment and destruction of ungodly men"
(2 Peter 3:3–7 NASB).

It would seem a worthy goal to get more familiar with the Hebrew names of the God of Israel. Following is a short compilation of some of God's Names:

- Yeshua (Jesus, the Beatitudes, Matt. 5)
- The Lord Yeshua (the Lord Jesus, Rev. 22)
- Yeshua the Messiah (Jesus Christ, 1 John 1)
- ADONAI, God (the LORD God)
- the angel of ADONAI (the angel of the LORD)
- ADONAI your God (the LORD your God)
- God of Ya akov (God of Jacob)
- ADONAI ELOHIM (LORD GOD)
- ADONAI Tzva'ot (LORD of hosts)
- ADONAI ELOHIM Tzva'ot (LORD GOD of Hosts)
- ADONAI Shamah (the LORD is there)
- ADONAI Eloheinu (our LORD and our God)
- ADONAI, God of heaven's armies (Lord God, the Almighty)
- Adonai ELOHIM Elohei-Tzva'ot (Lord GOD, the God of hosts)
- ADONAI Elyon (LORD Most High)
- HaKadosh (Holy One)
- Ruach HaKodesh (Holy Spirit)
- El Elyon (God Most High)
- El Shaddai (God Almighty, All-Sufficient God)
- El Yisrael (God of Israel)
- El Hakkadosh (Holy God)
- El Gibbor (Mighty God)
- El Kanno (Jealous God)
- El Hannora (Awesome God)
- El Hashamayim (God of the Heavens)
- El Rachum (God of Compassion)
- El Malei Rachamim (God Full of Mercy)
- El Channun (Gracious God)

Drawn from the *Complete Jewish Bible, An English Version of the* Tanakh *(Old Testament) and* B'rit Hadashah *(New Testament)* [Ed., David Stern, Clarksville, Maryland: Jewish New Testament Publications, 1998]; the New American Standard Bible; and hebrew4christians.com.

PREFACE: CONTENDING FOR THE FAITH

While I endeavor to conduct an honest examination of teachings that lead away from the Bible, it is not my intention to put down individuals. (Notwithstanding, the Holy Spirit may move in one's conscience and cause one to move in a more holy direction.) In the spirit of Jude 3, wherein we are enjoined to contend for the Christian faith, I have attempted to show how a variety of non-Christian teachings are not only unbiblical but actually false. I believe that ecumenical, or interfaith, work is repugnant, the province of wishy-washy thinkers and those professing Christians who refuse to stand up for the call of *Sola Scriptura* that served men well during the Protestant Reformation. I have studied four foreign languages and lived in Taiwan for five years, so I very much enjoy good people of different kinds. That said, I also want to explore the beauty and courage of great thinkers such as John Knox, Samuel Adams, and Noah Webster.

We in the United States of America have a rich Judeo-Christian heritage, one worth remembering and carrying on. I was once chastised by a friend in Taipei (a fellow American) for keeping my Christian stance in the face of the myriad Buddhist temples and practices that are prevalent in Taiwan. I told him something like, "I didn't come to Taiwan to give up my God."

That is still my position. I have firsthand experience with the ways of the world, but I believe that the God of Israel is ready to forgive and save; that He is the only true and living God; that He is the only way to salvation; and that He is mighty and holy. Jesus' ways are holy, and He is higher than us; therefore it is we who must conform to Him, not the other way around (as so many humanists seem to think).

We would do well to read from 2 Peter 3:

> Know this first of all, that in the last days mockers will come with their mocking, following after their own lusts, and saying, "Where is the promise of His coming? For ever since the fathers fell asleep, all continues just as it was from the beginning of creation." For when they maintain this, it escapes their notice that by the word of God *the* heavens existed long ago and *the* earth was formed out of water and by water, through which the world at that time was destroyed, being flooded with water. But by His word the present heavens and earth are being reserved for fire, kept for the day of judgment and destruction of ungodly men. But do not let this one *fact* escape your notice, beloved, that with the Lord one day is like a thousand years, and a thousand years like one day. The Lord is not slow about His promise as some count slowness, but is patient toward you, not wishing for any to perish but for all to come to repentance. … [A]ccording to His promise we are looking for new heavens and a new earth, in which righteousness dwells. Therefore, beloved, since you look for these things, be diligent to be found by Him in peace, spotless and blameless, and regard the patience of our Lord *as* salvation; just as also our beloved brother Paul, according to the wisdom given him, wrote to you, as also in all *his* letters, speaking in them of these things, in which are some things hard to understand, which the untaught and unstable distort, as *they do* also the rest of the Scriptures, to their own destruction. … [B]e on your guard so that you are not carried away by the error of unprincipled men. (2 Peter 3:3–9, 13b–16, 17b NASB)

We must be on guard (2 Peter 3, Ephesians 4 and 6, 1 John 4). The enemy is real, and he is on the prowl to see who he can destroy. All men are locked in a spiritual battle, and it is a Christian's job to side with the good, with the light, with Jesus Christ. This is not a race for the fainthearted. False teachings need to be exposed in love and with a view toward winning souls for Christ.

Let us savor the truthfulness of 1 John 4:1–3: "Beloved, do not believe every spirit, but test the spirits to see whether they are from God, because many false *prophets* have gone out into the world. By this you know the Spirit of God: every spirit that confesses that Jesus Christ has come in the flesh is from God; and every spirit that does not confess Jesus is not from God; this is the *spirit* of the antichrist, of which you have heard that it is coming, and now it is already in the world" (NASB).

We are called to test the spirits, to see which are from God and which are from the antichrist. The false teachers are many, and it would seem good to put up flags that lead back to the true faith in Jesus Christ. In this spirit, I hope that this work can be of some help in leading unbelievers to the true faith and in strengthening the resolve of those who already believe.

One who contends for the faith (Jude 3) will run into opposition. It is good to be gentle but not at the expense of truth:

> Then Peter opened his mouth, and said, "Of a truth I perceive that God is no respecter of persons: But in every nation he that feareth him, and worketh righteousness, is accepted with him. The word which God sent unto the children of Israel, preaching peace by Jesus Christ: (he is LORD of all:) That word, I say, ye know, which was published throughout all Judaea, and began from Galilee, after the baptism which John preached; how God anointed Jesus of Nazareth with the Holy Ghost and with power: who went about doing good, and healing all that were oppressed of the devil; for God was with him. And we are witnesses of all things which he did both in the land of the Jews, and in Jerusalem; whom they slew and hanged on a tree: Him God raised up the third day, and shewed him openly; not to all the people, but unto witnesses chosen before of God, even to us, who did eat and drink with him after he rose from the dead. And he commanded us to preach unto the people, and to testify

that it is he which was ordained of God to be the Judge of quick and dead. To him give all the prophets witness, that through his name whosoever believeth in him shall receive remission of sins." (Acts 10:34–43 KJV)

Wartburg Castle, near Eisenach, Germany, became a refuge for Martin Luther.

INTRODUCTION: THE IMPORTANCE OF DISCERNMENT

What is the importance of discernment? King Solomon, son of David, addresses the matter in Proverbs:

> The fear of the LORD is the beginning of knowledge; fools despise wisdom and instruction. ... Wisdom shouts in the street ... "How long O naïve ones, will you love being simple-minded? And scoffers delight themselves in scoffing and fools hate knowledge? Turn to my reproof. ... [T]hey will not find me, because they hated knowledge and did not choose the fear of the LORD ... [s]o they shall eat of the fruit of their own way and be satiated with their own devices. ... But he who listens to me shall live securely and will be at ease from the dread of evil."

> For if you cry for discernment, lift your voice for understanding; if you seek her as silver and search for her as for hidden treasures; then you will discern the fear of the LORD and discover the knowledge of God. ... Discretion will guard you, understanding will watch over you, to deliver you from the way of evil, from the man who speaks perverse things; from those who leave the paths of uprightness ... who delight in doing evil and rejoice in the perversity of evil. ... To deliver you from the strange woman, from the adulteress who flatters with

her words; that leaves the companion of her youth and forgets the covenant of her God; for her house sinks down to death and her tracks *lead* to the dead; none who go to her return again…

My son, give attention to my wisdom, incline your ear to my understanding; that you may observe discretion and your lips may reserve knowledge. For the lips of an adulteress drip honey and smoother than oil is her speech; but in the end she is bitter as wormwood. … Her feet go down to death, her steps take hold of Sheol. … Keep your way far from her and do not go near the door of her house, or you will give your vigor to others and your years to the cruel one; and strangers will be filled with your strength and your hard-earned goods *will go* to the house of an alien; and you groan at your final end. … Let your fountain be blessed, and rejoice in the wife of your youth. *As* a loving hind and a graceful doe, let her breasts satisfy you at all times; be exhilarated always with her love. For why should you, my son, be exhilarated with an adulteress and embrace the bosom of a foreigner?

Say to wisdom, "You are my sister," and call understanding *your* intimate friend; that they may keep you from an adulteress, from the foreigner who flatters with her words. (Prov. 1:7, 20a, 22–23a, 28b–29, 31, 33; 2:3–5, 11–13a, 14, 16–19a; 5:1–4a, 5, 8–11a, 18–20; 7:4–5 NASB)

I was once chastised by a friend (a fellow American) in Taipei for keeping my Christian stance in the face of the myriad Buddhist temples and Buddhist practices that are so much in evidence around Taiwan. I told him, "I didn't come to Taiwan to give up my God."

Discernment stems from a fear of the Lord; knowledge; wisdom; understanding; and discretion.

It is worth noting that both the sweet-talking adulteress and the flattering foreigner are singled out for their capacity to seduce, deceive, and destroy. My sense is that this warning to avoid them operates on a literal as well as a spiritual level. An adulteress can be a literal woman who destroys men's lives by seducing them into fornication; she can also be a false teaching, church, or spirit that wrecks people's lives by causing them to walk away from the light of Jesus Christ and into the darkness of the enemy (Satan).

Likewise, a flattering foreigner can be a person from a foreign nation who enamors his hosts but seeks their destruction surreptitiously (e.g., a Communist spy), or it can be one who has left the faith of the true and living God and seeks to lure others into unbelief (e.g., a Jesuit secret society member, Buddhist, Taoist, Confucianist, Communist, atheist, Hindu, Mohammaden, Mormon, Unitarian). The Jesuit secret society members mouth about morality and arrogate power to themselves but work ardently to undermine the true church (2 Corinthians 11); Buddhists seduce by playing at being peaceful; the Taoists try to dazzle with their paisley-style, teardrop-like symbol and conceits about interconnectedness (that end in empty philosophy); the Confucianists try to woo with a gross overestimation of their own personal virtue; Communists wield all the persuasion of a butcher knife and a hit team; atheists try to seduce with a vicious brand of prideful ingratitude; Hindus worship all manner of things; Mohammadens worship the moon and death; Mormons are led by a false story and a false prophet; and Unitarians avoid doctrine.

At the literal level, it is imperative that one avoid the woman who would seduce him into fornication or the foreigner who would trick him with syrupy words or the smarmy foreign government that serves up deceitful (and flattering) diplomatic propaganda designed to assuage and distract while it plans a military attack; spiritually speaking, we must avoid false teachings and false churches.

A king is supposed to be able to discern between good and evil. Against the backdrop of Absalom, who had been on the run after killing his brother Amnon, King David was faced with whether to spare the remaining son of the woman from Tekoa. She said, "[F]or as the angel of God, so is my lord the king to discern good and evil" (2 Sam. 14:17b NASB). Truly, national leaders are called on to discern between good and evil.

Our friend is Israel, and we should, as a people, befriend the friends of Israel and eschew the enemies of Israel (Genesis 12 and Zechariah 2, 12, and 14). Furthermore, we should eschew countries such as China and Russia and much of the Islamic world because their authoritarian forces treat beautiful Christians to undiluted brutality.

In Ezekiel, we see that God expects of His people spiritual purity—there is nary a glimmer of the so-called any-god-will-do diversity that has taken hold throughout the Western world:

> The LORD said to me, "Son of man, ... You shall say to the rebellious ones, to the house of Israel ... Enough of all your abominations, O house of Israel, when you brought in foreigners, uncircumcised in heart and uncircumcised in flesh, to be in My sanctuary to profane it, even My house, when you offered My food, the fat and the blood; for they made My covenant void—this in addition to all your abominations. And you have not kept charge of My holy things yourselves, but you have set foreigners to keep charge of My sanctuary. ... No foreigner uncircumcised in heart and uncircumcised in flesh, of all the foreigners who are among the sons of Israel, shall enter My sanctuary." (Ezek. 44:5a, 6a, 6c–8, 9b NASB)

Clearly, God wants His people to maintain His standards, not to be in the thrall of foreigners who often carry with them false teachings. The diversity policy doesn't look so pure in light of Ezekiel 44. The Mohammedans have wreaked havoc in many Western countries, trying to dismantle the influence of Christendom in countries such as Israel, Holland, France, England, and the United States and striving to put in place the abominable Sharia law and the terrible influence of the moon god. The Chinese have brought with them a pronounced sense of moral relativism, atheism, Confucianism,

Taoism, Buddhism, and almost ubiquitous depictions of the dragon symbol, injecting confusion into Western schools, institutions, and society at large. The East Indians have undergirded the New Age movement with Hindu yoga and blasphemous notions of becoming godlike. And the Latinos have brought in a large dose of Roman Catholic paganism.

Is there an anti-Bible, spiritual angle to the diversity policy? Yes. Diversity policy has the slobber of the dragon all over it.

We should remember the lesson of King Solomon. In 1 Kings 3:9, the king asked for discernment: "Give therefore thy servant an understanding heart to judge thy people, that I may discern between good and bad: for who is able to judge this thy so great a people?" (KJV)

Solomon got off to a good start, but there were, of course, conditions of purity that would apply to Solomon just as they applied to his father, David: "[I]f ye shall at all turn from following me, ye or your children, and will not keep my commandments and my statutes which I have set before you, but go and serve other gods, and worship them: then will I cut off Israel out of the land which I have given them; and this house, which I have hallowed for my name, will I cast out of my sight; and Israel shall be a proverb and a byword among all people" (1 Kings 9:6–7 KJV).

Solomon developed a personal policy of sexual diversity, having seven hundred wives and three hundred concubines. His policy led him astray from the Lord:

> But king Solomon loved many strange women, together with the daughter of Pharaoh, women of the Moabites, Ammonites, Edomites, Zidonians, and Hittites; of the nations concerning which the LORD said unto the children of Israel, Ye shall not go in to them, neither shall they come in unto you: for surely they will turn away your heart after their gods: Solomon clave unto these in love. And he had seven hundred wives, princesses, and three hundred concubines: and his wives turned away his heart. For it came to pass, when Solomon was old, that his wives turned away his heart after other gods: and

The wise king got enveloped by his feelings—literal fornication and spiritual fornication led to the dividing up of his kingdom.

his heart was not perfect with the LORD his God, as *was* the heart of David his father. For Solomon went after Ashtoreth the goddess of the Zidonians, and after Milcom the abomination of the Ammonites. And Solomon did evil in the sight of the LORD, and went not fully after the LORD, as *did* David his father. Then did Solomon build a high place for Chemosh, the abomination of Moab, in the hill that *is* before Jerusalem, and for Molech, the abomination of the children of Ammon. And likewise did he for all his strange wives, which burnt incense and sacrificed unto their gods." (1 Kings 11:1–8, KJV)

Solomon's "sexual diversity program" led to a "religious diversity program." The result of all that open-minded mushiness? The wise king was enveloped by his feelings—literal fornication and spiritual fornication led to the dividing up of his kingdom. Jeroboam, king of Israel, worshipped other gods at the groves and made molten images. Rehoboam, king of Judah, built high places, images, and groves on the high hills and under green trees; allowed sodomites to be in the land; and did the same abominations that were the habit of the nations that the Lord cast out before the children of Israel.

By the time of Isaiah's prophetic ministry (740–700 BC), Hoshea, king of Israel, would not listen to godly exhortation; therefore, Israel was destroyed by the Assyrians in 722 BC. But Hezekiah, king of Judah, did right in the sight of the Lord, removing the high places, breaking the images, cutting down the groves, and destroying the brass serpent made by Moses, calling it Nehushtan. King Hezekiah prayed to God, asking that he and his people be delivered out of the hand of the Assyrian king, Sennacherib. God heard his prayer, and the angel of the Lord smote the encampment of 185,000 Assyrian soldiers.

Unfortunately, Hezekiah's successors were not his equal as servants of God, and Judah also was destroyed, this time by the Babylonians in 586 BC. (The Babylonian captivity, a punishment for disobedience, lasted from 606 BC to 536 BC). Of course, the Maccabees fought off the Greeks after Antiochus Epiphanes defiled the temple and went on to rededicate the temple, but by 70 AD, Herod's temple was destroyed by the Roman general Titus, and the Jews were soon dispersed. Not until 1948 was Israel re-formed as a fulfillment of Ezekiel 36–37.

So how long-lasting were the effects of King Solomon's sins? It's a valid question. Perhaps a lesson from Solomon's sexual escapades would be that wisdom must be coupled with discretion to ensure that one not only knows what to do but actually does that which is right in the sight of the Lord. For instance, according to Ezekiel 44, a Judeo-Christian people should beware of flattering foreigners, who seduce with sweet propaganda and the thrall of false idols all the while sharpening their butcher knives. Ezekiel 3 should compel believers to warn their brethren about an advancing attack by lying, flattering foreigners.

The discerning of spirits is one of the gifts of the Holy Spirit enumerated in 1 Corinthians 12. It is listed right in between two other gifts of the Spirit: prophecy and diverse kinds of tongues. The discerning of spirits is a gift, an ability if you will, that leads inexorably to John's exhortation that Christians test the spirits to see which are from God and which are from the antichrist.

The stakes are high. Why have the American people countenanced the despicable Babylonian, Egyptian, and worldly practice of putting up Ashteroth poles such as the Washington Monument, a euphemism for the largest Egyptian obelisk in the world, one that is strangely 555 feet tall, showing a clear obsession with the number 5 and resonating a demonic quality that stems from Lucifer's five blasphemous conceits in Isaiah 14 as well as the five-pointed pentagram? Why have Americans put up with the juxtaposition of the Capitol Building (which mimics Roman architecture and resembles an excited breast) and the Washington Monument, which resembles an erect male member? Sexualized architecture is perverse and on the wrong side of Romans 1, which warns that we must worship the Creator, not created things. The enshrining (in stone, no less) of sexual uncleanness in our nation's capital is wrong—another religious diversity program gone wrong.

Why have Americans winked at evidence that numerous American presidents have worshipped the owl

> "The discerning of spirits" is one of the gifts of the Holy Spirit enumerated in 1 Corinthians 12. It's listed between two other gifts of the Spirit—prophecy and diverse kinds of tongues.

god Molech at California's Bohemian Grove? Why is there no investigation into the tiny owl in the upper right hand corner of the front of the dollar bill? Even though some laugh off the Bohemian Grove activity, no one can lucidly disagree that there's an owl secretly placed on the front of the dollar bill—an owl with all its secret hoots in the middle of the night when none are watching. (Notice they didn't secretly put a blue jay or a hummingbird on the dollar.) Baal-Ashteroth worship and Molech-Chemosh worship are strictly forbidden as abominations in the Old Testament, something that is well known in occultic circles, and the placement of anti-Christian abominations on the American dollar is a clear message from the occultists that they will have their day in squashing the Christian influence in the United States.

Federal Reserve personnel often lecture about the need for free trade (more dumbing down, this time letting in the Trojan horse of giving American wealth to Communist dictators in the name of diversity). Fed apparatchiks like to say that if someone (e.g., a Communist slave-labor sweatshop) is making a t-shirt for less, we have to buy t-shirts from them! But that's just wrong. We should trade with our allies, strengthening ourselves by strengthening our allies. The not-so-federal Federal Reserve (another linguistic trick) loves to manage the actual federal government's money. "For the love of money is a root of all sorts of evil, and some by longing for it have wandered away from the faith and pierced themselves with many griefs" (1 Tim. 6:10 NASB).

How did Americans allow wandering evildoers to wrest away the levers of trade and prosperity in this country? Has the American church become the lukewarm church of Laodicea, a church so numb from watching intrigue on TV that its members can no longer differentiate between disturbing events playing out on TV and nation-slaying events happening in real life?

Sexualized architecture is perverse, and on the wrong side of Romans 1, which warns that we must worship the Creator, not the created things.

Why do we allow our nation's independence to be mocked on the back of the dollar bill? The date 1776, expressed in Latin letters on the back of the dollar, is enmeshed in a scene that involves an Egyptian pyramid (Egypt being a symbol in the Bible of the unbelieving world);

the eye of Lucifer (a symbol of the antichrist); a solar blaze representing the sun-god worship that is the hallmark of the Roman Catholic pagan church; the words *Novus Ordo Seclorum,* which mean "New World Order" (another anti-Christian, secret-society nod to the worldly system of the antichrist); and the satanic triangle.

As if that were not enough evidence of an anti-Christian, anti-American conspiracy (a bankers' conspiracy) to overthrow the country, how about the obsession with the number 13 on the back of the one-dollar bill? It appears that the Federal Reserve, which was founded in secret on an island off Georgia in 1910 (and codified in 1913), is mocking our nation's independence and saying that the globalist bankers will take away America's freedom and subordinate her. Why would Americans allow a secretly devised organization to run their money supply?

The pyramid has thirteen levels, and the only thing left to do, according to the occultic scene on the back of the dollar, is to put in place the capstone (represented as a satanic triangle, the eye of Lucifer, and the solar blaze). In other words, the only thing left to complete Satan's world system (described in Revelation 13) is to put on the final antichrist (anti-Christian) touches! (Could that explain the regular cameos of the eye of Lucifer in so many corrupt movies put out by Hollywood in recent decades?) Also having thirteen elements are the stripes on the flag, the stars above the eagle's head, the arrows in the eagle's talons, and the leaves in the eagle's talons! The occultists are very serious about foisting their hellish, freedom-overthrowing program on society.

The media get very excited about ridiculing what they call conspiracy theories. Of course, if they can keep the specter of the secret-society boys' actual conspiracies to the realm of mere theory, then they are in the clear. If, however, people stop letting the Latin-loving, Romanism-loving occultists obstruct their vision, then the actual conspiracies become evident. Such hidden symbols and secret messages are the province of the enemy; the thrill

> Has the American church become the lukewarm church of Laodicea, a church so numb from watching intrigue on TV that its members can no longer differentiate between icky things happening on TV and nation-slaying things happening in real life?

of the masquerade is normal operating procedure for Satan because, after all, he masquerades as an angel of light (2 Corinthians 11).

Satan's minions clearly enjoy a chortling banking conspiracy that is hidden in plain sight as well. And isn't it strange that the US Treasury Department pulls so heavily from Federal Reserve personnel, ensuring that whatever is infecting the Fed then infects the entire US economy, rendering the country weak and therefore newly dependent on a new world order?

A broad blanket of naïveté has settled over America. It's as if the prosperity has congealed in all the wrong places: instead of praising the God of Israel for the many blessings He has bestowed, many Americans have gone the route of self-congratulations, mumbling something about the "American Dream" as if one has only to dream it to make it so.

But some dreams are nightmares, and the increasingly godless American Dream may turn out to be like Nebuchadnezzar's dream, in which the Babylonian king was forewarned by dream (and by the prophet Daniel) that his kingdom was about to be destroyed (Daniel 2). In other words, if Americans can only envision or dream of a godless state, then God will give them over to their godless devices (Romans 1). If Americans are so undiscerning that they accept the godless expressions all over their dollar bill and their nation's capital, then at some point their consciences will be so seared that it will be easier to laugh off warnings (such as this book) rather than simply study the meaning of the dollar bills in their own pockets! My purpose is hardly to bring up sensational topics for the sake of titillating—on the contrary, I do not find our country's demise to be titillating, and my purpose is to spur on Americans to stand up for their country and for the Christian faith.

We've seen briefly how the rise and fall of nations can be linked to a king's (and a people's) unwillingness to call a spade a spade and stand on the side of the good—on the side of the living God, the God of Israel. Discernment, and acting on that discernment, is important. The stakes are high.

All in the body of Christ have had struggles—some experience backsliding, some lethargy, and some indifference. Whatever the case, God's Word is nourishing, capable of making us mature, that is to say, discerning of good and evil:

> Concerning [Christ] we have much to say, and *it is* hard to explain, since you have become dull of hearing. For though by this time you ought to be teachers, you have need again for someone to teach you the elementary principles of the oracles of God, and you have come to need milk and not solid food. For everyone who partakes *only* of milk is not accustomed to the word of righteousness, for he is an infant. But solid food is for the mature, who because of practice have their senses trained to discern good and evil. (Heb. 5:11–14 NASB)

Many believers have grown soft or weary, and others have never matured. One who is dull of hearing, an infant in the faith, and unaccustomed to the word of righteousness is a prime candidate for succumbing to the wiles of the devil. The enemy is on the prowl; let us therefore take of meat, discern between good and evil, and stride into the light of Jesus.

So who is the strange woman the United States should avoid? In late 2011, esteemed prophecy scholar Irvin Baxter posited that the four horses of Zechariah 6 and Revelation 6 could be Roman Catholicism (white horse), communism (red horse), capitalism (black horse), and Islam (pale or green horse). I take Baxter's analysis seriously. Of course, I'm for vigorous trade with real allies, but if capitalism at its worst is indiscriminate, amoral, globalist trade, then I would be against that. Those four horses, and Jew haters of all stripes, comprise the strange woman that Christian America should oppose.

> If Americans can only envision, or dream of, a godless state, then God will give them over to their godless devices (per Rom. 1).

Chapter One

ARGUING FOR ABSOLUTE TRUTH

That we henceforth be no more children, tossed to and fro, and carried about with every wind of doctrine, by the sleight of men, and cunning craftiness whereby they lie in wait to deceive (Eph. 4:14 KJV).

This know also, that in the last days perilous times shall come. For men shall be lovers of their own selves, covetous, boasters, proud, blasphemers, disobedient to parents, unthankful, unholy, without natural affection, trucebreakers, false accusers, incontinent, fierce, despisers of those that are good, traitors, heady, highminded, lovers of pleasures more than lovers of God; having a form of godliness, but denying the power thereof: from such turn away. For of this sort are they which creep into houses, and lead captive silly women laden with sins, led away with divers lusts, ever learning, and never able to come to the knowledge of the truth. (2 Tim. 3:1–7 KJV)

In the contemporary atmosphere in which any ill-conceived, dastardly, or even satanic idea can masquerade under the mantle of respectability, many Americans have lost their footing. Moral relativism is the norm, and truth is too often considered a bad word. Relativists have held their convocations and have convinced themselves there's no truth, only a subjective stew pot of inklings and preferences. Without even studying the Bible, the relativists have pushed for an amalgamation of all beliefs (all except for Bible-based Christianity). This amalgamation allows the relativists to portray themselves as open and magnanimous (even though their position is neither). This approach, when applied uncritically and bigotedly, also allows them to portray the Bible-believing Christian as too narrow, even problematic in today's superficially inclusive world.

Many today have worshipped so long at the altar of relativism that they get offended when it is suggested they should repent and give their hearts to Jesus. After all, they reason, if they have descended through random processes from salamanders, how could they be sinners?

"I can have whatever size mocha I want," the moral relativist declares, "with the exact proportion of coffee to chocolate that I want and whatever amount of whipped cream that I want! And to boot, I'll take one part Roman Catholicism because they know pomp and ceremony; one part Unitarianism because it's against doctrine; one part Buddhism because they have kung-fu monks; one part Taoism because it's foreign and they have a chic logo; one part agnosticism because it's contrarian; one part atheism because it's self-centered; and two parts self-help psychology because the emphasis is on me—and make that to go!"

So how do we know how important—even crucial—it is to seek the truth and not just settle for a personally concocted mixture of belief systems? We find, for instance, that Jude had strong feelings about staying close to the true faith: "I felt I had to write and urge you to contend for the faith that was once for all entrusted to the saints. For certain men whose condemnation was written about long ago have secretly slipped in among you. They are godless men" (Jude 1:3–4 NIV).

Jude lays it on the line. He's not about to mince words about those who drag their friends and cohorts into unbelief; he simply calls them godless men. But Jude didn't stop there. In verse 8, he says this:

> These dreamers pollute their own bodies, reject authority and slander celestial beings … [They] speak abusively against whatever they do not understand … Woe to them! They have taken the way of Cain … These men are

blemishes at your love feasts, eating with you without the slightest qualm—shepherds who feed only themselves. They are clouds without rain, blown along by the wind; autumn trees, without fruit and uprooted—twice dead. They are wild waves of the sea, foaming up their shame; wandering stars, for whom blackest darkness has been reserved forever … These men are grumblers and faultfinders; they follow their own evil desires; they boast about themselves and flatter others for their own advantage. But, dear friends, remember what the apostles of our Lord Jesus Christ foretold. They said to you, "In the last times there will be scoffers who will follow their own ungodly desires." These are the men who divide you, who follow mere natural instincts and do not have the Spirit. (Jude 1:8, 10–13, 16–19 NIV)

Jude speaks in the clearest of terms. He contends for the one true faith based on the teachings of our Lord Jesus Christ. Jude calls those who reject Christ godless men, dreamers who pollute their own bodies, rejecters of authority and slanderers of celestial beings, followers of Cain, badmouthers of what they don't understand, clouds without rain, fruitless and uprooted trees, end-time scoffers, and dividers of men. Jude employs a stark vocabulary, one not colored by political nuance or social niceties. Clearly, for Jude the truth was just that important—important enough to warrant the clearest of terms and unambiguous analogies to drive home his exhortations. A fruitless tree or a tree toppled: these certainly are not what people want to be like. Who wants his or her life to be fruitless?

> Jude lays it on the line. He doesn't play patty-cake with those that pull others into unbelief—he simply calls them godless men.

Peter continues along with the same strand:

First of all, you must understand that in the last days scoffers will come, scoffing and following their own evil desires. They will say, "Where is this coming he promised? Ever since our fathers died, everything goes on as it has

> since the beginning of creation." But they deliberately forget that long ago by God's word the heavens existed and the earth was formed out of water and by water. By these waters also the world of that time was deluged and destroyed. By the same word the present heavens and earth are reserved for fire, being kept for the day of judgment and destruction of ungodly men … The Lord is not slow in keeping his promise, as some understand slowness. He is patient with you, not wanting anyone to perish, but everyone to come to repentance. (2 Peter 3:3–7, 9 NIV)

Peter specifically describes the character of the scoffing in the last days. The scoffing would embody an evolutionary character, marked by deliberately forgetting the biblical creation story and substituting that geological cousin to the theory of evolution—that is to say, the theory of uniformitarianism. In short, Charles Lyell's theory of uniformitarianism says that the earth's processes happen at a uniform rate; it supposes that canyons came about by the slow and steady erosion of stream, rain, and wind, rather than by the power of a God-directed catastrophic flood.

Noah's Ark brought mankind from the pre-Flood era to the post-Flood era.

"Lyell proposed that the geologic layers simply resulted from natural processes visible today—gradual erosion and sedimentation," says James Perloff, author of *Tornado in a Junkyard: The Relentless Myth of Darwinism*. "In other words, sedimentary rock had [supposedly] been formed just as rain erodes a mountain, and a river leaves deposits in a delta—drip by drip, grain by grain ... But geology, unlike chemistry and physics, deals with past events that the scientist cannot reproduce. Geologic activity is not a constant, like the speed of light. It can occur slowly, but also rapidly, as during a flood, earthquake, or volcano. Lyell, however, minimized the impact of catastrophic events."[1]

Lyell, in spinning his theory of uniformitarianism, didn't just minimize the Noahic flood of the Bible; he deliberately forgot it.

Indeed, as Scott M. Huse points out in his book *The Collapse of Evolution*, "With the doctrine of uniformitarianism, Peter's ancient prophecy has at last been fulfilled before our own eyes."[2] Watch public television (shows such as *Nova*) or the National Geographic Channel and you are likely to be force-fed a steady diet of the theories of evolution and uniformitarianism: a bee is said to be millions of years old, a rock the same, and everything is characterized as being much older than what the Bible says.

According to 2 Peter 3, last-days scoffers will forget the Noahic Flood as well as the biblical story of creation. Sure enough, today, last-days scoffers forget the Flood and biblical creation—yet another prophecy fulfilled.

Once again, in 2 Peter 3, we see that the last-days scoffers would promote flood-rejecting notions that have come to be known as the theory of uniformitarianism—that is, they would deliberately forget the biblical story of creation and the Noahic flood. Also in 2 Peter 3, we see that the last-days scoffers would live up to their names, saying, "Where is this coming he promised?" And sure enough, evolutionists and uniformitarianists are known for taking no small delight in mocking the prophesied coming of the Lord Jesus Christ. So we can see that the various aspects of this prophesy already have come true. This should do more than give pause to the evolutionists and uniformitarianists; it should make them believers in Jesus Christ and His Word.

We should also remember from 2 Peter 3 that the Lord's coming will take place and that the delay of the Lord's coming reflects His patience and love for all: "The Lord is not slow in keeping his promise, as some understand slowness. He is patient with you, not wanting anyone to perish, but everyone to come to repentance" (2 Peter 3:9 NIV). The Lord over all creation loves us and is waiting so that we will have time to give our hearts and minds to Him and to encourage others to do the same.

British paleontologist L. Merson Davies captures the current climate very aptly:

> Here, then, we come face to face with a circumstance which cannot be ignored … Namely, the existence of a marked prejudice against the acceptance of belief in a cataclysm like the Deluge. Now we should remember that, up to a hundred years ago, such a prejudice did not exist … as a general one, at least. Belief in the Deluge of Noah was axiomatic, not only in the Church itself … but in the scientific world as well. And yet the Bible stood committed to the prophecy that, in what it calls the "last days," a very different philosophy would be found in the ascendant; a philosophy which would lead men to regard belief in the Flood with disfavor, and treat it as disproved, declaring that "All things continue as from the beginning of the creation" (2 Peter 3:3–6). In other words, a doctrine of Uniformity in all things (a doctrine which the apostle obviously regarded as untrue to fact) was to replace belief in such cataclysms as the Deluge.[3]

We are exhorted to contend for the faith (Jude 3), and we must not be wandering stars, trees without fruit, clouds without rain, shepherds who feed only themselves, dreamers who pollute their own bodies, followers of Cain, or wild waves of the sea that foam up their shame. We are exhorted to contemplate God's creation and the lesson of the Noahic flood; we must not be as scoffers who follow their own evil desires, deliberately forgetting God's creation and the lesson of the Noahic flood (2 Peter 3). There is truth and there is falsehood, and we should seek truth.

In Col. 2:8, Paul sets out this injunction: "See to it that no one takes you captive through hollow and deceptive philosophy, which depends on human tradition and the basic principles of this world rather than on Christ" (NIV). And in 1 Tim. 4:1–2, 7, and 16, Paul notes this: "The Spirit clearly says that in later times some will abandon the faith and follow deceiving spirits and things taught by demons. Such teachings come through hypocritical liars, whose consciences have been seared as with a hot iron. ... Have nothing to do with godless myths and old wives' tales; rather, train yourself to be godly. ... Watch your life and doctrine closely. Persevere in them, because if you do, you will save both yourself and your hearers" (NIV).

Liberal universities across these United States are dotted with tarot card readers and fortune tellers of all kinds; yoga instructors who have fallen prey to the Hindu untruths that underpin yoga; martial arts instructors who sell Taoist untruths and other false Eastern mystical philosophies; anthropologists who make pronouncement after pronouncement about the ridiculous and contrived ape-man scenarios; biologists who intimate that we're all in the same big, happy family tree with nematodes and nudibranchs; geologists who will teach anything but the reshaping of the earth's surface by the Noahic flood; interfaith mumbo-jumbo halls that hold all belief systems to be equal and valid (except for Bible-believing Christianity); and pundits of various hues who praise or tolerate satanic expressions and sexual wantonness and anti-Semitism in the name of misappropriated free expression. The Holy Spirit foretold that in the later times some would abandon the faith and follow deceiving spirits (demons) (1 Timothy 4); everywhere we look we can see this prophesy has come true. One is instructed to watch his or her life and doctrine closely and to protect his or her conscience lest it be broken and of no effect.

> From 1 Timothy 4, we know that in the later times some will abandon the faith and follow deceiving spirits (demons)— yet another prophecy fulfilled.

In 2 Tim. 3:1–7, Paul says this:

> There will be terrible times in the last days. People will be lovers of themselves, lovers of money, boastful, proud,

abusive, disobedient to their parents, ungrateful, unholy, without love, unforgiving, slanderous, without self-control, brutal, not lovers of the good, treacherous, rash, conceited, lovers of pleasure rather than lovers of God—having a form of godliness but denying its power. Have nothing to do with them. They are the kind who worm their way into homes and gain control over weak-willed women, who are loaded down with sins and are swayed by all kinds of evil desires, always learning but never able to acknowledge the truth." (NIV)

Furthermore, in 2 Tim. 4:3–4: "For the time will come when men will not put up with sound doctrine. Instead, to suit their own desires, they will gather around them a great number of teachers to say what their itching ears want to hear. They will turn their ears away from the truth and turn aside to myths" (NIV).

This certainly rings true! These foretellings should reverberate in the heads of all who read them, so true are they to the facts of today, bearing out as they do the power of prophecy fulfilled. Go to the self-help section in most bookstores nowadays and read

> American news channels seem bent on providing both sides of every event as if every issue is too complicated for a national consensus to ever be achieved. So baby-killing and sodomy and fornication are debated and laughed off but rarely criticized, and the truth is rarely acknowledged.

a seemingly endless list of how to actualize this or that inner potentiality, as if the answers to life lie within the wicked human heart! Indeed, as Jeremiah stated long ago, "The heart is deceitful above all things and beyond cure. Who can understand it?" (Jer. 17:9 NIV).

Jeremiah's clear words are an indictment against psychotherapy, which purports to understand and solve problems of the heart and mind, and humanistic positivism, which professes that man can cure his ills and, indeed, his sins by relying on his own strength and understanding. The idea that people are now lovers of themselves and of pleasure hardly needs substantiating. The popular culture is swimming in the adulation of celebrities, and the celebrities, for their part, churn out a steady stream of false modesty and smarmy attempts at depth of character that include the Buddhist palms-together salutation. Indeed, many people are "always learning but never able to acknowledge the truth" (2 Tim. 3:7 NIV).

American news channels seem bent on providing both sides of every event as if every issue is too complicated for a national consensus to ever be achieved. So homosexuality, abortion, and fornication are debated and laughed off but rarely criticized, and the truth is rarely acknowledged. "For the time will come when men will not put up with sound doctrine" (2 Tim. 4:3 NIV).

Sure enough, in September 2002 on the TV show *The Factor*, the Catholic host summarily dismissed an evangelical, Scripture-quoting Christian as a religious fanatic. Perhaps the host of *The Factor* forgot to factor in that the God of Israel, whom his guest was quoting, actually created the very mouth that the host uses to make a living. People will turn from the truth and surround themselves with "teachers" who say "what their itching ears want to hear" (2 Tim. 4:3 NIV).

Throughout the 1990s, TV pundits constantly screamed that the United States was the only remaining superpower, without any apparent compunction—stroking the itching ears of Americans with what they supposedly wanted to hear and setting them up for a fall. Suffice it to say that the prophetic words of 2 Timothy 3–4 have been fulfilled in spades. These prophecies deserve our attention and should inspire everyone with the power and majesty of the God of Abraham, Isaac, and Jacob.

In 2 John 7 and 9–11, we read this: "Many deceivers, who do not acknowledge Jesus Christ as coming in the flesh, have gone out into the world. Any such person is the deceiver and the antichrist. ... Anyone who runs ahead and does not continue in the teaching of Christ does not have God; whoever continues in the teaching has both the Father and the Son. If anyone comes to you and does not bring this teaching, do not take him into your house or welcome him. Anyone who welcomes him shares in his wicked work" (NIV). One needs to have Christ's teaching to have God, and any who deny that Jesus Christ was a man are deceivers and antichrists. As we read in 1 John 4:15, "If anyone acknowledges that Jesus is the Son of God, God lives in him and he in God" (NIV).

Referring to those in the churches of Colosse and Laodicea, Paul says this in Col. 2:2–4 and 8: "My purpose is that they may be encouraged in heart and united in love, so that they may have the full riches of complete understanding, in order that they may know the mystery of God, namely, Christ, in whom are hidden all the treasures of wisdom and knowledge. I tell you this so that no one may deceive you by fine-sounding arguments. ... See to it that no one takes you captive through hollow and deceptive philosophy, which depends on human tradition and the basic principles of this world rather than on Christ" (NIV).

And James gave us this: "If any of you lacks wisdom, he should ask God, who gives generously to all without finding fault, and it will be given to him. But when he asks, he must believe and not doubt, because he who doubts is like a wave of the sea, blown and tossed by the wind" (James 1:5–6 NIV).

In Eph. 4:7 and 11–14, we find a similar exhortation:

> But to each one of us grace has been given as Christ apportioned it. ... It was he who gave some to be apostles, some to be prophets, some to be evangelists, and some to be pastors and teachers, to prepare God's people for works of service, so that the body of Christ may be built up until we all reach unity in the faith and in the knowledge of the Son of God and become mature, attaining to the whole measure of the fullness of Christ. Then we will no longer be infants, tossed back and forth by the waves, and blown here and there by every wind of teaching and by the cunning and craftiness of men in their deceitful scheming." (NIV)

These verses emphasize the importance of asking God for wisdom and believing the Word of God. James offers an instructive analogy that illustrates the folly of not heeding God's Word: "Anyone who listens to the word but does not do what it says is like a man who looks at his face in a mirror and, after looking at himself, goes away and immediately forgets what he looks like" (James 1:23–24 NIV).

Evolutionists have not humbly accepted the Word and therefore deceive themselves. Unable to follow the Word, evolutionists are like people who look in the mirror and then walk away forgetting what they look like. True enough, James' words were prophetic, for we have modern-day evolutionists who forget what they look like. They'd rather see themselves as derived from accidental chimps instead of seeing themselves as part of the creation of the God of the Bible.

I have tried to show, in a clear Scriptural way, that there is one truth—that contained in the Bible and in the teachings of our Lord Jesus Christ—and that disbelief is the broad way to ruin.

Chapter Two

DEBUNKING THE HOAX OF EVOLUTION

Knowing this first, that there shall come in the last days scoffers, walking after their own lusts, and saying, Where is the promise of his coming? For since the fathers fell asleep, all things continue as they were from the beginning of the creation. For this they willingly are ignorant of, that by the word of God the heavens were of old, and the earth standing out of the water and in the water: Whereby the world that then was, being overflowed with water, perished: But the heavens and the earth, which are now, by the same word are kept in store, reserved unto fire against the day of judgment and perdition of ungodly men. But, beloved, be not ignorant of this one thing, that one day is with the Lord as a thousand years, and a thousand years as one day. The Lord is not slack concerning his promise, as some men count slackness; but is long-suffering to us-ward, not willing that any should perish, but that all should come to repentance. But the day of the Lord will come as a thief in the night; in the which the heavens shall pass away with a great noise, and the elements shall melt with fervent heat, the earth also and the works that are therein shall be burned up. (2 Peter 3:3–10 KJV)

Life is not a wishy-washy mash of uncertainty. There are, in fact, compelling signposts that point to a true worldview, one that has the God of Israel at the center and emphasizes the importance of the relationship between man and God. Blue is not red; panthers are not toads; Douglas firs are not pumpkins; cold is not hot; people are not apes; and the road to the New Jerusalem is not the same as the road to destruction. False religions lead to death, not life, and the theory of evolution brings ruination.

The Bane of Secular Education and Secular Media

Americans are force-fed the evolutionary message at just about every turn. As Jeremy Walter says in the book *In Six Days: Why Fifty Scientists Choose to Believe in Creation*:

> Public education introduced the sciences of the space program, but also proclaimed as fact the four-and-a-half-billion-year age of the earth and that life had gradually evolved over millions of years from a single-cell organism, supposedly formed by chance in a primeval ocean. Students were compelled to accept the evolutionary model of earth history, as is the case for most people educated in this century. The ancient writings of Genesis were relegated as outdated and allegorical, and most Christian students reconciled an immature faith in God and the Bible with a casually contrived version of the "day-age" interpretation of the creation account.[1]

Even a casual survey of popular television will bear out the overwhelming evolutionary bias. The National Geographic Channel has been a mouthpiece for evolutionary theory, featuring the following proclamation on September 21, 2002: "The great white shark has ruled the oceans for tens of millions of years." So there you have it, bombastically proclaimed by the National Geographic Channel, with all the weight of some of the world's best photographers behind it.

In September 2002, the National Geographic Channel's *Explorer* program told an unwary public that lemurs split from apes millions of years ago—more bombast. The idea that the National Geographic Channel can tell one what happened millions of years ago is laughable.

The National Geographic Channel's *Close-Up* program (Oct. 10, 2002) featured a fossilized Tyrannosaurus rex named Sue. After Sue was moved to the Field Museum in Chicago, curators cleaned dirt or debris from her big skull, and the narrator solemnly said that they were cleaning millions of years of the dirt (or whatever) off Sue.

Regarding the origin of Arizona's famous Antelope Canyon, the National Geographic Channel's *This Week* program (Oct. 18, 2002) posited that the slot canyon probably began with a crack in the sandstone and assumed its beautifully sculpted shape only after millions of years of erosion from floods. A narrator solemnly pronounced that flash floods represent Mother Nature's attempt to cleanse herself and start anew.

Thus, we have yet another glib and unrigorous endorsement of uniformitarianism and old-earth conceptions spiced with a dash of nature worship. In the National Geographic Channel's *Greatest Natural Wonders of the World* program (Oct. 19, 2002), the unwary viewer was told that the Colorado River carved out the Grand Canyon in just a few million years and that the Grand Canyon's oldest rocks are nearly two billion years old; that 20,000 years ago ice filled the Yosemite Valley nearly to the top of Half Dome; that the Himalayan peaks started rising up thirty million years ago; and that the Great Barrier Reef evolved over hundreds of thousands of years. On top of this, the narrator solemnly announced that in Australia, one can sense the great age of the earth, and that humans have only been a part of earth's history for a relatively trivial duration.

Confronting Mainstream Journalism's Proevolution Bias

TIME magazine featured an artist's imaginative drawing of an "ape-man" on the cover, and next to this "ape-man" contrivance were the ungodly words, "How Apes Became Human." The feature article offers more evolutionary pablum: "Paleontologists have suspected for nearly 200 years that bipedalism was probably the key evolutionary transition that split the human line off from the apes, and fossil discoveries as far back as Java Man in the 1890s supported that notion. The astonishingly complete skeleton of Lucy, with its clearly apelike skull but upright posture, cemented the idea a quarter-century ago."[2]

Bipedalism was key for splitting the human line off from the apes? Java Man supported the notion, and Lucy cemented the idea? The bones that Eugene Dubois thought were the Java Man were in fact, according to Scott M. Huse's *The Collapse of Evolution,* collected over a range of some seventy feet. It is therefore quite a stretch to suppose that Java Man's bones were even from one and the same creature.[3] Indeed, in James Perloff's *Tornado in a Junkyard,* we learn that Rudolph Virchow, the father of modern pathology, believed that Java Man was none other than a giant gibbon and that "the thigh bone has not the slightest connection with the skull." Reportedly, Dubois was absent when the Java Man fossil remains were dug up, and diagrams of the site were only made once the excavation was finished—conditions that would invalidate a modern dig.[4] Moreover, Huse notes that a second Java Man discovery turned out to be the knee bone of a no-longer-extant elephant.[5]

"It should be mentioned," Huse says, "that the knee joint that was used to 'prove' that Lucy walked upright was found more than 200 feet lower in the strata and more than two miles away!"[6] Perloff adds, "The assumption that two-footed mobility establishes human kinship is groundless. Gorillas occasionally walk bipedally; Tanzanian chimpanzees are seen standing on two legs when gathering fruit from small trees; Zaire's pygmy chimpanzee walks upright so often that it has been dubbed 'a living link.' … For that matter, birds are bipedal—therefore human?"[7]

If Java Man and Lucy were both charades, and evolutionary buzzwords such as bipedalism have lost their luster, then the theory of evolution should lose steam.

A recent star among the ape-man contenders was found in the Middle Awash region of Ethiopia and goes by the moniker

> Joseph Lister, namesake of Listerine and developer of antiseptic surgery, believed in Jesus the Christ. Swishing and swabbing are good practices, but they can only do so much. One can get really clean by repenting, receiving Jesus as one's Lord and Savior, and letting the Great Physician cleanse away the sins.

Ardipithecus—we'll call him Ardi for short. Like Java Man and Lucy, Ardi has his problems. Regarding Ardi, *TIME* notes that anthropologist Donald Johanson is "dubious about categorizing the 5.2 million-year-old toe bone with the rest of the fossils: not only is it separated in time by several hundred thousand years, but it was also found some 10 miles away from the rest."[8] I totally share Johanson's misgivings about Ardi.

But such misgivings didn't stop *TIME* from issuing still more proevolution dogma in statements such as "It's already clear that eastern Africa was bubbling with evolutionary experiments 6 million years ago."[9] Perhaps all this talk about Ardi of the Middle Awash is itself a wash. Anthropologist Tim White has been quoted as saying, "The problem with a lot of anthropologists is that they want so much to find a hominid that any scrap of bone becomes a hominid bone."[10]

In a similar vein, biochemist Michael Behe, author of *Darwin's Black Box,* says this about Darwin's theory of evolution: "Because the popular media likes to publish exciting stories, and because some scientists enjoy speculating about how far their theories might go, it has been difficult for the public to separate fact from conjecture. ... But ... if you search the scientific literature on evolution, and if you focus your search on the question of how molecular machines—the basis of life—developed, you find an eery and complete silence."[11]

Paleontologists who want to understand the hoary past would do well to take a page from famed agriculturalist George Washington Carver, who attributed his success to the Bible, saying, "In all thy ways acknowledge Him and He shall direct thy paths."[12] Similarly, Joseph Lister, developer of antiseptic surgery and the namesake for Listerine mouthwash, said, "I have no hesitation in saying that in my opinion there is no antagonism between the Religion of Jesus Christ and any fact scientifically established."[13]

Perloff points out that "Dr. Larry Vardiman, chairman of the Physics Department at the Institute for Creation Research, doesn't buy evolution. ... His technical book, *The Age of Earth's Atmosphere: A Study of the Helium Flux Through the Atmosphere,* makes a strong case that helium accumulation limits the Earth's age to about 10,000 years."[14] If Vardiman is even close to being right, then we can say goodbye to TIME's assertion that "it's already clear that eastern Africa was *bubbling with evolutionary experiments 6 million years ago"* (italics mine).

"When I was young, my embryo went through an elephant phase, followed by another elephant phase. If another smooth-talking pseudobiologist says I went through a salamander phase, I might have to throw my weight around, and you don't want to see that!"

Huse notes, "The Bible speaks clearly of man as a special creation, entirely unrelated to the animal kingdom by any sort of evolutionary connection (Genesis 1; 1 Cor. 15:39). Far from being an evolutionary accident of nature, man is the crown of creation, made in the very image of God (Gen. 1:26–27)." Furthermore, he says, "The Bible tells us that some 'shall turn away their ears from the truth, and shall be turned unto fables' (2 Tim. 4:4); and again that some are 'ever learning, and never able to come to the knowledge of the truth' (2 Tim. 3:7)."[15]

How many concocted ape-men will have to be discredited before imagination-rich paleontologists and sensational publications get down to the serious business of understanding God's creation as God's creation? And when will the humanistically inspired charade of evolution let go its grip on science and society?

More Bias in Mainstream Journalism

The July 22, 2002, issue of *TIME* introduced a new candidate to be the hominid-type missing link. I've redacted the article as follows: "My guess is that *Sahelanthropus* is the first of what will turn out to be a whole handful of apes and ape-like creatures living throughout Africa 6 or 7 million years ago."[16] Famed anthropologist Tim White has said, "This *[Sahelanthropus]* fossil is the closest we've got to the common ancestor."[17]

The *TIME* reporters say "there seems little doubt, at least, that *[Sahelanthropus]* was truly a hominid," and that "it almost certainly dates from very near that crucial moment in prehistory when hominids began to tread an evolutionary path that diverged from that of chimps, our closest living relatives."[18]

One *"my guess is that,"* one *"this is the closest we've got,"* one *"there seems little doubt that,"* and a couple *"almost certainly's"* are not exactly the stuff that confidence is made of. But such wishy-washy bad-science propaganda is exactly what the so-called hunt for hominids is made of. Yet for all of the *TIME* reporters' hedging over *Sahelanthropus,* they just matter-of-factly call the chimpanzee our closest living relative. And the evolutionary brainwashing goes on.

The Noahic flood changed the surface of the earth very dramatically. Many canyons and other rock formations stand as testaments to the power of the worldwide flood.

The article quotes White as saying that "if you think of Africa as a giant place where human ancestors existed for the past 7 million years, you have to get lucky to find places where environmental conditions allowed them to live and where the geological conditions allowed them to be preserved."[19] If, on the other hand, one thinks that Lucy is a charade, and that human ancestors go back to the creation of Adam and Eve, then Africa becomes a giant place where one can discern some six thousand years of earth history.

The evolutionists and uniformitarianists toss around a million years here and a billion years there, change the age of the earth on a regular basis, and show that they really do put a premium on "getting lucky" instead of doing serious scientific work.

Evolutionary Beliefs Not Based on Science

Many assume that in any controversy, the issues must be complex and best left to the experts. In the case of evolutionary theory, many who say they believe it can't really explain why. They've been bamboozled through a potent mixture of bad science and unbelief. Henry M. Morris lays it out for us in his essay "The Conflict of the Ages":

> The late Isaac Asimov, who was president of the American Humanist Association and one of the most prolific science writers of our time, was a bitter opponent of creationism. He refused to debate any creationist publicly, but he wrote against creationism vigorously in his publications. Asimov, who is said to have produced more than 500 books covering every field of science, probably knew science as well as anybody. What he said, in case you have any questions about what humanism really is: "I am an atheist, out and out." Humanism is basically an esoteric form of atheism. He went on to say: "Emotionally, I'm an atheist—I don't have the evidence to prove that God doesn't exist. But I so strongly suspect He doesn't that I don't want to waste my time."

> Now if anybody would have any scientific evidence against God, it would seem that Isaac Asimov would. But he admitted that he didn't; and if he didn't, then nobody does. ... Science is supposed to be what you can see, but no one has ever seen any evolution take place. As long as people have been looking at changes in biological organisms, no one has ever seen a new species evolve. No one has ever seen evolution from simple to complex take place anywhere in the whole universe in all human history, and nobody knows how evolution works to this very day...
>
> Dr. Colin Patterson of England, a great evolutionist, has said, in effect, that no one has ever seen a new species come into existence by natural selection. Nobody knows how it works; nobody has ever seen it happen. If we go to the fossil record, there are no evolutionary transitional forms there, either. Evolution is even contrary to the laws of thermodynamics, the basic laws of science. There is no scientific evidence for evolution whatsoever. People don't believe in evolution because of science. In spite of science, they believe in evolution because emotionally they don't want to believe in God.[20]

In his essay "The Denial of the Obvious," John D. Morris makes much the same case:

> Darwin [wrote] in a letter on May 22, 1860 [the following]: "I had no intention to write atheistically. But I own that I cannot see as plainly as others do, and as I should wish to do, evidence of design and beneficence on all sides of us. There seems to me too much misery in the world. I cannot persuade myself that a beneficent and omnipotent God would have designedly created the ichneumonidae (ie, parasite) with the express intention of their feeding within the living bodies of caterpillars, or that a cat should play

with mice. [Thus] I see no necessity in the belief that the eye was expressly designed."

Thus, we see that Darwin's acceptance of evolution was not because of scientific reasons but for theological reasons. He plainly saw the prominence of death, pain, and suffering engulfing the living world. He saw extinction, mutation, cancer, and parasites, and rightly reasoned that the God of the Bible would not have created things in this fashion. But ... the world that Darwin observed, and that [which] we observe, is not the world as God created it. Refusing to acknowledge the effects of the Curse [on the creation], and how Adam's rebellion ruined God's "very good" creation, he wrongly chose to deny God as Creator.[21]

Physical chemist A. J. Monty White noted that there is circular reasoning when it comes to the age of rocks and evolution: "The age of the rock is determined from the age of a fossil, the age of which in turn is determined by evolution; the proof of evolution is the age of the rocks in which the fossil is found. ... I became convinced (and still am convinced) that people believe in evolution because they choose to do so. It has nothing at all to do with evidence. Evolution is not a fact, as so many bigots maintain. There is not a shred of evidence for the evolution of life on earth."[22]

George Wald, winner of the 1967 Nobel Peace Prize in science, revealed his motive for believing in evolution when he said, "When it comes to the origin of life on this earth, there are only two possibilities: creation or spontaneous generation (evolution). There is no third way. Spontaneous generation was disproved 100 years ago, but that leads us only to one other conclusion: that of supernatural creation. We cannot accept that on philosophical grounds (personal reasons); therefore, we choose to believe the impossible: that life arose spontaneously by chance."[23]

James Perloff points to the dishonest quality of evolutionary science: "How do evolutionists justify their estimate of billions of years? Their greatest argument is probably Darwinian theory itself. Chance and natural selection would require eons to develop life forms. After one buys that argument, all evidence that doesn't fit is rejected. As British physicist H.

S. Lipson observed in *Physics Bulletin:* 'In fact, evolution became in a sense a scientific religion; almost all scientists have accepted it and many are prepared to "bend" their observations to fit in with it.'"[24]

Historically, casual observations gave rise to the theory that perhaps fruit flies come from banana peels, maggots come from manure, bees come from dead calves, etc. However, this theory was rightly debunked by more careful observers, as Scott M. Huse notes: "Spontaneous generation was disproved by the careful studies of [Francesco] Redi (1688), [Lazzaro] Spallanzani (1780), [Louis] Pasteur (1860), and [Rudolph] Virchow (1858). … They proved that when matter was presterilized and sealed off from possible biological contamination, no life arose; hence, no spontaneous generation. The work of these men and others [has] established the law of biogenesis: life comes only from preexisting life and will only perpetuate its own kind."[25]

As a result of Ernst Haeckel's fantastical and fraudulent drawings of supposedly identical-looking animal and human embryos, biology classrooms throughout the world were infected with the lie that people came from animals. As Perloff notes, "Students were taught that the human embryo manifested reminders of man's past, such as 'gill slits' from the fish stage of evolution. Actually, the 'gill slits' evolutionists thought they saw were simply clefts and pouches which, as the embryo grows, develop principally into structures of the ear, jaw and neck."[26] In fact, as Perloff notes, "The human fetus is fully human at every stage. … It seems the height of pretense that a theory—a fraudulent one, at that—was designated a 'law', as if it had been established with the certainty of gravity. But this is symptomatic of Darwinism, where speculative opinions routinely masquerade as facts."[27]

And as Dr. Sabine Schwabenthan wrote, "Fetoscopy makes it possible to observe directly the unborn child through a tiny telescope inserted through the uterine wall. … The development of the child—from the union of the partners' cells to birth—has been studied exhaustively. As a result, long-held beliefs have been put to rest. We now know, for instance, that man, in his prenatal stages, does not go through the complete evolution of life—from a primitive single cell to a fish-like water creature to man. Today it is known that every step in the fetal developmental process is specifically human."[28]

One bizarre and sickening outgrowth of Haeckel's imagination was the belief that people were saddled with vestigial organs or half-organs that more properly belonged on an animal. Perloff explains:

> One reason why so many tonsillectomies were previously performed was the false belief that tonsils were "vestigial." Today it is recognized that the tonsils have an immune function. The thyroid gland, pituitary gland, thymus, pineal gland, and coccyx, also once considered useless, are now known to have important functions. ... Darwin had said that organs evolve over eons; a structure might therefore be incipient—on its way to becoming full-fledged. The "vestigial" idea thus posed quite a dilemma for evolution: Was a functionless organ "incipient" and on its way in, or "vestigial" and on its way out? The discovery that our organs *are* fully functional resolved the predicament, and suggested that Darwinism itself should be classed as vestigial.[29]

More Evidence Against Evolution

The following statements convey much of the heft, weight, depth, and breadth of the case against evolution. One needs to understand the variety and strength of the objections to evolution to see that the objections come from all angles and disciplines and all types of learned men and women. It's good to be fully armed in the battle against evolution; one can be, and should be, comfortable in the knowledge that the rejection of evolution is a lucid, historical, and altogether cogent response to the world around us.

> One can, and should, be comfortable in the knowledge that rejecting evolution is a lucid, historical, and cogent response to the world around us.

In 1978, Arthur Koestler noted that "in the meantime, the educated public continues to believe that Darwin has provided all the relevant answers by the magic formula of random mutation plus natural selection—quite unaware of the fact that random mutations turned out to be irrelevant and natural selection a tautology."[30] In *American Biology Teacher*, Norman Macbeth wrote that "Darwinism has failed in practice. The whole aim and purpose of Darwinism is to show how modern forms descended from ancient forms, that is, to construct reliable phylogenies (genealogies or family trees). In this it has utterly failed. ... Darwinism is not science."[31]

Gregory Alan Pesely, a philosophy professor, noted that "one of the most frequent objections against the theory of natural selection is that it is a sophisticated tautology. ... What is most unsettling is that some evolutionary biologists have no qualms about proposing tautologies as explanations. One would immediately reject any lexicographer who tried to define a word by the same word, or a thinker who merely restated his proposition, or any other instance of gross redundancy; yet no one seems scandalized that men of science should be satisfied with a major principle which is no more than a tautology."[32]

And in the same vein, geneticist Conrad Waddington of Edinburgh University offered this: "There, you do come to what is, in effect, a vacuous statement: Natural selection is that some things leave more offspring than others; and you ask, which leave more offspring than others; and it is those that leave more offspring; and there is nothing more to it than that."[33]

Max Planck, a Nobel Prize winner and modern physics pioneer, wrote that "there is evidence of an intelligent order of the universe to which both man and nature are subservient. ... Wherever we look, we find no evidence as far as we can see of any conflict between science and religion, but only complete agreement on the decisive issues instead. ... Side by side, science and religion wage a constant, continuing and unrelenting struggle against skepticism and dogmatism, against disbelief and superstition. The battle cry, the goal of this struggle, has been and will always be: Forward to God."[34]

This ain't your gran'pappy. Gibbons were specially made for climbing and swinging.

And David Raphael Klein put it well: "Anyone who can contemplate the eye of a housefly, the mechanics of human finger movement, the camouflage of a moth, or the building of every kind of matter from variations in arrangement of proton and electron, and then maintain that all this design happened without a designer, happened by sheer, blind accident—such a person believes in a miracle far more astounding than any in the Bible."[35]

James Perloff points out the obvious but with a vital point in mind: "We can drop sugar, flour, baking powder, and an egg on the floor—but they won't turn into a cake by themselves. We have to mix and bake them according to a recipe. Throwing steel, rubber, glass and plastic together doesn't make a car. It takes skillful engineering."[36]

The magazine *Nature* quoted astronomer Fred Hoyle as saying that the odds of higher life forms coming about by chance are roughly the same as the odds that "a tornado sweeping through a junk-yard might assemble a Boeing 747 from the materials therein."[37]

British philosopher G. K. Chesterton says that "it is absurd for the evolutionist to complain that it is unthinkable for an admittedly unthinkable God to make everything out of nothing, and then pretend that it is *more* thinkable that nothing should turn itself into everything."[38]

Ernst Chain, a Nobel Prize–winning biochemist, put it this way: "I have said for years that speculations about the origin of life lead to no useful purpose as even the simplest living system is far too complex to be understood in terms of the extremely primitive chemistry scientists have used in their attempts to explain the unexplainable that happened [supposedly] billions of years ago. God cannot be explained away by such naïve thoughts."[39]

As Perloff says:

Matter is not intrinsically informative. To say that a human cell was built by its chemicals is like saying a book was written by its paper and ink, or that a typewriter

> A dragonfly's compound eye has 30,000 lenses called ommatidia, enabling the insect to survey its whole neighborhood at once. Such awesome structures provide evolution-slaying evidence for "irreducible complexity" specifically, and for creationism generally.

was constructed by the iron in its frame. Functional design requires more than matter—it takes intelligence. ... Caryl P. Haskins' comments in *American Scientist* were understated: "Did the [genetic] code and the means of translating it appear simultaneously in evolution? It seems almost incredible that any such coincidence could have occurred, given the extraordinary complexities of both sides and the requirement that they be coordinated accurately for survival." Which came first? Not likely the genetic code, if there was nothing to translate it. That would be like books existing before there were people to read them. But why would translation devices evolve first, if there was no genetic code to read? This is yet another irreducible complexity.[40]

In 1988, Dr. Wolfgang Smith, who has taught at MIT and UCLA and has written on many scientific topics, said that "[macroevolution] is totally bereft of scientific sanction. Now, to be sure, given the multitude of extravagant claims about evolution promulgated by evolutionists with an air of scientific infallibility, this may indeed sound strange. And yet the fact remains that there exists to this day not a shred of bona fide scientific evidence in support of the thesis that macroevolutionary transformations have ever occurred."[41]

Zoologist Albert Fleischmann of the University of Erlangen in Germany declared that "the Darwinian theory of descent has not a single fact to confirm it in the realm of nature. It is not the result of scientific research, but purely the product of imagination. ... The theory ... can no longer square with practical scientific knowledge, nor does it suffice for our theoretical grasp of the facts. ... No one can demonstrate that the limits of a species have ever been passed. These are the Rubicons which evolutionists cannot cross."[42]

And Dr. T. N. Tahmisian of the US Atomic Energy Commission said in 1959, "Scientists who go about teaching that evolution is a fact of life are great con-men, and the story they are telling may be the greatest hoax ever. In explaining evolution, we do not have one iota of fact."[43]

In 1987, Swedish biologist Soren Lovtrup noted, "I believe that one day the Darwinian myth will be ranked the greatest deceit in the history of science."[44]

In 1988, Louis Bounoure, former director of the Strasbourg Zoological Museum and later director of research at the French National Center of Scientific Research, noted, "Evolutionism is a fairy tale for grown-ups. This theory has helped nothing in the progress of science. It is useless."[45]

Dr. Robert Etheridge, a world-renowned paleontologist at the British Museum, has said, "Nine-tenths of the talk of evolutionists is sheer nonsense, not founded on observation and wholly unsupported by facts. This museum is full of proofs of the utter falsity of their views. In all this great museum, there is not a particle of evidence of the transmutation of species."[46]

Dr. Wernher von Braun, father of the US space program with NASA, wrote the following letter to the California State Board of Education in 1972:

> [T]he scientific method does not allow us to exclude data which lead to the conclusion that the universe, life and man are based on design. To be forced to believe only one conclusion—that everything in the universe happened by chance—would violate the very objectivity of science itself. Certainly there are those who argue that the universe evolved out of a random process, but what random process could produce the brain of a man or the system of the human eye? … Many men who are intelligent and of good faith say they cannot visualize a Designer. Well, can a physicist visualize an electron? The electron is materially inconceivable and yet it is so perfectly known through its effects that we use it to illuminate our cities, guide our airlines through the night skies and take the most accurate measurements. What strange rationale makes some physicists accept the inconceivable electrons as real while refusing to accept the reality of a Designer on the ground that they cannot conceive Him? …
>
> I endorse the presentation of alternative theories for the origin of the universe, life and man in the science classroom. It would be an error to overlook the possibility that the universe was planned rather than happened by chance.[47]

And finally, Fleischmann brings us an eloquent refutation of evolution: "I reject evolution because I deem it obsolete; because the knowledge, hard won since 1830, of anatomy, histology, cytology, and embryology, cannot be made to accord with its basic idea. The foundationless, fantastic edifice of the evolution doctrine would long ago have met with its long-deserved fate were it not that the love of fairy tales is so deep-rooted in the hearts of man."[48]

Love and Morality Are No Accident

C. S. Lewis makes a common-sense, if eloquent, point about the nonsensical nature of evolutionary theory. He states:

> If the solar system was brought about by an accidental collision, then the appearance of organic life on this planet was also an accident, and the whole evolution of man was an accident, too. If so, then all our thought processes are mere accidents—the accidental by-product of the movement of atoms. And this holds for the materialists' and astronomers' as well as for anyone else's. But if their thoughts—ie, of Materialism and Astronomy—are merely accidental by-products, why should we believe them to be true? I see no reason for believing that one accident should be able to give a correct account of all the other accidents.[49]

Indeed, why should an accidental paleontologist be trusted to tell us about the supposedly accidental origin of man? Why should an accidental geologist be trusted to tell us about the supposedly accidental origin of the shape of the earth? And why should an accidental atheist be trusted to tell us about the inconsequence of supposedly accidental thoughts on God? Why trust John Lennon if he accidentally lulled people into a stupor with his accidental musicality and accidentally urged people to imagine there's no heaven and no hell in his song "Imagine"? Is a woman's sensual design an accident, or is it possible that woman was designed by a loving creator who is revealed in the Holy Bible and that she was made with procreation and joy and beauty in mind? God's purposeful designs are consistent with the love we feel as people. But how about evolution? Is evolution consistent with the love that we feel and see?

This just in: Tigers reproduce and give rise to other … tigers! In other words, tigers come from other tigers and, ultimately, from God's hand. The cats that leapt off Noah's Ark were imbued with fantastic God-given DNA that has made it possible for us to enjoy cats such as cougars, tigers, lions, jaguars, and cheetahs—not to mention tabbies and Siamese. Tigers don't hold sit-ins to discuss new techniques in striping, coloring, and other camouflage configurations; they don't hold year-end assessment meetings on the relative benefits of retractable claw design. They are part of God's creation, and they will be gentler during the millennial reign of Christ.

Australian chemist Stephen Grocott clearly thinks that love is not compatible with evolution:

> Does my heart melt when I think of my wife simply because I want to propagate more and I want her to look after my little two-legged gene-bundles? When I witnessed the births of my two children, did I cry because those babies meant my gene line would continue? … [Y]ou can believe in a Creator who describes himself as love and says that He made us in His image, able to discern right from wrong, and able to love both Him and others for no logical reason other than that is the way we were made. Yes, you can believe that your life has no higher purpose than to propagate the species and then die, but in your heart and head, does that fit with the world you see?[50]

Irreducible Complexity and Marvels of God's Creation

Evolution makes no sense. How could all of the beautifully engineered systems around us have just popped up—poof—from out of nowhere and with no real purpose? "The complexity of the simplest imaginable living organism is mind-boggling," Stephen Grocott says. "You need to have the cell wall, the energy system, a system of self-repair, a reproduction system, and means for taking in 'food' and expelling 'waste,' a means for interpreting the complex genetic code and replicating it, etc., etc. The combined telecommunication systems of the world are far less complex, and yet no one believes they arose by chance."[51]

"Some scientists believe that the aggregate (schizocroal) eyes of some trilobites were the most sophisticated optical systems ever utilized by any organism," says Australian geologist Andrew Snelling. "The schizochroal eye is a compound eye, made up of many single lenses, each specifically designed to correct for spherical aberration, thus allowing the trilobites to see an undistorted image under water. The elegant physical design of trilobite eyes also employs Fermat's principle, Abbe's sine law, Snell's laws of refraction, and compensates for the optics of birefringent crystals."[52]

Biochemist Michael Behe addressed the topic of gradual evolution:

> Darwin knew that his theory of gradual evolution by natural selection carried a heavy burden: "If it could be demonstrated that any complex organ existed which could not possibly have been formed by numerous, successive, slight modifications, my theory would absolutely break down...."
>
> From Mivart's concern over the incipient stages of new structures to Margulis' dismissal of gradual evolution, critics of Darwin have suspected that his criterion of failure had been met. But how can we be confident? What type of biological system could not be formed by "numerous, successive, slight modifications"?
>
> Well, for starters, a system that is irreducibly complex. By *irreducibly complex* I mean a single system composed of several well-matched, interacting parts that contribute to the basic function, wherein the removal of any one of the parts causes the system to effectively cease functioning. An irreducibly complex system cannot be produced directly (that is, by continuously improving the initial function, which continues to work by the same mechanism) by slight, successive modifications of a precursor system, because any precursor to an irreducibly complex system that is missing a part is by definition nonfunctional.[53]

Behe critiques a paper by T. Cavalier-Smith, which appeared in 1978 in the journal *BioSystems:*

> The paper does not try to present a realistic, quantitative model for even one step in the development of a cilium in a cell line originally lacking that structure. Instead it paints a picture of what the author imagines must have been significant events along the way to a cilium. These imaginary steps are described in phrases such as "flagella [long cilia are frequently called 'flagella'] are so complex

> that their evolution must have involved many stages"; "I suggest that flagella initially need not have been motile, but were slender cell extensions"; "organisms would evolve with a great variety of axonemal structures"; and "it is likely that mechanisms of phototaxis [motion toward light] evolved simultaneously with flagella."
>
> The quotations give the flavor of the fuzzy word-pictures typical of evolutionary biology. The lack of quantitative details—a calculation or informed estimation based on a proposed intermediate structure of how much any particular change would have improved the active swimming ability of the organism—makes such a story utterly useless for understanding how a cilium truly might have evolved.[54]

Behe hits the nail on the head, calling the claims of evolutionary biology so many "fuzzy word-pictures." Straight talk from a hard-hitting chemist. Does it get any better? When one observes a bird in flight or notices the ease with which rain slides off a bird's feathers, one must admit that birds are indeed very good. It's fascinating how kestrels are so good at flying in bursts of speed followed by modulated dips and bobs, all part of God's design for them to handle the rigors of finding prey in bush-speckled desert regions.

Welsh mathematician Andrew McIntosh also thinks that birds are birds are birds. Imagine that! His analysis is detailed and rigorous:

> A feather is a marvel of lightweight engineering. Though light, it is very wind-resistant. This is because there is a clever system of barbs and barbules. Each barb of a feather is visible to the naked eye and comes off the main stem. What is not generally realized is that on either side of the barb are further tiny barbules which can only be seen under a microscope. These are of different types, depending on whether they are coming from one side of the barb or the other. On one side of the barb, ridged barbules will emerge, while on the other side, the barbules

will have hooks. Thus, the hooks coming out of one barb will connect with ridges reaching in the opposite direction from a neighboring barb. The hooks and ridges act like "velcro," but go one stage further, since the ridges allow a sliding joint, and there is thus an ingenious mechanism for keeping the surface flexible and yet intact.

The next time you see a flight feather on the ground, remember it is a marvel of lightweight, flexible, aerodynamic engineering…

Not until all the hook and ridge structure is in place is there any advantage, even as a vane for catching insects! Unless one invokes some "thinking ahead" planning, there is no way that chance mutations could produce the "idea" of the cross-linking of the barbules to make a connecting lattice. Even if the chance mutation of a ridge/hook occurs in two of the barbules, there is no mechanism for translating this "advantage" to the rest of the structure. This is a classic case of irreducible complexity which is not consistent with slow evolutionary changes, but quite consistent with the notion of design.

But that is not all. Even if one had the feather, the delicate lattice structure would soon become frayed, unless there was also oil to lubricate the sliding joint made by the hooked and ridged barbules. Most of us realize that once the barbs of a feather have been separated, it is difficult to make them come back together. The feather becomes easily frayed in the absence of oil, which a bird provides from its preening gland at the base of its spine. Some of this oil is put on its beak and spread throughout the feathers, which for a water bird also gives waterproofing of its surface (thus, water slides off a duck's back). Without the oil the feathers are useless, so even if a supposed land-dwelling dinosaur got as far as wafting a wing, it would be no use after a few hours!

As one might expect, however, the story does not end there either, for a bird can fly only because it also has an exceedingly light bone structure, which is achieved by the bones being hollow. Many birds maintain skeleton strength by cross members within the hollow bones. Such an arrangement began to be used in the middle of [the twentieth] century for aircraft wings and is termed the "Warren's truss arrangement." Large birds, such as an eagle or a vulture, would simply break into pieces in midair if there were some supposed halfway stage in their skeletal development where they had not yet "developed" such cross members in their bones.

Furthermore, birds breathe differently. The respiratory system of a bird enables oxygen to be fed straight into air sacs, which are connected directly to the heart, lungs, and stomach, bypassing the normal mammalian requirement to breathe out carbon dioxide first before the next intake of oxygen. Human beings breathe about 12 times a minute, whereas small birds can breathe up to about 250 times a minute. This is thus a perfect system for the high metabolic rate[s] of birds, which use up energy very quickly. In fast forward flight particularly, birds could not sustain exhaling against the oncoming airstream. Note also that birds are warm-blooded, which presents a vast biological hurdle for those who maintain a reptile ancestry for birds.

Consider the wing-flapping motion of a bird. This motion requires a bird to have strong wing muscles, with a forward-facing elbow joint to enable the foreshortening of the wing used much in the upward stroke of most species, and in the dive of birds of prey. The versatility of the swivel joint at the base of the wing, coupled with the elbow joint on the wing itself and the smooth feather structure overlaying all, leads to great flexibility in the aerodynamics of the wing. Lift and drag can be balanced with instant movements, which in aircraft still require comparatively cumbersome changes of flap and ailerons.

Suppose we have an "almost" bird with all the above structures—namely feathers, preening gland, hollow bones, direct respiration, warm blood, swivel joint, and forward-facing elbow joint—but no tail! Controlled flight would still be impossible. Longitudinal stability can only be achieved with a tail structure, which most small boys soon realize when making paper airplanes! But what possible advantage do all of the above have for any land-based "almost" bird?

Such a creature would be easy prey to any hunting animal. In the list of mechanisms (feathers, preening gland, etc.), all are essential. Attempt to drop one and the whole project fails! The tail is essential, and with the tail must come another muscle to operate the variable small, but all-important wing surface—for instance, holding the plumage spread out and downwards when coming in to land. In other words, the tail is no use as a static "add-on." It must have the means of altering its shape in flight. All these mechanisms are controlled by a nervous system connected to the on-board computer in the bird's brain, all pre-programmed to operate within a wide envelope of complicated aerodynamic maneuvers. ...

[Hummingbirds] have the ability to beat their wings at up to 80 beats per second and, as is well known, can hover, fly backwards, forwards, and sideways with ease. ... Speeds of 50 miles an hour are commonplace for these flying marvels. Fuel must be replenished very quickly because of the great turnover of energy. Consequently, the bird must feed on a food which can be broken down quickly into energy.

All this is achieved by feeding on the nectar of flowers, which requires the ability to hover and a thin long beak to get into the flower (e.g., a fuchsia for the rufous hummingbird). The bird also has a special tongue with two furrows, enabling the nectar to be stored on it. The long tongue goes in and out of the bill, at an unbelievable rate of 13 times per second and, when retracted, is curled up at the back of the head.

One can envisage the odd scenario of the supposedly half-evolved hummingbird either with the ability to hover and a sparrow beak, unable to feed, or the long beak but no ability to hover, which would mean flying into the flower with no ability to stop! All the requirements must be there to begin with.

The extreme maneuverability of hummingbirds is due to their having the ability to swivel the wing through a much greater angle than other birds. Consequently, the hummingbird can produce a power stroke on the upward motion of the wing as well as the downstroke, and the motion of the wing tip of a hummingbird in flight sweeps out a figure eight as the joint swivels round some 90 degrees first in one direction, and then about 90 degrees in the other direction. Further rotation is possible which means that the wing can thus beat a power stroke in any direction, with small asymmetries enabling sideways movements as well.

Flight cannot be explained by supposed evolutionary change. The attempts to find any transitional forms have all failed. *Archaeopteryx* has been shown to have fully developed flight feathers (thus, no half-bird). ... The evidence is overwhelming that birds have always been birds, and is entirely consistent with their being created right at the beginning on day 5, just as the Bible says.

It is not scientific to argue, on the one hand, for the obvious design of a Boeing 747, and then rule design "out of court" when considering the far more versatile flight of an eagle, falcon, or the remarkable hummingbird. Modern minds within the secular media are presenting an unscientific duality of thought when praising engineering complexity in man-made machines, but presenting the complexity in the world around us (of often far greater intricacy than man-made machines) as due to a gigantic unplanned cosmic experiment, with no Creator.[55]

Hummingbirds demonstrate the creationist principle of irreducible complexity. Their wingtips trace out a figure eight, making it possible for them to hover, and their long beaks are perfectly structured for extracting nectar from deep inside a flower—without both capabilities operating simultaneously, they would not be able to hover and extract as they do. They were created by the God of Jacob with both capabilities from the get-go, as ready-to-go hummingbirds. Hummingbirds are well known for reproducing and giving rise to other hummingbirds!

McIntosh is, I think, more than generous when he gives us the phrase "unscientific duality of thought" to describe the secular media's habit of going ape (pun intended) over man's devices and inventions while explaining away God's creation as a "gigantic unplanned cosmic experiment." One could say the secular media's prejudice against God's creation is unholy and irreverent, bringing stain on society and the land. Newsmagazines that gush over new innovations in bomber technology while relegating the wonders of long-distance whale communications to the realm of random happenstance (ie, evolution) do more than create a duality of thought; they push their readers further into the pit of despair that is selfishness and godlessness.

Bearing in mind the irreducibly complex nature of a bird's wing, we see another example of irreducible complexity from James Perloff:

> Blood clotting swings into action when we get cut. Its multi-step process utilizes numerous proteins, many with no other function besides clotting. Each protein depends on an enzyme to activate it. So which evolved first—the protein or the enzyme? Not the protein; it cannot function without the enzyme to switch it on. But why would the enzyme have come first?—without the protein, it serves no purpose. The system is irreducibly complex. ... Furthermore, after a clot forms, the proteins which produced it must be *in*activated by other substances—otherwise the rest of the person's blood would start to coagulate. Step-by-step evolution of clotting is inconceivable: in the trial and error stage, organisms would have either bled to death or clotted to death.[56]

Horticulturist Angela Meyer maintains that plants could not have come about by evolutionary chance because the sustaining factors in the life of a plant are so complex and interwoven. The key point is that the complex weave of sustaining factors is such that when you take away one there's no longer sustenance.

> "The extravagance of shape variation, color, and patterns of flowers is a clear expression of a divine artist."
> —Angela Meyer, Horticulturist

Meyer also relates the importance of divine artistry in the plant world:

> Controlling factors, such as temperature, day length, light quality, and various hormones, act upon the flowering process to different degrees, depending on the species, plant age, position, growing conditions, and season. The whole system is not at all well understood by us mere humans—although we attempt to modify and maximize the system to our benefit in horticulture. This is all so complex and so interdependent that these systems cannot have come about gradually by chance. All plant life systems must have been complete and operative at the same moment in time—on day 3. It is also significant that for pollination and seed distribution, many plant species need animals which were created on days 5 and 6. A thousand-year gap between the days would not provide for the survival of many plants. ... In addition, the extravagance of shape variation, color, and patterns of flowers is a clear expression of a divine artist.[57]

Careful consideration of a scant few of God's wondrous creations is sufficient to see the hand of God at work. Scott M. Huse points to the wonder contained in the unassuming sea slug, which is able to eat stinger-laden sea anemones:

> One of the most fascinating stories in nature is what the sea slug does with the poor anemone's stinging cells. The undigested cells are swept along through ciliated tubes that are connected to the stomach and end in pouches. The stinging cells are arranged and stored in these pouches to be used for the sea slug's defense! And so, whenever the sea slug is attacked, it defends itself using the stinging cells that the ill-fated anemone manufactured for its own protection.

> This incredible relationship completely defies evolutionary explanation. First of all, in order to prevent the stinging cells from exploding, the sea slug would have to evolve some sort of chemical means to temporarily neutralize them. The sea slug would also have to evolve a new digestive system, which would digest the tissues of the anemone but not the stinging cells. The sea slug would also have to cleverly evolve the sophisticated ciliated tubes and pouches as well as a highly complex mechanism for arranging, storing, and maintaining the stinging cells. Finally, and contrary to evolutionary expectations, the anemone would have to endorse the sea slug's plans by refraining from evolving countermeasures.[58]

Even plants and animals can be fast allies in God's wondrous design. Huse elaborates:

> Another fascinating relationship, which has been observed in nature, concerns the Bull's Horn Acacia tree of Central and South America. This tree is furnished with large hollow thorns that are inhabited by a species of ferocious stinging ants. Small bumps on the tree also supply food to the tree. The tree, for its part of the bargain, receives complete protection from all animal predators and plant competitors. The ants viciously attack any and all intruders. But the truly remarkable aspect of this symbiotic relationship is the fact that these ants are gardeners! They make regular raids in all directions from their home tree, nipping off every green shoot that dares to show its head near their tree. As a result, this particular tree always has plenty of sunlight and space, which is a rarity in the tropical jungle where the competition for such things is intense. Experiments have shown that when all of the ants are removed from one of these trees, the tree dies within two to fifteen months.[59]

Migratory instincts are beyond amazing in my book. In the late German summers, lesser white-throated warblers (parent birds, that is) take off for Africa, leaving their young behind. A few weeks later, the young lesser white-throated warblers take off and fly instinctively across thousands of miles over land and sea to rejoin their parents. This would seem, on the face of it, to speak of a programming of sorts that comes standard with the issuance of a new bird out of its mother's egg. Perhaps the bird aficionados can convene a meeting and rename these the *greater* white-throated warblers, as theirs is no mean feat.

> Either the plovers eat some special clovers or they're simply programmed, in a manner of speaking, to know how to find their summer spot and their winter spot.

Moreover, the golden plover flies about eight thousand miles from Hudson Bay to Argentina, traversing roughly two thousand miles over the sea. Either the plovers eat some special clovers or they're simply programmed, in a manner of speaking, to know how to find their summer spot and their winter spot.

Barn swallows fly nine thousand miles from northern Canada to Argentina, and arctic terns fly fourteen thousand miles every year to the opposite pole and back. It seems those terns are smooth as a rabbit's back and make all the right turns. As Huse points out, "The piecemeal development of such an instinct seems highly improbable because migratory instincts are useless unless perfect. Obviously, it is of no benefit to be able to navigate perfectly across only half an ocean."[60] Birds' direction-finding is clearly a miracle of God's creation.

Mutations

Mutations, despite all the hullabaloo surrounding them, are nasty—anything but the wondrous agents of positive change that evolutionists wish them to be. Even the conflicted evolutionist Theodosius Dobzhansky couldn't help but take pot shots at the central role mutations play in the evolutionist worldview: "[A] majority of mutations, both those arising in laboratories and those stored in natural populations, produce deteriorations of viability, hereditary diseases, and monstrosities. Such changes, it would seem, can hardly serve as evolutionary building blocks."[61]

Dr. Lee Spetner, who got his doctorate in physics from MIT, looked at the problems of evolutionist concepts of mutation in his book *Not by Chance! Shattering the Modern Theory of Evolution*. He put it this way: "But in all the reading I've done in the life-sciences literature, I've never found a mutation that added information. ... All point mutations that have been studied on the molecular level turn out to reduce the genetic information and not increase it."[62]

And Dr. A. E. Wilder-Smith noted the following in his book *The Natural Sciences Know Nothing of Evolution*: "If water is poured onto a text written in ink, this text will thus be modified or partly smudged; but never is fundamentally new information added to the text in this manner. The chemistry of *mutations* in the genetic code information has an effect similar to that of water on our text. Mutations modify or destroy already existing genetic information, but they never create new information. They never create, for example, an entirely new biological organ such as an eye or ear."[63]

Biochemist Ernst Chain shared a Nobel Prize for his work on penicillin, and he was moved to offer this regarding the process of mutation:

> To postulate, as the positivists of the end of the [nineteenth] century and their followers here have done, that the development and survival of the fittest is *entirely* a consequence of chance mutations, or even that nature carries out experiments by trial and error through mutations in order to create living systems better fitted to survive, seems to me a hypothesis based on no evidence and irreconcilable with the facts. ... These classical evolutionary theories are a gross oversimplification of an immensely complex and intricate mass of facts, and it amazes me that they were swallowed so uncritically and readily, and for such a long time, by so many scientists without a murmur of protest."[64]

Trumpeter swans in flight. Need I say more? The next time someone calls you a birdbrain, the appropriate response would be, "Why, thank you." The swans make man's best flying machines look like child's play. They are well built for the ground, water, and air; masters of paddling, waddling, and their specialty—flying. In the complete absence of salamander-swan hybrids, it appears that swans come from other swans, and before that, God's hand. The Salamander-Swan School of Flight has not gotten off the ground and, in the absence of intermediate forms, the swans have been cleared to fly as God's creatures, as swans from the hand of the God of Israel. Hallelujah!

Perloff also offers a nice synopsis of mutations:

> [I]f life began as a single cell, then the entire living world around us resulted from mutations. This explanation faces serious difficulties, however. Mutations are almost universally *harmful*. In human beings, they are classed as "birth defects." They often result in death or sterility. People today suffer from more than 4,000 disorders caused by gene mutations. Down's syndrome, cystic fibrosis and sickle cell anemia are familiar examples...
>
> Rarely, babies are born with congenital heart disorders, making blood shunt to the wrong place. There is no known case of mutations improving circulation. Hemoglobin—the blood's oxygen-carrying component—has over forty mutant variants. Not one transports oxygen as well as normal hemoglobin.
>
> To accept evolution, we must believe that human blood circulation—a wonder of engineering—was actually *constructed* by chance mutations, when actual observation demonstrates they do nothing but damage it. [To accept evolution,] we must believe that mutations built the human brain and every other feature of life on Earth.[65]

Reproduction After Kinds

Each part of creation has its own scope of variegating leeway beyond which it does not go. That's why there are pink flamingos but no purple flamingos, brown bears but no pink bear,

"I have roses that bloom pretty steadily for six months in the year, but I have none that will bloom twelve, and I will not have. In short, there are limits to the development possible...."
—Luther Burbank, Plant Breeder

and zebras with black-and-white striped coats but no zebras with black parallelograms against a yellow background.

Luther Burbank, a famous American plant breeder, put it thusly:

> I know from my experience that I can develop a plum half an inch long or one two-and-a-half inches long, with every possible length in between, but I am willing to admit that it is hopeless to try to get a plum the size of a small pea, or one as big as a grapefruit. ... I have roses that bloom pretty steadily for six months in the year, but I have none that will bloom twelve, and I will not have. In short, there are limits to the development possible, and these limits follow a law. ... Plants and animals all tend to revert, in successive generations, toward a given mean or average.[66]

Interestingly, when fruit flies were bred so that the number of bristles on their bodies went well above or well below the normal number, they became sterile—there are limits for variation. As Perloff says, "Breeders of dogs and horses have isolated animals with traits they thought desirable. This has given rise to new varieties, but not species. In nature's parallel, a few animals sometimes become geographically isolated. The population they sire inherits their particular genes and thus their characteristics. That is essentially what happened to Darwin's finches—after becoming sequestered on islands, they individuated from other finches, but no 'new species' emerged."[67]

Creation scientist Walter Lammerts became known as the "Father of Modern Rose Breeding," owing to his having produced such scintillating rose varieties as the Charlotte Armstrong and Queen Elizabeth. Botanist George Howe underlines the importance of Lammerts' spiritual orientation in pioneering new varieties: "Many of Lammerts' horticultural colleagues believed in gradual evolution, involving long spans of time. But as a creationist Lammerts assumed that whatever variation is possible will occur in the present and rapidly. It was to this underlying supposition that he attributed his achievements in plant breeding. His evolution-minded friends felt there was little chance of effecting any immediate change. Ironically, it was Lammerts, the creationist, who proceeded to find those changes and to use them in developing new roses!"[68]

Let's see how the Bible puts it in Gen. 1:

> Then God said, "Let the land produce vegetation: seed-bearing plants and trees on the land that bear fruit with seed in it, according to their various kinds." And it was so. The land produced vegetation: plants bearing seed according to their kinds and trees bearing fruit with seed in it according to their kinds. And God saw that it was good. And there was evening, and there was morning—the third day. ...
>
> And God said, "Let the water teem with living creatures, and let birds fly above the earth across the expanse of the sky." So God created the great creatures of the sea and every living and moving thing with which the water teems, according to their kinds, and every winged bird according to its kind.
>
> And God saw that it was good. God blessed them and said, "Be fruitful and increase in number and fill the water in the seas, and let the birds increase on the earth." And there was evening, and there was morning—the fifth day.
>
> And God said, "Let the land produce living creatures according to their kinds: livestock, creatures that move along the ground, and wild animals, each according to its kind." And it was so. God made the wild animals according to their kinds, the livestock according to their kinds, and all the creatures that move along the ground according to their kinds. And God saw that it was good.
>
> Then God said, "Let us make man in our image, in our likeness, and let them rule over the fish of the sea and the birds of the air, over the livestock, over all the earth, and over all the creatures that move along the ground."

> So God created man in his own image, in the image of God he created him; male and female he created them. God blessed them and said to them, "Be fruitful and increase in number; fill the earth and subdue it. Rule over the fish of the sea and the birds of the air and over every living creature that moves on the ground."
>
> Then God said, "I give you every seed-bearing plant on the face of the whole earth and every tree that has fruit with seed in it. They will be yours for food. And to all the beasts of the earth and all the birds of the air and all the creatures that move on the ground—everything that has the breath of life in it—I give every green plant for food." And it was so. God saw all that he had made, and it was very good. And there was evening, and there was morning—the sixth day.[69] (NIV)

Evolutionists search in desperation for some proof of their godless and terrible theory yet they will be thwarted. God's creatures reproduce after their kinds, and that's that. My own view of chimps, gorillas, and other primates is pretty straightforward: they interest me in much the same way other parts of God's creation do. That is to say, I'm awed by the strength of their hands and arms, and when it comes to the strength in the back of a gorilla—forget about it. The frenzied whooping of chimps is intriguing; the sidling gait of gorillas is interesting to watch; and the climbing and swinging abilities of some of the smaller primates are simply captivating and enthralling. They're powerful, beautiful, and complex, yet I don't see a long lost great-great-gran'pappy when I look into their eyes.

As Jack Cuozzo says in his essay "The Fire Builders":

> Faith in God's love has been buried with artifacts taken out of graves and subsequently filed away deep within museum cabinets, never to be shown to the public. It has been washed away by scrub brushes scouring red-ochre from Neanderthal remains so they wouldn't reveal contemporaneity with more modern bones. It has been molded away by artificial plastic or plaster replacement of

> bone that is not faithful to the dimensions of the original specimen. ... Once chemical and biological evolution is taken for granted, the unmistakable message from human paleontology is that many animals had to die so that men and women could live. Natural selection, which is the agent of death ... has been the scalpel blade that has carved mankind out of the rough substance of its animal predecessors. Presumably, many apes and hominids died so men and women could eventually have physical life as humans. Therefore, it is my belief that this ... paleontological gospel ... has been offered to mankind to detract from the clear message of the Bible; that is, Christ had to die so that men and women can live. He died and rose again so that we can have eternal spiritual life and at the pinnacle of our existence, eternal physical life in the resurrection."[70]

Clearly, humanistic attempts to doctor up bone finds so they look more like imaginary ape-men has been one of the stains on evolutionary practices. But evolutionists have shown a willingness to paint imaginary transitional forms between any number of plants and animals based on less than scanty evidence. In the May 1999 *National Geographic* article "From Fins to Feet," writer Kerri Westenberg struggles to present a picture of how ancient fish developed feet and climbed toward shore, if not onto the shore. In the process, Westenberg shows how she has been sucked into the baseless construct of evolutionism.

Westenberg's evolution-friendly portrayal of footprints on a shoreline on Valentia Island, Ireland, supposes that the prints are evidence of some kind of a proto-salamander or fish-salamander or whatever. Keeping in mind that "tetrapod" is a wiggly and wishy-washy word that is defined in *The American Heritage Dictionary of the English Language* as a creature with four feet, four legs, or four leg-like appendages, Westenberg states: "[The] dearth of fossils has long frustrated specialists because tetrapods supposedly made one of the greatest breakthroughs in the history of life on Earth, one that made possible the evolution of humans. By developing those four limbs they became the first large animals able to crawl out of the water, where life first evolved, onto dry land. ... I try to imagine what this animal would have looked like, but I conjure up only an unclear image of a fish with limbs. The creature left no bones, only clues that could be deduced from the tracks."[71]

First of all, there's not a dearth of fossils. There are millions of fossils crowding natural museums worldwide, and evolutionists like to use the ruse of "not enough fossils" to cover for all their bad science and lack of transitional forms. Westenberg wants us to believe that this is a breakthrough, yet even she unwittingly reveals her lack of assurance when she says, "I try to imagine what this animal would have looked like, but I conjure up only an unclear image."[72]

Continuing with her uncritical portrayal of the alleged land-discovering tetrapods, Westenberg creates a picture of many specialists agreeing on a scenario for how tetrapods could have approached land: "[Hans Christian Bjerring] thinks that [a certain tetrapod] evolved in swamps clogged with water plants. 'It isn't easy to swim around thick vegetation,' he explains. Fins became limbs, he maintains, because they made it easier to maneuver through the swampy mire. In fact, he doubts that [said tetrapod] ever actually stepped foot on land. Many specialists now agree."[73] That's about as convincing as saying a skier's feet became skis because the skis made it easier to maneuver on the slopes.

To me, theories about fish becoming swamp capable, and eventually land capable, are a crock. "If I could find even a toe of a tetrapod," Westenberg says, "my mind's eye could turn it into a salamander-like creature the size of a crocodile, a predator lurking in those woods."[74] Ah, yes, her mind's eye! Where have we heard such imagination-laden ruminations before? Her comment is eerily reminiscent of the Nebraska Man find, in which desperate paleontologists wanted

> "[W]e find no trace of any animal forms which are intermediate between the various major groups or phyla.... If we are willing to accept the facts we must believe that there never were such intermediates, or in other words that these major groups have from the very first borne the same relation to each other that they bear today."
> —Austin H. Clark, Zoologist, Smithsonian Institution

the world to believe that a tooth—what turned out to be a pig's tooth—could be interpreted and finally painted into an ape-man.

After witnessing how New Jersey police officer Del Szatmary could go to Red Hill, Pennsylvania, look at markings on a rock, and see in them important new evidence for the supposed evolution of arachnids (e.g., spiders, scorpions), Westenberg was moved to pronounce this veritable evolutionary rhapsody: "By now I can walk a site like Red Hill and see a piece of a tree and imagine a Devonian forest there. I have no trouble envisioning Szatmary's arachnid poised on the foliage of that forest."[75]

The General Sherman Tree (a giant sequoia) in California's Sequoia National Park. God's eternal power and Godhead can be clearly seen by the things He has made (Rom. 1:20). This tree is amazing—even more amazing is the one who made it. "For by Him all things were created, *both* in the heavens and on earth, visible and invisible, whether thrones or dominions or rulers or authorities—all things have been created through Him and for Him. He is before all things, and in Him all things hold together" (Col. 1:16–17 NASB).

Summing up her foray into the imaginary adventures of evolutionism, Westenberg offers this: "I have learned that limbs probably evolved for something totally different than what we, descendents of tetrapods, use them for. But that's how evolution works. Something evolves that solves one problem and opens up a world of new possibilities."[76]

Coming back to earth, we should consider the words of Professor N. Heribert-Nilsson of Lund University in Sweden who has studied the subject of evolution for more than forty years: "The fossil material is now so complete that the lack of transitional series cannot be explained by the scarcity of the material. The deficiencies are real, they will never be filled."[77]

Austin H. Clark, the famous zoologist of the Smithsonian Institution, has popped the illusion of transitional forms this way:

> The complete absence of any intermediate forms between the major groups of animals, which is one of the most striking and most significant phenomena brought out by the study of zoology, has hitherto been overlooked, or at least ignored. ... [W]e find no trace of any animal forms which are intermediate between the various major groups or phyla. ... If we are willing to accept the facts we must believe that there never were such intermediates, or in other words that these major groups have from the very first borne the same relation to each other that they bear today.[78]

Theistic Evolution a Sham

The Holy Bible is not a vehicle for the theory of evolution. Indeed, so-called theistic evolution is untenable. Scott M. Huse elaborates:

> Theistic evolutionists claim to believe in God and the Bible, while at the same time maintaining that all life has evolved from inorganic chemicals. But in adopting this unholy alliance, theistic evolutionists are forced to depart from, contradict, and compromise numerous biblical essentials. ... Simply stated, the theory of biological evolution asserts that

nonliving matter somehow gave rise to simple living organisms that subsequently reproduced and diversified, generating all life-forms. According to this belief, all bacteria, plants, animals, and humans have arisen by mere chance from a single, remote ancestor that somehow came into existence. All of this is supposed to have occurred accidentally without the benefit of any intelligence or planning. The basic premise of this "molecule-to-man" theory is that hydrogen gas, given enough time, will eventually turn into people. Diametrically opposed to this viewpoint, biblical creationism postulates an initial special creation by God through which all the laws, processes, and entities of nature were brought into existence as described in the Book of Genesis.[79]

The fable of evolution is incompatible with the Bible. In the Bible, the world was created in six days, whereas evolutionists claim the world evolved over many eons. In the Bible, life first appears on land, whereas evolutionists claim life began in the oceans. In the Bible, there are fixed and distinct kinds, whereas evolutionists claim life-forms are continually morphing into different kinds. And in the Bible, man's body originated from the dust of the earth, whereas, according to evolution, man derived from monkeys and a bunch of other organisms. Evolution is a sham. Yeshua (Jesus) is the Word; the Rock of Salvation; the Way, the Truth, and the Life; and the Creator.

CHAPTER THREE

AMERICA'S SOCIAL DECLINE

Righteousness exalteth a nation: but sin is *a reproach to any people (Prov. 14:34 KJV).*

There is a way that seemeth right unto a man, but the end thereof are the ways of death (Prov. 16:25 KJV).

Pride goeth *before destruction, and a haughty spirit before a fall (Prov. 16:18 KJV).*

Were not the Ethiopians and the Lubim an immense army with very many chariots and horsemen? Yet because you relied on the Lord, He delivered them into your hand. For the eyes of the Lord move to and fro throughout the earth that He may strongly support those whose heart is completely His. You have acted foolishly in this. Indeed, from now on you will surely have wars (2 Chron. 16:8–9 NASB).

Modern-day America is in free fall. Diversity reigns supreme, and there's little sense of a social core anymore—and without a social core, there can be no nationalism. Spiritually, the any-god-will-do crowd has swelled in size and become militant, champing for any chance to feign being offended in order to diminish the profile and influence of Christianity throughout the land.

As people have flirted with atheism, pantheism, and interfaithism, the level of sobriety and decency has gone down. Taking care of the poor and needy is often not a top priority for the atheist—he has his nice house and that's as it should be, or so he thinks. Families spend very little time together anymore—the nuclear family sort of disappears after the kids grow up and take jobs.

Many materialistic family members look down on struggling family members, leaving them in shanties, beat-up campers, or homeless. Where is the fabric? And whatever happened to the extended family? Cousins and aunts and uncles may as well be Martians given the amount of interest that is paid to them.

Filling the void once occupied by church, family gatherings, and nationalism are glamorized sports, lascivious and anti-American TV programming, and a deep malaise that stems from kowtowing to too many foreign dictatorships and ignoring our very own Judeo-Christian heritage and US Constitution.

Much Was Better in the Old America

Social commentator Os Guinness has noted that "our Puritan forebears ... [were] perhaps the most literate people in the history of the world, [and] they gained their ideas and shaped their tough-minded thinking from one chief source—the sermon. Historian Harry Stout of Yale University estimates that the average New Englander heard seven thousand sermons in a lifetime—about fifteen thousand hours of concentrated listening."[1] And sure enough, when we look to the old founding fathers for instruction, we find there is plenty there for edification.

A lawyer and the first chief justice of the United States, John Jay was unabashed in his description, in 1824, of the strong Christian influence in the United States:

> A zeal unknown to many preceding ages has recently pervaded almost every Christian country, and occasioned the establishment of institutions well calculated to diffuse the knowledge and impress the precepts of the gospel both at home and abroad. The number and diversity of these institutions, their concurrent tendency to promote these purposes, and the multitudes who are cordially giving them aid and support, are so extraordinary, and so little analogous to the dictates of human propensities and passions, that no adequate cause can be assigned for them

> but the goodness, wisdom, and will of HIM who made and governs the world.
>
> We have reason to rejoice that such institutions have been so greatly multiplied and cherished in the United States; especially as a kind Providence has blessed us, not only with peace and plenty, but also with the full and secure enjoyment of our civil and religious rights and privileges. Let us, therefore, persevere in our endeavors to promote the operation of these institutions. ... Their unexampled rise, progress and success in giving light to the heathen, and in rendering Christians more and more "obedient to the faith," apprise us that the great Captain of our salvation is going forth, "conquering and to conquer" and is directing and employing these means and measures for that important purpose.[2]

Jay did not pull any punches. His reference to the heathen would seem to point to those unsaved non-Christian peoples with whom the Puritans came into contact. As bearers of the Gospel, Jay and company endeavored to bring the light of the Word of God to people generally, and for that his modern-day countrymen ought to be grateful.

Jay was four-square behind the establishment of institutions calculated to spread the gospel both in the United States and abroad. His clear and courageous writings drew a distinction between light and darkness, between a saving knowledge of the gospel of Jesus Christ and the wicked ways of darkness. By Jay's reckoning, the bubbling up of many pro-gospel institutions in the early days of the United States was a sure sign of God's hand—indeed, providence—at work. In fact, so sure was Jay of the Bible's importance that he declared that "except the Bible there is not a true history in the world."[3] How refreshing are the words of these founding fathers who exuded boldness and didn't suffer from the disease of *political correctness* (a socialist code phrase for those who would trample America's Biblical heritage in the name of diversity).

Jay puts the lie to the mythology that has encumbered mankind throughout its development. Playing the part of apologist, he notes that myth, fable, and idolatry are ultimately incapable of rendering man knowledgeable about his present state and future destiny:

> After the astonishing catastrophe at Babel, men naturally divided into different associations, according to their languages; and migrating into various regions, multiplied into distinct nations. Tradition, doubtless, still continued to transmit these great truths from generation to generation; but the diminution of longevity, together with the defects and casualties incident to tradition, gradually rendered it less and less accurate. These important truths thus became, in process of time, disfigured, obscure, and disregarded. Custom and usage continued the practice of sacrifices, but the design of their institution ceased to be remembered. Men "sought out many inventions" and true religion was supplanted by fables and idolatrous rites. Their mythology manifests the inability of *mere* human reason, even when combined with the learning of Egypt, and the philosophy of Greece and Rome, to acquire the knowledge of our actual state and future destiny, and of the conduct proper to be observed in relation to both.[4]

Like Jay, Benjamin Rush, a signer of the Declaration of Independence and the first founding father to call for free public education, also had little patience for myths, fables, and idols in the schoolhouse: "The only foundation for a useful education in a republic is to be laid in religion. Without this, there can be no virtue, and without virtue there can be no liberty. The only means of

> "The only foundation for a useful education in a republic is to be laid in religion. Without this, there can be no virtue, and without virtue there can be no liberty. The only means of establishing and perpetuating our republican forms of government ... is the universal education of our youth in the principles of Christianity by means of the Bible...."
> —Benjamin Rush, Founding Father

establishing and perpetuating our republican forms of government … is the universal education of our youth in the principles of Christianity by means of the Bible; for this divine book above all others favors … respect for just laws. Without religion, I believe that learning does real mischief to the morals and principles of mankind."[5]

Rush was inclined to think that an unbiblical education would do mischief to the morals and principles of mankind. Any cursory look at the current American education system shows that Rush was downright prescient: the chic, antiwhite ethnic studies have for decades rendered college graduates increasingly ignorant of the broad sweep of US history and increasingly vulnerable to foreign sabotage; the abortion advocates have made our society brutal and idolatrous; the interfaith gurus have cowed some Christians into relativistic psychobabble; the fornication lobby has done terrible damage; filth and perversion and horror of unspeakable proportions have swamped our televisions, movie screens, radio airwaves, books, magazines, and newspapers, while effete men and puffed-up feminists try to justify perversion in the name of free speech; and opponents of Christianity have been systematically tearing down sections of the Christian quilt that once made America strong.

> "And the more I know of the circumstances of America, I am sorry to say it, the more reason I find to be apprehensive of Popery. Bless me! Could our ancestors look out of their graves and see so many of their own sons, decked with the worst of foreign superfluities, the ornaments of the whore of Babylon, how would it break their sacred Repose!"
> —Samuel Adams (1768), Boston Tea Party Organizer

The honorable Samuel Adams played a pivotal role in galvanizing support for the Boston Tea Party and for the break with Britain that the Tea Party so vividly implied. He also had little patience for the compromising ways of Catholicism, as he noted in 1768:

> And the more I know of the circumstances of America, I am sorry to say it, the more reason I find to be apprehensive of Popery. Bless me! Could our ancestors look out of their

> graves and see so many of their own sons, decked with the worst of foreign superfluities, the ornaments of the whore of Babylon, how would it break their sacred Repose! But amidst my gloomy apprehensions, it is a consolation to me to observe, that some of our towns, maintain their integrity, and show a laudable zeal against Popery. To do honor to those towns as much as in my power, I intend to publish a list of them.[6]

Adams wanted to protect the settlers against the predations of popery, against the devious ornamentation of the Great Whore of Babylon. It seems Adams understood that Revelation 17, with its description of the Great Whore of Babylon, stands as a warning against the spiritual whoredom of the Roman Catholic Church. (The identity of the Roman Catholic Church as the Great Whore of Babylon is well demonstrated in Dave Hunt's book *A Woman Rides the Beast*.) In effect, Adams cared deeply about protecting settlers from bad doctrine such as that in the Roman Catholic Church, and he also cared enough about the goal of making a clean start of it in this new land that he saw fit to break away from British designs. Adams strove for sensible alliances and good doctrine.

Jay took a more oblique approach to the matter of maintaining good doctrine. Nevertheless, in 1823, he oozed wariness about Catholic control and positively brimmed with a zeal for spreading the gospel:

> Our Redeemer having directed that the Gospel should be preached throughout the world, it was preached accordingly; and being witnessed from on high, "with signs and wonders, and with divers[e] miracles and gifts of the Holy Ghost," it became preponderant, and triumphant, and effulgent. But this state of exaltation, for reasons unknown to us, was suffered to undergo a temporary depression. A subsequent period [of Roman Catholic control] arrived, when the pure doctrines of the Gospel were so alloyed by admixtures, and obscured by appendages, that its luster gradually diminished, and like the fine gold mentioned by the prophet, it became dim.

Since the Reformation, artifice and error have been losing their influence on ignorance and credulity, and the Gospel has been resuming its purity. We now see Christians, in different countries, and of different denominations, spontaneously and cordially engaged in conveying the Scriptures, and the knowledge of salvation, to the heathen inhabitants of distant regions. So singular, impressive, and efficient is the impulse which actuates them, that without the least prospect of earthly retribution [compensation], they cheerfully submit to such pecuniary contributions, such approbations of time and industry, and, in many instances, to such hazards and privations, and such derelictions of personal comfort and convenience, as are in direct opposition to the propensities of human nature.[7]

Noah Webster, a founding father and early American educator, laid out in explicit terms in 1836 the importance of Christianity to both education and government at large:

"The opinion that human reason, left without the constant control of divine laws and commands, will preserve a just administration, secure freedom and other rights, restrain men from violations of laws and constitutions, and give duration to a popular government, is as chimerical [unlikely] as the most extravagant ideas that enter the head of a maniac...."

—Noah Webster (1836), Early American Educator

In my view, the Christian religion is the most important and one of the first things in which all children, under a free government, ought to be instructed. ... No truth is more evident to my mind than that the Christian religion must be the basis of any government intended to secure the rights and privileges of a free people. The opinion that human reason, left without the constant control of divine laws and commands, will preserve a just administration, secure freedom and other rights, restrain men from violations of laws and constitutions, and give duration to a popular government, is as chimerical [unlikely] as the most extravagant ideas that enter the head of a maniac...[8]

Webster's notion has been proved amply: without a proper reverence for the Christian faith, government will produce tyranny.

Legal precedents have left a clear trail of America's Christian upbringing. *Charleston v Benjamin* established in 1846 that "Christianity has reference to the principles of right and wrong. ... It is the foundation of those morals and manners upon which our society is formed; it is their basis. Remove this and they would fall. ... [Morality] has grown upon the basis of Christianity. ... The day of moral virtue in which we live would, in an instant, if that standard were abolished, lapse into the dark and murky night of pagan immorality."[9] *People v Ruggles* established in 1811 that "the morality of the country is deeply [reliant] upon Christianity. ... [We are] people whose manners ... and whose morals have been elevated and inspired ... by means of the Christian religion."[10]

Old America Was Blessed for its Christian Aims

Again, we turn to John Jay for insight into the early impulses and conditions among the white settlers. In essence, Jay's point is that preaching the gospel to those in darkness is good, and to be sure, he and his cohorts were very much involved in that pursuit:

> We know that a great proportion of mankind are ignorant of the revealed will of God, and that they have strong claims to the sympathy and compassion which we, who are favored with it, feel and are manifesting for them. To the most sagacious among the heathen it must appear wonderful and inexplicable that such a vicious, suffering being as man should have proceeded in such a condition from the hands of his Creator. Having obscure and confused ideas of a future state, and unable to ascertain how far justice may yield to mercy or mercy to justice,

they live and die (as our heathen ancestors did) involved in darkness and perplexities.

By conveying the Bible to people thus circumstanced we certainly do them a most interesting act of kindness. We thereby enable them to learn, that man was originally created and placed in a state of happiness, but, becoming disobedient, was subjected to the degradation and evils which he and his posterity have since experienced. The Bible will also inform them, that our gracious Creator has provided for us a Redeemer, in whom all the nations of the earth should be blessed—that this Redeemer has made atonement "for the sins of the world," and thereby reconciling the Divine justice with the Divine mercy, has opened a way for our redemption and salvation; and that these inestimable benefits are of the free gift and grace of God, not of our deserving, nor in our power to deserve. The Bible will also animate them with many explicit and consoling assurances of the Divine mercy to our fallen race, and with repeated invitations to accept the offers of pardon and reconciliation.[11]

Coming here to this new land took immense courage, faith, and stamina on the part of the settlers from Europe. There was plenty of room to share land and resources had the whites and the Indians acted with goodwill in spite of their natural wariness and fear of one another. As for slavery—another stick used by the self-serving liberal elites and multiculturalists to try to disenfranchise Americans of their good heritage—Jay wrote the following in 1822:

> Throughout many generations there have been professing Christians, who, under the countenance and authority of their respective governments, treated the heathen inhabitants of certain countries in Africa as articles of commerce; taking and transporting multitudes of them, like beasts of burden, to distant regions; to be sold, and to toil and die in slavery. During the continuance of such

Testing the Spirits

a traffic, with what consistence, grace, or prospect of success, could such Christians send missionaries to present the Bible, or preach the Christian doctrines of brotherly kindness and charity to the people of those countries? ... It will be recollected that many influential individuals deeply interested in the slave-trade, together with others who believed its continuance to be indispensable to the prosperity of the British West India Islands, made strenuous opposition to its abolition, even in the British parliament. Delays were caused by it, but considerations of a higher class than those which excited the opposition finally prevailed, and the parliament abolished that detestable trade. Well-merited honor was thereby reflected on the Legislature; and particularly on that excellent and celebrated member of it, whose pious zeal and unwearied perseverance were greatly and conspicuously instrumental to the other nations who are in a similar predicament, and must tend to encourage them to proceed and act in like manner. ... Let us therefore persevere steadfastly in distributing the Scriptures far and near, and without note or comment. We are assured that they "are profitable for doctrine, for reproof, for correction, for instruction in righteousness."[12]

Jay all too clearly was an abolitionist and sought to rid the American scene of slavery. And true to his convictions, he remained exuberant about the possibilities for spreading the gospel of Jesus Christ.

A Turning Point

One of the factors leading to Rome's ruination was a general coarsening of Roman society, a moral laziness and fatuousness that led to corruption and weakness. Samuel Adams, for one, viewed the matter of Biblical virtue as pivotal in the destiny of a nation, as he stated in 1776:

Revelation assures us that "Righteousness exalteth a nation"—Communities are dealt with in this world by the wise and just Ruler of the Universe. He rewards or punishes them according to their general character. The diminution of public virtue is usually attended with that of public happiness, and the public liberty will not long survive the total extinction of morals. "The Roman Empire," says the historian, "*must* have sunk, though the Goths had not invaded it. Why? Because the Roman virtue was sunk." Could I be assured that America would remain virtuous, I would venture to defy the utmost efforts of enemies to subjugate her.[13]

In a similar vein, John Jay noted in 1825 that Christian countries were lowered and debased by the artful designs of unholy souls to pull people away from Scripture and into a secular haze:

It is to be regretted that comments of a very [impious] character and description have caused errors to germinate and take root in Christian countries. Some of these were fabricated by individuals, who, finding that they could not carry their favorite propensities and habits with them through the "narrow way" prescribed by the Gospel, endeavored to discredit Christianity by objections which exhibit stronger marks of disingenuous, than of correct and candid reasoning. By artfully and diligently encouraging defection from Scripture, and from Scripture doctrines, they gradually introduced and spread that contempt for both, which in the last century was publicly displayed in impious acts of profaneness and in dreadful deeds of ferocity.[14]

Those who pulled people away from Scripture did so because they were protecting selfish "propensities and habits" that were at odds with Scripture. In the book *Pale Blue Dot,* astronomer Carl Sagan argues that the earth is just another pale blue dot in the innumerable galaxies that make up the universe, in effect denying the specialness of our planet under God's merciful design. Such selfish, pseudo-scientific thinking has broken many intellectual foundations in academia, and the results are disastrous. Nowadays, we see evolutionists, homosexuals, abortionists, and fornicators using disingenuous arguments in an attempt to discredit the supremacy of Scripture so that they may proceed blithely in the pursuit of their abominable propensities and habits—indeed, habits such as viewing man as a relative of apes and abalones, viewing the earth as an accidental speck in the universe, mocking holy matrimony, condoning fornication, killing babies, etc.

Our founding fathers saw the importance of Biblical virtue and training for the guidance of these United States. Pride goes before destruction (Prov. 16:18). Pride says we're great, when in fact it is the God of Abraham, Isaac, and Jacob who is great. Pride says that we are the masters of our own destinies because we invented the Ford Mustang and the Dodge Viper and the computer and the Internet, when in fact it is the God of the Bible who gives us strength and wisdom, and yea, the very marrow and blood and water that are necessary for life itself. Pride says that we're big and safe, protected by oceans and land borders that contain benign neighbors, when in fact our borders are being violated by Chinese hackers and saboteurs, Chinese spies, Chinese criminal gangs, Chinese surveillance networks, Muslim terrorists, Roman Catholic instigators, Mexican *La Raza* invaders and, undoubtedly, Communist-UN forces.

Perhaps nobody can say exactly when the tide turned in America. My simple sense of it is that when there's a pandemic effect of godless and unrepentant behavior in a country, there is a serious consequence awaiting that country. One barometer of the weakening of the American people would be affluence and consumerism. Robert Bork, author of *Slouching Towards Gomorrah: Modern Liberalism and American Decline,* noted that after the 1940s affluence has made its home in America and that in its train has come sensual boredom. "Affluence brings with it boredom," Bork says. "Of itself, it offers little but the ability to consume, and a life centered on consumption will appear, and be, devoid of meaning. Persons so afflicted will seek sensation as a palliative, and that today's culture offers in abundance. ... Technology and its entrepreneurs supplied the demand with motion pictures, radio, television, and videocassettes, all increasingly featuring sex and violence. Sensations must be steadily intensified if boredom is to be kept at bay."[16] Wanton sex and violence steadily increased as people strove to keep boredom at bay—I'd say that well summarizes much of the recent "advance" on the American scene.

Krishna, one of many false gods. The Satanic hand sign shown by Krishna is consistent with the horned Goat of Mendes, an occult favorite, as well as Molech, which is a horned god alternately represented as an owl and as a horned bull's head atop a man's body. "The embrace that smothers" is an embracing of every foul thing that floats by—indeed, in the 1960s, American society was primed by tear-it-all-down-man social anarchy, hallucinogenic drugs, rampant fornication, Satanic rock-and-roll lyrics, New Age philosophies, and flirtation with Communism. Let's remember Paul's admonitions so that we would not fall prey to the wiles of the enemy: "But I am afraid that, as the serpent deceived Eve by his craftiness, your minds will be led astray from the simplicity and purity *of devotion* to Christ. ... No wonder, for even Satan disguises himself as an angel of light" (2 Cor. 11:3, 14 NASB).

It seems there's just no decency anymore. At the 45th Annual Grammy Awards in February 2003, No Doubt singer Gwen Stefani shook her fanny around, this way and that, while the backup singers behind her did pelvic thrusts in unison. To say the music was sexualized would be an understatement: it would be more accurate to say the sexual motions were set to music.

At the same Grammy Awards, Eminem rapped about losing yourself in the music, and as he sang, his hand kept returning to his crotch area. For his efforts, he got a standing ovation from much of the audience.

Those two acts featured pelvic thrusts and crotch grabs, all with the full approbation of the television czars. The suggestion of sex is almost ubiquitous in American society, and violence in the media is a stench that seems to fill the nostrils only to double back and fill the nostrils again. And into this nauseating and shameful mix is inserted many film producers' blasphemous habit of using the Lord's name in vain.

The proliferation of sin in America should make Americans tremble. As a people, we need to call each other to task and condemn such exuberant orgies of filth, horror, and vacuous self-obsession. Bork says:

> A culture obsessed with technology will come to value personal convenience above almost all else, and ours does. … Among [the] consequences … is impatience with anything that interferes with personal convenience. Religion, morality, and law do that, which accounts for the tendency of modern religion to eschew proscriptions and commandments and turn to counseling and therapeutic sermons; of morality to be relativized; and of law, particularly criminal law, to become soft and uncertain. Religion tends to be strongest when life is hard, and the same may be said of morality and law. A person whose main difficulty is not crop failure but video breakdown has less need of the consolations and promises of religion."[17]

For many, morality has become passé, and personal feelings are paramount in the "search for meaning." Psychological mush and wafty therapy sessions are substituted for Bible-based history, Bible prophecy, and the power of God's Word.

One barometer would describe the transition point as the development of affluence in the late 1940s and onward. Another angle of consideration could put the transition point at the period between the wars in Korea and Vietnam, that is to say, during the late 1950s and early 1960s. If American boys were proud to be Americans in the Korea conflict, they were disillusioned during the Vietnam War. In Bork's words:

> American youth went willingly, if not gladly, to Korea, while they demonstrated against Vietnam, marched on the Pentagon, threw blood on draft records, fled to Canada and Sweden, and denounced "Amerika." Something in our culture, or at least the culture of our youth, had changed between the two wars. ... The generation that fought in Korea had not grown up with affluence. Many had served in World War II or grew up during the war. The middle-class youths who were asked to fight in Vietnam were of a pampered generation, one that prized personal convenience above almost all else. The prospect that their comfortable lives might be disrupted, or even endangered, by having to serve their country in Vietnam was for many intolerable. Thus, the student protests wound down when the draft ended. ... We know of the tortures and murders in the re-education camps. ... The almost complete indifference of American antiwar radicals to the terrible fate of the South Vietnamese after the Communists' victory demonstrates that the protests were not motivated by concern for the people of Vietnam.[18]

In the sixties, many youths zoned out on drugs, and with the zeal of utopian flower power, they rebelled against the establishment, calling cops "pigs" and scoffing at the need for a robust national defense. Some of them cozied up to the idea of Maoist communism, this at a time when Mao's forces were fresh off the slaughter of tens of millions of Chinese. Flower power, Mao power, and utopian revolution were in the ascendant. Practical matters such as making lands safe against Communist dictators seemed far away and abstruse, especially when under the influence of psychedelic shirts, miniskirts, braless blouses, and mushrooms. Bork cites the mood among some leftist college students in the sixties:

> [F]our-square against anti-Communism, eight-square against American culture, twelve-square against sell-out unions, one-hundred-twenty square against an interpretation of the Cold War that saw it as a Soviet plot and identified American policy fondly. In short, they rejected America. Worse, as their statement of principles made clear, they were also four-square against [recognizing] the nature of human beings and features of the world that are unchangeable. That is the utopian impulse. It has produced disasters in the past, just as it was to do with the Sixties generation.[19]

Certainly, the response to the music of the sixties was almost lemming-like in its mania. The cultic response to the Beatles, the Grateful Dead, and the Rolling Stones was a signal that American virtue was in free fall. But the Fab Four were supposedly bigger than life, and there's no question that millions of American teenagers in the sixties were in their thrall, even as George Harrison flirted with Hinduism and other Eastern mysticism. Many in the generation that popularized the Beatles movie *The Yellow Submarine* (thought to be the movie version of an acid trip) threw down their country's godly heritage, picked up the marijuana pipe, and worshipped all manner of false teachers that wandered in from the Far East.

The clips of Elvis Presley gyrating really convey the asinine; in Presley's obvious thirst to become larger than life, he became a shocking and ostentatious character that was clearly intended to reel in impressionable girls in the same way that barely clad rock nymphs now reel in impressionable young men.

Bork further clarifies the turning point represented by the tie-dyed, utopian generation from the sixties:

> [T]he Sixties radicals ... prized individualism so greatly that it turned them into egalitarian conformists. ... What made them egalitarians was also their rejection of

Hillary has expressed an interest in "human reconstruction" and "remolding [Western] society" in her Wellesley and Texas speeches, respectively. Journalist Michael Kelly noted that her Wellesley and Texas speeches suffered from "intellectual incoherence and the adolescent assumption that the past does not exist and the present needs only your guiding hand to create the glorious future." What could be the connection between Hillary's revolutionary, utopian tones, her high-profile women's "rights" work in China, and her doting attention to Peking dictators as Secretary of State? Strange how the U.S. seems more Chinese and more authoritarian all the time! Who might the mentors in authoritarianism (communism) be?

> American culture and bourgeois morals. Since none of them aspired to an aristocracy or to asceticism, they had to reject bourgeois hierarchies and morals from the other direction. This translated as foul language, sexual promiscuity, marijuana and hard drugs, and disdain for the military and for conventional success. Since these were the only "authentic" ways to think and behave, the student radicals eagerly became what Harold Rosenberg once characterized as a "herd of independent minds." ... In the Sixties the spirit and the exaltation expressed at Port Huron played out across the country and produced a massive lurch to the left among university students. SDS [ie, the leftist group Students for a Democratic Society] grew from 600 members in 1963 to over 100,000 in 1968, but then collapsed in 1969 into hostile factions and in the end consisted only of a small group of Maoists.[20]

Foul language, sexual promiscuity, marijuana and hard drugs, and disdain for the military and conventional success: does that sound familiar? That describes the American popular culture of the twenty-first century almost to a tee, the only difference being that success is back in favor. Maybe the social rebellion was mostly about the desire to have sex without restrictions, and all the jazz about drugs and altered frames of mind and Maoist conceits were really just ploys and distractions.

Potter Stewart was the only one of the nine to bring extended federal Constitutional experience to his appointment on the Supreme Court, and sure enough he was the only one of the justices to object to removing prayer and Bible reading from the public schools. Stewart alone acted as a judge, not developing new political policies but rather upholding legal precedent. Remember the name: Supreme Court Justice Potter Stewart.

Like a good lemming, Hillary Rodham characterized the movement that was afoot in the sixties. As the student commencement speaker at Wellesley in 1969, she said she and her peers were interested in "human reconstruction"; that the acquisitive and competitive corporate life was not for them; and that they were "searching for more immediate, ecstatic and penetrating mode[s] of living." Later, as the wife of President Clinton, Rodham gave a speech in Texas in which she said that "remolding society certainly in the West is one of the great challenges facing all of us," and that we needed "a society that fills us up again and makes us feel that we are part of something bigger than ourselves." Bork characterized Rodham's Texas speech as "a religious feeling without structure," while journalist Michael Kelly noted that her Wellesley and Texas speeches suffered from "intellectual incoherence and the adolescent assumption that the past does not exist and the present needs only your guiding hand to create the glorious future."[21]

In effect, the transition point that debased America during the late 1950s and early 1960s had to do with affluence, consumerism, boredom, promiscuous sex, drugs, rock-and-roll music, psychological mush, counseling and therapy, intellectual incoherence, badly crafted utopian ideals, leftist and Communist leanings, anti-Americanism, and anti-Christian energies. Indeed, as the famed economist Friedrich Hayek has noted, "The mood of [the West's] intellectual leaders has long been characterized by disillusionment with its principles, disparagement of its achievements, and exclusive concern with the creation of 'better worlds.'"²²

In 1962, the Supreme Court justices strode onto the scene and took prayer out of public schools in their ruling on the case of *Engel v Vitale*. In so doing, they repudiated nearly two hundred years of Supreme Court rulings that were largely consonant with Christian principles. As David Barton points out, eight of the nine justices on the 1962–63 Supreme Court were appointed after much political (not judicial) experience. Chief Justice Earl Warren had been California's governor for ten years; Justice Hugo Black had been a US Senator for ten years; Justice Felix Frankfurter had been an assistant to the Secretary of Labor and also helped found the American Civil Liberties Union; Justice Arthur Goldberg had been the Secretary of Labor; and Justice William Douglas had been chairman of the Securities and Exchange Commission.²³ Justice Potter Stewart was the only one of the nine to bring extended federal Constitutional experience to his appointment on the Supreme Court and, sure enough, he was the only one of the justices to object to removing prayer and Bible reading from the public schools. Stewart alone acted as a judge, not developing new political policies but rather upholding legal precedent.²⁴ Politicians ignored godly jurisprudence, and from the Supreme Court acted like social reorganizers (stealth revolutionaries) in taking Christian prayer out of the schools.

Social Ills

In the early 1960s, there were a lot of drugs floating around, putting young people into altered states and generally tearing up the fabric of the culture. Tom Wolfe, author of *The Electric Kool-Aid Acid Test*, tried to capture the spirit of the budding American drug culture on the tip of his deft pen. He put it in the following way:

> Actually, there were a lot of kids in the early 1960s who were ... yes; attuned. I used to think of them as the Beautiful People because of the Beautiful People letters they used to write their parents. They were chiefly in Los Angeles, San Francisco, New York City, these kids. They had a regular circuit they were on, and there was a lot of traffic from city to city. Most of them were from middle-

class backgrounds, but not upper bourgeois, more petit bourgeois, if that old garbanzo can stand being written down again—homes with Culture but no money or money but no Culture. ... [Somehow] there was enough money floating around in the air so that one could do this thing, live together with other kids—Our own thing!—from our own status sphere, without having to work at *a job,* and live on our own terms—Us! And people our age!—it was ... *beautiful,* it was a ... *whole feeling,* and the straight world never understood it, this thing of one's status sphere and how one was only nineteen, twenty, twenty-one, twenty-two or so and not starting out helpless at the bottom of the ladder. ... I suppose the Beautiful People identified with the Beat Generation excitement of the late 1950s, but in fact there was a whole new motif in their particular bohemian status sphere: namely, psychedelic drugs. El ... Es ... Dee ... se-cret-ly...

Timothy Leary, Alpert, and a few chemists like Al Hubbard and the incognito "Dr. Spaulding" had been pumping LSD out into the hip circuit with a truly messianic conviction. LSD, peyote, mescaline, morning-glory seeds were becoming the secret new *thing* in the hip life. A lot of kids who were into it were already piled into amputated apartments, as I called them. The seats, the tables, the beds--none of them ever had legs. Communal living on the floor, you might say. ... They had no particular philosophy, just a little leftover Buddhism and Hinduism from the *beat* period, plus Huxley's theory of opening doors in the mind. ...

At [Ken] Kesey's the days began—when? There were no clocks around and nobody had a watch. The lime light would be sparkling down through the redwoods when you woke up. [And there were] the everlasting visitors ... friends of friends of friends, curiosity seekers, some of them, dope seekers, some of them, kids from Berkeley, you could never tell. ... They live in—*La Honda!*

At *Kesey's!* Their place is called the Nest. ... Everything is totally out front in the Nest—no secrets, no guilt, no jealousies, no putting anyone down for anything: "... a plural marriage— ... 'Ain't anybody here but us gods'—so how could anyone be offended? Bacchanalia, unashamed swapping, communal living ... everything."[25]

LSD, other psychedelics, and pot were just some of the mind-altering substances used and abused during the druggie revolution in the early 1960s. It's interesting to note that, according to Wolfe, these drug users had no particular philosophy except for "a little leftover Buddhism and Hinduism." Apparently, the drug users' inspiration was about the excitement of unfettered sex, free time, and ungodly self-absorption. At any rate, any intellectual or spiritual cause had only the appearance of an inarticulate veneer to Wolfe, who has proven himself to be no small observer of the American scene.

At Ken Kesey's (LSD experimenter and author of *One Flew Over the Cuckoo's Nest*) place outside of Eugene, Oregon, apparently the drug-culture adherents held a utopian ideal that they would work it all out, that there would be no room for criticism or pointing out the need for repentance and salvation. This free-sex mentality, prettied up with a tacit stricture to avoid criticism (criticism being a drag, man), undoubtedly was encouraged by the Hindu and Taoist habits of relativistic thought.

Throughout the 1960s and well into the 1970s, drug-dependent hippies hung out in rural spots, painted flowers on their VW buses, wore tie-dyed psychedelic shirts to match their psychedelic mind tripping, and skulked around barefoot in the trees, leaving the stench of feces in their midst. Middle-class cool cats from Marin County, California, drove into San Francisco to score pot and other drugs and competed to see who could pay the most homage to the Grateful Dead, a band that glorified death with its famous skeleton logo and laced tunes with blasphemous language. At colleges throughout the country, students lit up their marijuana cigarettes and chortled to the tunes of Neil Young and other hipster singers. The marijuana and psychedelics of the sixties and seventies gave way to amphetamines such as speed and cocaine in the eighties and then crystal meth and heroin in the nineties. It's an ongoing tale of romance with altered states, spurred on by the false promise of a neverending party.

Of course, drug taking and drug selling is an equal-opportunity habit that has wreaked havoc across color lines in this country, but Ken Hamblin has been a keen observer of the black inner-city experience as it relates to drugs. "[T]here is an underground commerce run by the gangs and thriving in Dark Town," Hamblin says in his book *Pick a Better Country: An Unassuming Colored Guy Speaks His Mind About America*. "In addition to their enterprise of crime, which they justify in connection with their alleged crusade for social justice, the black gangs view drug sales as their legitimate industry."[26]

Hamblin argues that some blacks have been held captive by the "Myth of the Hobbled Black." He observes, "They have been brainwashed by a line of propaganda from groups like the black political caucuses, the Nation of Islam, and the NAACP to believe the myth. Armed only with a perception of the wrongs perpetrated against them, and with no knowledge of the history of the successful struggle to right those wrongs, they cannot grasp the promise of the American Dream. That forward-thinking message is not being sent to the children in Dark Town."[27]

Hamblin also opines on the topic of out-of-wedlock births:

> Having a baby out of wedlock particularly in your teen years, used to be shameful and stigmatizing, just as poverty and welfare once were. Pregnant girls were banished in a hush from school, sometimes to a home for unwed mothers, sometimes out of town to live with a relative. They were outcasts because they had failed to meet the standards of the community. But today, inch by inch, step by step, with the aid of prominent voices like Toni Morrison's, we have allowed these community standards to be dismantled. … We began tearing down the stigma of illegitimate births on TV talk shows hosted by supposedly compassionate liberals like Phil Donahue. They provided a credible platform for the psychobabble of so-called experts who bemoaned the trauma we inflict on

innocent bastard babies when we stigmatize their immoral and primitive mothers.[28]

Of course, there is a balance by which standards can be protected and unmarried mothers and their kids can also be supported.

Many liberals would have us believe that premarital sex is just dandy. Americans have largely done away with the terms "living in sin" and "shacking up," and many now prefer such euphemisms as "living together with one's partner" to describe a premarital sexual relationship. Wardell Pomeroy, author of *Boys and Sex,* has even likened premarital intercourse to a prepurchase test drive of a car![29]

Pomeroy's viewpoint is widespread, but the test-drive analogy cheapens the value of sex. "Looking under the hood" before marriage puts the emphasis on the physical, ignoring the fact that we're primarily spirit beings. Liberal groups such as Planned Parenthood bandy around that word "parenthood" and cop a degree of respectability from its use, and the word "planned" makes the organization sound like a group of serious planners. Unfortunately, what they plan is so-called safe sex, which is largely a euphemism for premarital sex with birth-control devices so as to ensure that a baby won't be produced inconveniently. They plan for premature and ungodly sex, but hold out the option of abortion as a safety valve if their badly laid plans should "go awry" and actually produce a baby.

It would be wise to remember that abortion is really just a euphemism for Molech worship—the sacrificing of children to a false god—something that was strictly forbidden in the Old Testament. Child sacrifice is not a complicated issue; one has only to detangle it from all the modern jargon to see it for what it really is. King Josiah ordered Hilkiah the high priest and the second-order priests to put down Baal, sun, moon, planet, star, and Molech worship: "And [Hilkiah] defiled Topheth, which *is* in the valley of the children of Hinnom, that no man might make his son or his daughter to pass through the fire to Molech" (2 Kings 23:10 KJV). Remembering Lev. 18:21a, we read, "And thou shalt not let any of thy seed pass through *the fire* to Molech" (KJV).

Lest anyone think that such standards were the exclusive province of the Old Testament, perhaps we should revisit Acts 7:41–43: "And they made a calf in those days, and offered sacrifice unto the idol, and rejoiced in the works of their own hands. Then God turned, and gave them up to worship the host of heaven; as it is written in the book of the prophets, O ye house of Israel, have ye offered to me slain beasts and sacrifices *by the space of* forty years in the wilderness? Yea, ye took up the tabernacle of Moloch, and the star of your god Remphan, figures which ye made to worship them: and I will carry you away beyond Babylon" (KJV). If the Moloch worshippers were carried away beyond Babylon, then what will be the fate of a country such as the United States, that has not stopped the baby killing?

So severe is the teen sex problem that teen pregnancies are reputed to have increased several fold since 1962–63, and the United States has the highest incidence of teen motherhood of any country in the West, according to Barton. Sections of high schools, and even entire high schools in extreme cases, are being devoted to the care of pregnant students; half of all teen mothers go on welfare within a year of giving birth.[30] Billions of dollars are being siphoned off our economy due to an undisciplined society and unrestrained TV and radio executives (hacks) who promote fornication in their shows.

Dumbing Down Entertainment

"Some of our elites—professors, journalists, makers of motion pictures and television entertainment, et al.—delight in nihilism and destruction as much as do the random killers in our cities," Robert Bork says.[31] Is that possible? Could our elites be bad elites? Could our rich elites have their own interests in mind instead of the health, vigor, and godliness of our society?

Bork is right on the money, and though all of us get sucked into the drama and cleverness of TV advertisements now and then, we should be mindful that behind the dazzle is often a spirit of promiscuity, lying, cheating, hurting, and misleading. Since when did the Ad Council have a résumé that was all about the edification and strengthening of our nation? It's the Ad Council. They hawk stuff.

I agree with Bork's notion that certain smug elites delight in emptiness and destruction much like random killers do: if American brains are emptied and dumbed down by TV garbage and media lies, then the

Testing the Spirits

hawkers can sell their wares as if selling to idiots. Could it be that certain elites want to have big houses more than they want to sanctify the nation? Would they do that? Could a news anchor with a mellifluous voice and billowing breasts not be interested in the fiber and grit of our nation's Bible heritage? Could a national news anchor with a mellifluous voice and a nice head of hair be badly versed in the history of the Middle East, and could he not understand the importance of the US-Israel relationship?

Elitist moviemakers make sickening films about all manner of random and senseless violence, intended to titillate anyone who will shell out the bucks to see the filth, and then they turn around and say that movies don't affect people. Avaricious TV producers jump at the chance to follow the gory details of murders, accidents, missing-person cases, and the like—it's like having an ambulance chaser in your living room, complete with dramatic music and sexy collages of weird and gory scenes, all merged together as they are and flitting rapidly on the screen. All those flitting images and the color merging combine to create a visual delicatessen, even if the subject is tawdry and the story has little chance of advancing the common good. Could it be that the entertainment elites are no longer sober, no longer keeping their eyes on the Word of God?

Violence as entertainment is seemingly omnipresent on TV. Jay Leno, the liberal host of *The Tonight Show*, actually joked about the dead husband of Clara Harris (the notorious dentist from Texas who used her Mercedes to run over her husband in a fit of rage). Leno joked that Harris used to be the flat one before her breast-augmentation surgery—the sickening and reprehensible joke being that she had been flatter in the chest than she would have liked, but that her dead husband was the flatter of the two now that he'd been run over (Feb. 17, 2003 show). That kind of coarseness has led to a gradual deadening of the senses, and disgusting comics keep sneering all the way to the bank.

On the topic of violence as entertainment, Art Bell interviewed Chuck Barris, former *Gong Show* host, on the radio show *Coast to Coast* (Dec. 4, 2002). Barris said he thought American reality TV is going in the direction of trying to get a fatality on some reality TV segment, and Bell concurred, noting that already on a reality TV show a guy flipped off his bike, got impaled on a tree branch, and almost died. Bell pointed out that America's obsession with watching dangerous reality TV, such as *Fear*

Factor and *Survivor*, seems to be mimicking the Roman indulgence in coliseum violence from the period of Rome's decline.

One has only to watch extreme fighting, or ultimate fighting, to see how rampant is the fascination with extreme violence. I saw an extreme-fighting competition on TV in which one wrestler was on the ground trying to catch his breath, and the other fighter came over and kneed him in the head five times! The referee was supposed to stop the fight if one fighter couldn't fight back but, in this case, he allowed the unmoving, panting fighter to be brutally kneed in the head five times before stopping the fight.

Hollywood hubris knows few bounds and poses a major danger to our people because life does imitate bad art when we're not sober. It's well known that the killers in the Columbine High School massacre had been inspired by a violent movie. Moreover, the high-school killings come in waves, proving to any intelligent person that the sickos who pull off such horrific crimes are motivated by lurid and graphic television news. The argument about whether life imitates sick art should have been over a long time ago.

While interviewing hip-hop promoter David Mays, TV talk host Bill O'Reilly indicated he thought that Mays and his ilk get rich off mind-poisoning hip-hop lyrics that use bad language and glamorize the rude and coarse hip-hop subculture *(The O'Reilly Factor,* Feb. 18, 2003). Mays countered by saying that hip-hop music empowers kids from "the hood," kids who supposedly suffer from oppression under Euro-centric curricula. Mays was quick to call O'Reilly a racist, using the same bogus strategy that Ken Hamblin alludes to in regard to African-American looters who rationalize their crimes.

Finally, on *Nightline Up-Close*, a female cartoon character named Ceta was analyzed (Dec. 2, 2002). The character wears short skirts and has a bulging bosom and is, according to its producer, a black female version of the shock jock. Ceta embodies a credo called "ghetto fabulous," an "urban hip-hop slang thing" that relies on fur coats and big glasses and baggy jeans. But contrary to the claims of the character's producer, the ostentatiousness and vampiness of Ceta do not mesh with "good-home standard American values." Moreover, when the character's producer was describing her debt to her mother for making her education possible, she said that her mother "enabled that to take place" [sic]. Though the character's producer was less than well spoken, she would have us believe that one can glide effortlessly between street slang (with its attendant bad grammar) and good diction all in the same breath. Ceta's producer suggests that kids tune in to *Ceta's World* and hang out. And to think that hundreds of years ago, our people spoke good English and read the Scriptures in the original languages! While some social broadening makes sense in principle, diversity as a mantra should be rejected and standards should be maintained.

As Os Guinness has observed, "Why should anyone read Nathaniel Hawthorne and listen to William Shakespeare when modern life rewards a studious devotion to comic books, interactive technology, and MTV?"[32] Journalist Carl Bernstein has noted that we're trending toward becoming an idiot culture, a "sleizoid info-tainment culture" in which "the lurid and the loopy are more important than real news." He says, "For the first time in our history, the weird and the stupid and the coarse are becoming our cultural norm, even our cultural ideal."[33]

Ted Koppel, former host of ABC's *Nightline*, was similarly concerned about the decline of television. "How does one explain or, perhaps more relevant, guard against the influence of an industry which is on the verge of becoming a hallucinogenic barrage of images, whose only grammar is pacing, whose principal theme is energy?" Koppel once asked. "We are losing our ability to manage ideas; to contemplate, to think."[34] In the same vein, Neil Postman has said Las Vegas is the new metaphor for American character and aspiration, devoted as it is to entertainment all the time.[35]

Educational Ruin

While in college during the early eighties, I took an Asian studies class from an edgy Japanese-American professor. From my perspective, he sought to create a litany of white sins against Asians in this country to the exclusion of the larger picture of American development. He could go on and on about how a Chinese was murdered by Detroit whites who mistook the Chinese for a Japanese, taking him for an enemy of General Motors. That incident was, by dint of constant repetition, held out by the professor as being representative, and whites in the class were apparently supposed to come clean about their racist heritage.

I did extra credit work for the class, helping Asian immigrants in Oakland, California, improve their job interview skills. Even so, I felt that the professor was partial to the Asians in the class and gave whites short shrift both in class discussions and during office hours.

As someone who has lived in Asia for many years and experienced the virulent bigotry of Asians in their cultures, I can say that I consider that professor's brand of scholarship to be unbalanced and self-serving—indeed, multiculturalism at its worst. Robert Bork says:

> Scientific skepticism and rationality ... are dangerous to the Left because radical individualism and radical egalitarianism are pernicious points of view that cannot withstand empirical investigation and rational analysis. Most women's studies, racial and ethnic studies, and gay and lesbian studies are intellectual hoaxes, programs of propaganda and mutual support. ... Radical feminism is put in peril by scientific proof that some sex-role differences are inherent and cannot be dismissed as mere social constructs. To multiculturalists, empirical investigation is dangerous because it will demonstrate that not all cultures are equal in their capacity to equip their members for success in the modern world. Contrary to the claims of the multiculturalists, there are not different ways of knowing. There is one way and, though it is accessible to people of all cultures, it had its origins, or at least was brought to its fullest development, in Europe.[36]

Physicist Alan Sokal also believes in one way of knowing. That is to say, the physical laws that bind our environment are not subject to social engineering. In a clever ruse, he submitted an article to the magazine *Social Text* pretending to bring the science of physics under the constraints of social constructionism. "It has thus become increasingly apparent," Sokal posited sarcastically, "that physical 'reality,' no less than social 'reality,' is at bottom a social and linguistic construct."[37] Sokal's point is that the law of gravity cannot be socially engineered, and anyone who believes otherwise can put his ethnic-way-of-knowing theories to the test by jumping off a roof to see whether gravity is subject to ethnic and social interpretation.

It should be obvious by now that the antiwhite bias inherent in multiculturalism has led to a tendency to appease foreigners, including Russian and Chinese communists who oppose Christianity and free enterprise and Islamic fundamentalists who are pushing for the extension of Islamic law in the West. Moreover, the multiculturalism practiced in the West is not reciprocated: Asian cultures in particular enjoy Western movies and products, but they have no problem making foreigners second class in their cultures.

Bork, too, has lamented the trend of making American historical studies into a smorgasbord of cute little boutiques. "In college," Bork says, "my son was not offered a survey course in history and wound up studying such niches of history as the Weimar Republic. The college had given up on the idea that there was a central body of historical knowledge all educated persons should have. That is true across the board, not just in history. It will be a few years yet before America discovers what the decline of general knowledge means for our well-being."[38]

The esteemed Judge Robert Bork has observed that the National History Standards have been "politically correct." Contributions of the West have been trivialized or ignored while those of Africans and Indians have been magnified; males who have played important roles in our history, such as Jonas Salk, have been dropped out; whereas organizations and events that reflected poorly upon us have been stressed. For instance, McCarthyism gets 19 mentions to 17 for the Ku Klux Klan: it seems that McCarthy's warning about Communist intruders was bad, bad. Such marginalizing of the brave Mr. McCarthy has had the effect of paving the way for massive appeasement of Communist China. "Human reconstruction" sounds like what Mao and Pol Pot did, and "remolding [Western] society" sounds like what the communized National History Standards did. Upon reflection, it would seem that "politically correct" (an inherently vacuous term just like "hippies") is a stealth phrase for "politically communist."

That's interesting, because my high-school Modern Europe class (circa 1979 or 1980) also featured the Weimar Republic prominently, but an overview of Europe was lacking. The radical multiculturalists had already begun questioning the value of survey history courses. No big picture was required—only the small picture, which could then be utilized and extrapolated from by each group according to its own purposes.

Bork describes a recent version of the National History Standards that "prescribed a multicultural curriculum that minimized the achievements of Europeans and their descendants in America in order to focus attention on Africans and Indians." Students are instructed to consider the achievements of Aztec civilization but not the practice of human sacrifice. McCarthy and McCarthyism get nineteen mentions, the Ku Klux Klan seventeen. Harriet Tubman, a black who helped rescue slaves through the Underground Railroad, is mentioned six times. By contrast, Henry Clay and Ulysses S. Grant are each mentioned once. There is no mention at all of Daniel Webster, Robert E. Lee, Alexander Graham Bell, Thomas Edison, Albert Einstein, Jonas Salk, or the Wright Brothers. George Washington appears fleetingly but is not identified as our first president. The Sierra Club and the National Organization for Women get significant billing, but the first gathering of the US Congress is overlooked.

The National Standards were politically correct. The contributions of the West were trivialized or ignored, while those of Africans and Indians were magnified. Men who had played important roles in our history were dropped out; organizations and events that reflected poorly on us were stressed.[39]

Robert Hughes, author of *Culture of Complaint: The Fraying of America*, noticed that the decline in American education began with a deemphasis on rigor and an emphasis on feelings:

> For when the 1960s' animus against elitism entered American education, it brought in its train an enormous and cynical tolerance of student ignorance, rationalized as a regard for "personal expression" and "self-esteem." Rather than "stress" the kids by asking them to read too much or think too closely, which might cause their fragile personalities to implode on contact with college-level

demands, schools reduced their reading assignments, thus automatically reducing their command of language. Untrained in logical analysis, ill-equipped to develop and construct formal arguments about issues, unused to mining texts for deposits of factual material, the students fell back to the only position they could truly call their own: what they *felt* about things. When feelings and attitudes are the main referents of argument, to attack any position is automatically to insult its holder. ... [and every argument approaches] the condition of harassment, if not quite rape. ... Cycle this subjectivization of discourse through two or three generations of students turning into teachers, with the sixties' dioxins accumulating more each time, and you have the entropic background to our culture of complaint.[40]

So what has all this personal expression and self-esteem done for

> "Many old heroes have not survived the killing fields of the New History. Ultimate goal: Destroy patriotism, kill the love of country, demoralize the people, deconstruct America."
> —Pat Buchanan, Author
>
> Whatever happened to Washington and Lincoln's birthdays? Hillary's "human reconstruction" and "remolding of [Western] society" seem to be "deconstructing" America. Let us stop the trance, and say, "Be gone X, hello Madison," "be gone Mao, hello Adams," "be gone Marx, hello Jefferson."

America? Our schools require less learning, less data mining, but demand all kinds of feelings, preferably feelings of the liberal slant. The goal is to forget the white male and Christian contributions, fall silent under the mystique of science classes that mention million-year-old rocks and evolution, and become enamored with the feminist, multiculturalist, and homosexual agendas by which a black lesbian rapper is a profound thinker and Albert Sabin (developer of oral polio vaccine) is nobody.

Pat Buchanan takes a broad view of the recent developments in American education. "Many of the institutions that now have custody of America's past," Buchanan says, "operate on the principles of Big Brother's Ministry of Truth: drop down the 'memory hole' the patriotic stories of America's greatness and glory, and produce new 'warts-and-all' histories that play up her crimes and sins, revealing what we have loved to be loathsome and those we have revered to be disreputable, even despicable. Many old heroes have not survived the killing fields of the New History. Ultimate goal: Destroy patriotism, kill the love of country, demoralize the people, deconstruct America."[41] In fact, wart-filled liberals should come clean about the extent of their self-reviling, not to mention their ignorance of foreign countries, which they are only too happy to portray as idyllic foils to American treachery.

Two of the big sticks in the liberals' antiwhite, politically correct arsenal are the suffering of the Indians and the early American practice of slavery. As Hughes points out, "A PC book like Kirkpatrick Sale's *The Conquest of Paradise* makes [Christopher Columbus] more like Hitler in a caravel … landing like a virus among the innocent people of the New World. This new stereotype, a rebirth of Rousseauist notions about the Noble Savage, brings a new outfit of double standards into play. Thus the Taino of Puerto Rico become innocent creatures living in a state of classless nature, like hippies in Vermont when Kirkpatrick Sale and I were young, whereas in fact they liked to be carried around in litters by their slaves."[42]

I remember in the late 1980s (or thereabout) I attended a public lecture by an octogenarian Hopi man. He spoke at length about how the Hopi tradition had long ago known that white people were coming and that some degree of chaos would ensue. His talk was so flattering to his own people and extremely negative towards the whites in spite of all that modern America had afforded him and all Americans. It was quite stunning to see how none in the white audience challenged this man's interpretation of history. Personally, I feel that his talk was self-indulgent and not a little bit revisionist. He played to the audience's need to be wowed by a noble Indian, and the audience kept their part of the politically disingenuous bargain, eagerly throwing him fawning looks and meaningful nods at every turn.

Hughes has a slightly different view of the culture that was in place when the Europeans arrived centuries ago:

> [T]he historical evidence ... shows that the peoples of the Americas had been doing very nicely for centuries and probably for millennia, when it came to murder, torture, materialism, ecocide, enslavement and sexist hegemony. We may worry about the fate of the spotted owl, but the first men to arrive in prehistoric north America did not seem to have any qualms about their [role in the] extinction of its megafauna, which they accomplished in short order. The civilization of the Maya, the greatest to flourish in Central America before Columbus, reached its peak between 250 and 900 AD, at which point a puzzling event called the Mayan Hiatus occurred. It collapsed. Nobody from outside had conquered it. However, recent digs and the slow work of deciphering glyphs, particularly at the site of Dos Pilas in Guatemala, indicate that the classic period of the Maya was ruined by a continuous state of war between local rulers that began around 700 AD and devoured the whole economy and ecology of the Mayan empire by the 10th century. The Mayans fell by self-induced ecological collapse, caused by a devotion to unwinnable wars which was itself sustained by an obsession with ideology—the ideology of the transcendent god-king, viewed by his limestone-toting helots as the embodiment of the whole universe.
>
> Pre-Columbian Meso-America was not the Shangri-la that the anti-Columbians would like it to be. You cannot climb the Pyramid of the Sun at Teotihuacan near Mexico City and look down the vast symmetrical perspective of the Avenue of the Dead, abandoned in the 8th century for reasons we know nothing about, without sensing that the society that built them was a theocratic ant-state whose rigidity might have made Albert Speer faint. And try staring

> at the fangs of the Feathered Serpent and talking about the benign pastoral quality of life before whitey arrived. Aztec culture was messianic and invasive and imperialistic; it had been so ever since the Aztecs came down from the north, under the command of a charismatic ruler whose name translates as Hummingbird-on-the-Left, and slaughtered or enslaved the resident people around what is now Mexico City. ... [I]t is anachronistic to condemn or to justify the destruction of Aztec society by the Spanish *conquista*. It was an evil fate to be enslaved by 16th-century Spanish regidors. But it was no joke to be one of the countless thousands whose hearts were ripped out by the Aztec priests of Tenochtitlan in order that the sun might rise in the morning. The Spanish burned nearly all the written records of Aztec history, except for a few codices. But the Aztecs, when they conquered central Mexico, also destroyed all the records of the previous societies, so that there could be no history before theirs.[43]

Dave Hunt, author of *Occult Invasion: The Subtle Seduction of the World and Church,* also provides some needed perspective to counter the palpably disingenuous myth of prewhitey bliss in pre-Columbian societies:

> The picture being painted for us of the idyllic life of perfect harmony with nature and with one another supposedly lived by indigenous peoples before the evil white man came along is not true. Concerned by such lies, Jungleman, once a powerful shaman of the Yanomamo Indians of the Amazon, told the bitter truth about the lives of indigenous peoples in *Spirit of the Rainforest*. It is a tale of continual sexual perversion and abuse, warmongering, brutality, living in terror of human and spirit enemies; of curses, suffering, and death. It is a story, too, of deliverance through Jesus Christ into a whole new life of peace and joy and hope for eternity. ...

Consider [also] two young sisters, survivors of Oatman's wagon massacre in 1851. Their captivity by Apaches and sale into slavery to another tribe is recounted in agonizing detail. The two girls spent some years with their Native American captors performing slave labor. The younger sister died from starvation. Most interesting was the reaction of the girls' fellow "slaves" (the Indian squaws). Great was the women's amazement when they learned how civilly the white man lived with his wife. They expressed the vain hope that they might escape and join so kindly a society.

Or who could forget the cruel massacre at the Marcus Whitman Mission in the State of Washington? Entirely unprovoked, it reflected the Indians' tragic superstition that the god of these gentle missionaries had malevolently caused the deaths of some of their people. Indigenous peoples are as fallen and as prone to sin as are the rest of mankind.[44]

Relations between groups have been tense since ancient times, and not every issue points back to European-American malevolence. It's probably best to be engaged in ideas about love and justice and God—and thereby avoid making over every single environment using a racial cookie cutter or leveler, making over every town, corporation, and school to make them just like the others. As long as the channels of education and employment and social mixing are open and encouraged and as long as we're leaning toward God's Word, good things will happen.

One of the biggest trump cards used by the race wonks is the idea that contemporary

> Multiculturalism and diversity have been used as whips to shame European-Americans, to stultify Judeo-Christian institutions, to erase any remnant of American nationalism, and to render the country weak before a phalanx of enemies. Multiculturalism and diversity are full-fledged, destroy-from-within military weapons. Go back and re-read Sun Tzu's *The Art of War:* Warring is not all about explosions.

whites are inherently tied to the American slavery experience in a way that makes them suspect and morally indebted. But it is the race wonks themselves who are suspect and morally questionable as they neglect to report on white suffering at the hands of blacks, Hispanics, and Asians.

All around this country, whites are the target of prejudiced nonwhites, and that has gone unaddressed in the media. But such stories just don't make it into the African-American studies classes, nor do the antiwhite killings in Hawaii make it into the Asian-American studies classes. At the end of the day, multiculturalism is not about social justice, rather it's about political conquest by way of destroying American nationalism and rendering America defenseless. Can you say "divide and conquer"?

But in the end, if we're to lean toward God, we must seek truth and cultivate a spirit of forgiveness rather than play as though we're in a morality contest with the other races, always pointing fingers and exacting debts. A racially organized morality contest will lead us nowhere because the list of complaints on all sides would be endless. Keeping truth and the spirit of forgiveness at our side, perhaps we can forge a meaningful truce by which all of us can give others some consideration and affection. Multiculturalism and diversity have been used as whips to shame European-Americans, stultify Judeo-Christian institutions, erase any remnant of American nationalism, and render the country weak before a phalanx of enemies—the Roman Catholic generals; the Russian and Chinese Communists; the black-hearted, amoral trade fiends; and the anti-Jew, anti-Christian Islamic jihadists (ie, possibly the four horses of Zechariah 6 and Revelation 6).

In the case of American slavery, truth ought to proceed from some historical context. After all, we've all got ancestors from different countries, and even different continents, and if one looks back to our common roots in the sons of Noah (Shem, Japheth, and Ham) then one will have to admit that we're in this thing together. If any of us looks back far enough, we're bound to find some horse thieves or slave owners or other all-purpose scoundrels in our own family trees.

Hughes tackles the problem of American slavery head on, but not without a little historical perspective:

> Periclean Athens was a slave state, and so was Augustan Rome. Most of their slaves were Caucasian whites. ... The

word "slave" meant a person of Slavic origin. By the 13th century it spread to other Caucasian peoples subjugated by armies from central Asia: Russians, Georgians, Circassians, Albanians, Armenians, all of whom found ready buyers from Venice to Sicily to Barcelona, and throughout the Muslim world.

But the *African* slave trade as such, the black traffic, was a Muslim invention, developed by Arab traders with the enthusiastic collaboration of black African ones, institutionalized with the most unrelenting brutality centuries before the white man appeared on the African continent, and continuing long after the slave market in North America was finally crushed.

[B]y the first millennium BC Pharaoh Rameses II boasts of providing the temples with more than 100,000 slaves, and indeed it is inconceivable that the monumental culture of Egypt could have been raised outside a slave economy. For the next two thousand years the basic economies of sub-Saharan Africa would be tied into the catching, use and sale of slaves. The sculptures of medieval life show slaves bound and gagged for sacrifice, and the first Portuguese explorers of Africa around 1480 found a large slave trade set up from the Congo to Benin. There were large slave plantations in the Mali empire in the 13th-14th centuries and every abuse and cruelty visited on slaves in the antebellum South, including the practice of breeding children for sale like cattle, was practised by the black rulers of those towns which the Afrocentrists now hold up as sanitized examples of high civilization, such as Timbuktu and Songhay…

The image promulgated by pop-history fictions like *Roots*—white slavers bursting with cutlass and musket into the settled lives of peaceful African villages—is very far from the historical truth. A marketing system had been in place for centuries, and its supply was controlled by Africans.

Nor did it simply vanish with Abolition.

In 1865, the year the Civil War ended in the defeat of the South, Livingstone was in Zanzibar; he estimated that between 80,000 and 100,000 African slaves were brought down in chains from the interior by Arab and African slavers that year, loaded on the dhows and shipped off to Persia and the Arabian Gulf states.

Unlike the English and the Americans, neither the Arabs nor the African kings in the 19th century saw the smallest humanitarian reason to move against slavery. Slave markets, supplying the Arab emirates, were still operating in Djibouti in the 1950s; and since 1960, the slave trade has flourished in Mauritania and the Sudan. There are still reports of chattel slavery in northern Nigeria, Rwanda and Niger. Jean-Bedel Bokassa, emperor of the Central African Republic, whom a diamond-hungry Giscard d'Estaing ostentatiously embraced as his black brother at the time of his coronation in 1977, kept hundreds of slaves and from time to time arranged a massacre of them for his own amusement.

If, as H. Rap Brown once observed, violence is as American as apple pie, then slavery would seem to be as African as yams. ...

Africa, Islam and Europe all participated in black slavery, enforced it, profited from its miseries. But in the end, only Europe (including here, North America) proved itself able

Testing the Spirits

to conceive of abolishing it; only the immense moral and intellectual force of the Enlightenment, brought to bear on the hideous oppression that slavery represented, was able … to bring the trade to an end.⁴⁵

Much of the politically disingenuous education is driven by nonwhites and sappy whites and anti-Christians who would be happy to damage the Pilgrims' reputations and erode American purpose and resolve at the same time. Buchanan takes a deft swipe at guilt trippers such as Jesse Jackson and Al Sharpton when he says that "in Mauritania and Sudan today, slavery has returned, to the deafening silence of intellectuals who have built careers on the moral shakedown of America and the West."⁴⁶ The art of the pseudomoral shakedown, playing as it does on white gullibility, has become a well-contrived art form—and it pays very handsomely in some cases. Buchanan says:

> Civil rights has become a racket. All Americans of goodwill would offer a hand to alleviate the social catastrophe in black America. For, after all, African Americans are children of the same God and citizens of the same republic. But the Jacksons, Sharptons, and Bonds do not want our help. They want to bait us, for that is how they keep the pot boiling, the TV producers calling, and the federal and foundation grants rolling in. If Theodore Bilbo and Bull Conner are dead and gone, new white racists must be found, even if they have to be invented… ⁴⁷

Clearly our education should not be dragged down by the endless lists of grievances being churned out by the multiculturalist crowd; many of the multiculturalists are prejudiced propagandists anyway. High schoolers should be reading Nathaniel Hawthorne and Samuel Adams, not Malcolm X. We should seek to inculcate our children with a broad base of knowledge—indeed, a curriculum based on Bible truths, long-arching histories, and the kind of nationalism that would sever ties to dictatorships, rebuild American factories right here in America, and put the US Constitution back into the courts and back into the classrooms.

CHAPTER FOUR

EXPOSING THE CONCEITS OF THE NEW AGE

When thou art come into the land which the LORD *thy God giveth thee, thou shalt not learn to do after the abominations of those nations. There shall not be found among you* any one *that maketh his son or his daughter to pass through the fire,* or *that useth divination,* or *an observer of times, or an enchanter, or a witch, or a charmer, or a consulter with familiar spirits, or a wizard, or a necromancer. For all that do these things* are *an abomination unto the* LORD: *and because of these abominations the* LORD *thy God doth drive them out from before thee. (Deut. 18:9–12 KJV)*

For there are certain men crept in unawares, who were before of old ordained to this condemnation, ungodly men, turning the grace of our God into lasciviousness, and denying the only LORD *God, and our* LORD *Jesus Christ. I will therefore put you in remembrance, though ye once knew this, how that the* LORD, *having saved the people out of the land of Egypt, afterward destroyed them that believed not. And the angels which kept not their first estate, but left their own habitation, he hath reserved in everlasting chains under darkness unto the judgment of the great day. Even as Sodom and Gomorrah, and the cities about them in like manner, giving themselves over to fornication, and going after strange flesh, are set forth for an example, suffering the vengeance of eternal fire. Likewise also these* filthy *dreamers defile the flesh, despise dominion, and speak evil of dignities. ...*

But these speak evil of those things which they know not: but what they know naturally, as brute beasts in those things they corrupt themselves. Woe unto them! For they have gone in the way of Cain, and ran greedily after the error of Balaam for reward, and perished in the gainsaying of Core. These are spots in your feasts of charity, when they feast with you, feeding themselves without fear: clouds *they are without water carried about of winds; trees whose fruit withereth, without fruit, twice dead, plucked up by the roots; raging waves of the sea, foaming out their own shame; wandering stars, to whom is reserved the blackness of darkness for ever. And Enoch also, the seventh from Adam, prophesied of these, saying, Behold, the* LORD *cometh with ten thousands of his saints, to execute judgment upon all, and to convince all that are ungodly among them of all their ungodly deeds which they have ungodly committed, and of all their hard* speeches *which ungodly sinners have spoken against him. These are murmurers, complainers, walking after their own lusts; and their mouth speaketh great swelling* words, *having men's persons in admiration because of advantage. But, beloved, remember ye the words which were spoken before of the apostles of our* LORD *Jesus Christ; how that they told you there should be mockers in the last time, who should walk after their own ungodly lusts. These be they who separate themselves, sensual, having not the Spirit. (Jude 1:4–8, 10–19 KJV)*

The New Age is not new; rather it stems from a rebellion against godly thinking that started with Lucifer. (Lucifer's obsession with "I" took his eyes off the will of God, as related in Is. 14:12–15: "How art thou fallen from heaven, O Lucifer, son of the morning! *How* art thou cut down to the ground, which didst weaken the nations! For thou hast said in thine heart,

I will ascend into heaven, I will exalt my throne above the stars of God: I will sit also upon the mount of the congregation, in the sides of the north: I will ascend above the heights of the clouds; I will be like the most High. Yet thou shalt be brought down to hell, to the sides of the pit" (KJV).

Sin began with the pride and arrogance of Lucifer, extended into the hearts of Eve and Adam, and has infected mankind ever since. Therefore, the New Age is just another lie from Satan, the father of lies, a repackaging of a very ancient deceit—a lie that tells people they are great without God. If New Agers were to strive for truth in advertising, they would introduce themselves as Old-Age Deceivers.

New Age History

Many maps could be drawn that show the lineage of the New Agers. One such map starts with Immanuel Kant, the German philosopher from the 1700s. Kant came up with the idea of transcendental unity of apperception, or TUA as it is sometimes known. According to this feckless idea, reality itself is created by the mind. Tal Brooke explains:

> Suddenly, Kant's move of T.U.A. philosophically and epistemologically threw open the door not only for a knowledge independent of God, but it opened the way for mysticism, monism, and the pursuit of the occult. The nature of the mind, Kant argued, is to order the indeterminate stuff of sensation so that it can be perceived or known. This ordering takes place before the experience is possible. Therefore time, space, and causality are not "out there" in a real world; they are extended from the subject's mind. ... What we "know" is made possible not by God, not by the mind's penetration of a real world, but by the mind's projections of what we can know upon an essentially unknowable world.[1]

Subsequently, the Romantics embraced Kant's notion about the mind creating reality and ran with it. English Romantics such as Samuel Taylor Coleridge and Thomas Carlyle immersed themselves in a sense of newfound freedom—a freedom to act and perceive and experience by themselves and for themselves, unbothered by any sense of being responsible to the God of

Testing the Spirits

the Bible. Such self-indulgence didn't take long in spreading to the United States, where New England–based Transcendentalists such as Henry David Thoreau, Ralph Waldo Emerson, and Walt Whitman took the bait.

In his famous *Walden,* Thoreau said that "the universe constantly and obediently answers our conceptions. ... Let us spend our lives in conceiving them." Falling for the Kantian notion that the mind creates reality, Thoreau said, "I have read a Hindoo book. ... So the Soul, from the circumstances in which it is placed, mistakes its own character, until the truth is revealed to it by some holy teacher, and then it knows itself to be Brahma (God)."[2]

Some holy teacher, indeed! Thoreau had tossed aside the Christian principle of one loving God—the God of Abraham, Isaac, and Jacob—and instead pursued the quest of having his own soul manifest as a god; he had read a "Hindoo" book and was on the road to pantheism.

Thoreau made no secret of his antipathy toward Christianity. In his journal from December 15, 1841, he stated the following:

> The earth looks as fair this morning as the Valhalla of the gods. Indeed our spirits never go beyond nature. ... All [the] sounds and sights [of the woods] are elixir to my spirit. They possess a divine health. God is not more well. ... How much of my well-being, think you, depends on the condition of my lungs and stomach—such cheap pieces of Nature as they, which, indeed, she is every day reproducing with prodigality. ... I seem to see somewhat more of my own kith and kin in the lichens on the rocks than in any books. It does seem as if mine were a peculiarly wild nature, which so yearns toward all wildness.[3]

Thoreau was an articulate purveyor of the blasphemous notions of Eastern mysticism. According to this worldview, our spirits are beholden to the power of nature whereas, in fact, our spirits are beholden to the power of God, who is above nature. In his ecstasy over the sights and sounds of the woods, Thoreau mused that the woods themselves "possess a divine health" and that "God is not more well." What blasphemy! God created the trees and is certainly infinitely "more well" than the trees.

I also have a deep love of the trees, the woods, the forests, and the timbers. I, too, have lived for years amidst the trees, listening to the howls of the coyotes at night and marveling at the strangely beautiful creaking sound of timber rubbing against timber in a high wind. I have worked in the woods full time in boots and in various kinds of weather, marking off parcels of forest that were slated for sale, assessing the condition of the trees, and enjoying the grandeur of the woodland homes of eagles and bears. Yet for all my love of the timberlands, I never became one with the trees in some holistic and mystical frenzy.

Thoreau regarded God's creation—nature—as being on a par with God the creator. He blasphemously called his own lungs and stomach "cheap pieces of Nature," unaware as he was that his body was wonderfully and fearfully made by God—anything but cheap.

The Psalms remind us of God's power and majesty in His role as creator: "For you created my inmost being; you knit me together in my mother's womb. I praise you because I am fearfully and wonderfully made; your works are wonderful, I know that full well" (Ps. 139:13–14 NIV).

Thoreau pushes the idolatrous concept of Mother Nature instead of Father God. So idolatrous of nature was Thoreau that he was little moved by the stories of people in books, yet he was mightily moved by the lichens on the rocks. The lichens are a testimony to God the creator, yet Thoreau was so thoroughly entranced by the lichens themselves that he couldn't feel the power of God that undergirded the lichens, indeed the power of God that conceived of and gave life to the lichens!

Again, Thoreau was wont to push pantheism and take regular swipes at Christianity:

> I wish to meet the facts of life—the vital facts, which are the phenomena or actuality the gods meant to show us—face to face, and so I came down here. Life! Who knows what it is, what it does? ... The preacher, instead of vexing the ears of drowsy farmers on their day of rest, at the end of the week—for Sunday always seemed to me like a fit conclusion of an ill-spent week and not the fresh and brave beginning of a new one—with this one other draggletail and postponed affair of a sermon, from thirdly

to fifteenthly, should teach them with a thundering voice pause and simplicity.[4]

After all, Thoreau had read a "Hindoo" book, so he fancied himself an intellectual and from his New England hideaway declared that Christian sermons were vexing.

He favored becoming one with the lichens and preaching simplicity. He didn't want to be bothered with the Ten Commandments, just as he didn't want to be bothered with the third point or the fifteenth point of any given portion of Scripture. He just wanted to stare at the lichens on his own terms.

The subject of Thoreau is fairly personal to me. When I was young and living out in the woods near Mt. Shasta, California, there was a quotation of Thoreau's tacked to the wall of our utility room, a quote that basically urged people to walk to the beat of their own drummer. Nowadays, New Agers have their inner child and what not, whereas Thoreau had his own inner drummer. I had liked the sound of that quote growing up, but fortunately I've found out how self-indulgent and ungodly Thoreau's conceptions really were.

Merge with the lichens and be simple—that was Thoreau's message. That's a tad weird. I like lichens myself; the mosses that hang off the bark of old firs, hemlocks, and spruce are really exotic. But I have no intention of becoming one with the lichens. The way I see it, the lichens are lichens, and I am me, and the lichens are doing just fine the way they are without undergoing a merger with me. Nevertheless, Thoreau's desire to merge into oneness with lichens provides a tableau for the mystical occultism that undergirds the New Age. Brooke explains:

> Mysticism attached itself to the Romantic [and Transcendentalist] quest. To penetrate the secret world of "things in themselves" required an occult approach. Many adopted the attitude that ... the rational faculties were merely an obstacle to true knowledge. ... Ecstatic self-absorption into a mystical oneness with or through nature—most obvious in Wordsworth, Shelley, and Whitman—had become an almost conventional form of religious experience.

Nature began to be regarded as somehow divine. It was a tabloid for the sacred experience. Pantheism crept in. By the time the first translations of Hindu and Buddhist texts were made in the nineteenth century, there was an immediate influence on Western minds. Walt Whitman applauded these new mystical breakthroughs in his celebrated poem "Song of Myself." Whitman announced to the world: "Divine am I inside and out, and I make holy whatever I touch or am touched from."[5]

As nature came to be perceived as divine, supposedly the rocks became divine; the water drops became divine; and the lichens became divine, therefore pantheism had won an inroad. Transcendentalist writers saw themselves as divine and urged others to see themselves as divine also. Thoreau-esque space-out sessions put the emphasis on ecstatic experience, throwing rationality and reason—and yes, morality—to the wind.

Walter Pater, the British author of *The Renaissance*, delivered a blow to morality with the claim that "not the fruit of experience, but experience itself, is the end." Clearly, if experience is the goal without any reference to a moral compass, then everything goes and what used to be debauchery becomes merely another experience, another flavor if you will—and that was the point of the so-called Romantics and Transcendentalists. They wanted to run the back alleys of sensuality in the name of the newly kinged experience, all the while snubbing their noses at the fine heritage of Biblical strictures. Pater said one should experience things intensely and rejected any ideas which would require one to abandon the pursuit of intense experience.[6]

In 1875, a Russian occultist named Madame Blavatsky founded the Theosophical Society, and her book *Isis Unveiled* was a blatant attack on Christianity. Among other things, Blavatsky trotted out the blasphemous idea that Satan was creator. She noted that her message was given to her by Tibetan spirit masters that would surround her "as a misty cloud" and speak through her. "Someone comes and envelopes me as a misty cloud," she said, "and all at once pushes me out of myself and then I am not 'I' anymore … but someone else."[7] Demon possession is real, and demons speak a satanic, unholy message that is contrary to the Bible.

Testing the Spirits

Theosophists Annie Besant and Alice Bailey claimed to be channels for a so-called ascended master that went by the name of "The Tibetan" or "Djwhal Khul." Recently, Elizabeth Claire Prophet has also claimed to be a channel in the same line as the original Theosophists.

The Theosophists made themselves sitting ducks by opening up to the demonic realm and becoming channels for a coordinated set of satanic lies. The Theosophists' popularity in some circles shows the degree to which the very concept of evil has been scoffed at in American society, rendering people vulnerable to the lying schemes of demonic beings that are only too willing to take over a person's mind.

I once saw a bumper sticker that said "Altered State," a pun that brings to mind a state college dedicated to taking drugs. Getting high and going into an altered state was portrayed by the bumper sticker as funny and, by extension, worthwhile. This kind of cynical humor has a veneer of sophistication but, on closer examination, its hallmark is stupidity because what is being advocated could lead to diminished critical thinking abilities.

The Bible teaches that one needs to capture any evil thoughts that may flit across his or her mind, but much of America's pop culture has long advocated a fascination with evil instead, as though there's no real danger in evil images or ideas. Yoga-induced meditations that are accompanied by urgings to empty the mind, mind-altering foods such as mushrooms, and illicit drugs themselves have long conditioned Americans to flirt with

Understanding that evil exists can promote healthy levels of wariness (Gen. 3, Is. 14, Ez. 28, Jer. 17, Matt. 15). Unfortunately, New Agers routinely fall for tantalizing lies that hold up the human soul as wondrous and virtually untappable in all of its super-duper potentialities. Let us give ear to the weeping prophet: "Thus says the LORD, 'Cursed is the man who trusts in mankind, and makes flesh his strength, and whose heart turns away from the LORD.... The heart is more deceitful than all else and is desperately sick; who can understand it?' ... Those who turn away on earth will be written down, because they have forsaken the fountain of living water, even the LORD." (Jer. 17:5, 9, 13b, NASB) the disaster of mind alteration and demonic possession. Sadly, New Age adherents want desperately to think that they've latched onto something exotic and novel, unaware that they're rushing into the arms of demons.

What was so cool about James Dean, with his squinting but vacant poses and slothy demeanor? Nothing. And what was so cool about the groinal gyrations of Elvis Presley? Nothing. Instead of asking what's cool, we should ask, "What's good about such and such?" It's more important to be good than to pursue a vague and fruitless conception of cool. Indeed, in 1 John 4:1, we're told not to accept every spirit that floats by but rather to test the spirits to see which are from God. That may not be easily packaged on a bumper sticker, but we need to be sober in this modern age and not be drawn to ancient, devilish lies about the supposed pleasures of emptying (and losing) one's mind.

It is with a recognition that evil exists that one can be duly wary. Unfortunately, New Agers routinely fall for tantalizing lies that hold up the human soul as wondrous and virtually untappable in all its wonderful potentialities. Consider the over-the-top language of Pierre Teilhard de Chardin, sometimes counted as the father of the New Age: "Evolution … is a general condition to which all theories, all systems, all hypotheses must bow … a light illuminating all facts, a curve that all lines must follow."[8]

Provided one hasn't gone into a trance or emptied his mind recently, one ought to cringe at the bombastic sound of Teilhard de Chardin's imperious statement! Who is he to say that evolution, that senseless and unsupportable theory, must be bowed down to?

His statement has all the earmarks of brainwashing, yet many people submit to such bullying. He felt that some "new awareness" would reach a critical mass among the world's population, bringing men to an enlightened state he called the Omega Point.[9] Even his language has a satanic ring to it, for clearly the term "Omega Point" is a rip-off of Jesus' self-description as the Alpha and the Omega. If New Agers would spend more time reading the Word of God, they would know that it is Jesus who is the Alpha and the Omega, and they may be less inclined to accept Teilhard de Chardin's crafty language and starry-eyed claims about the ability of men to craft an upward-evolving and beautiful future.

Testing the Spirits

Teilhard de Chardin was involved in the dig at Piltdown, England, that produced bones that came to be publicized (by evolutionists) as those of a supposed ape-man called Piltdown Man. In 1912, some scientists doubted the relationship between the jaw and skull that had supposedly come from Piltdown Man. Then, lo and behold, when scientists said a canine tooth would resolve the question of the bones' interrelationship, none other than Teilhard de Chardin came up with a canine tooth—supposedly found while he was sitting on a gravel pile at the Piltdown site! How convenient and altogether suspicious!

As if that weren't enough for the beleaguered Piltdown Man, analysis in the 1950s revealed that Piltdown Man's teeth had been whittled down to give them a more human look and that the bones had been treated to make them look amazingly old. Then, in the 1980s, collagen testing proved that the jaw of Piltdown Man was actually that of an orangutan.[10]

Thus, old Tielhard de Chardin comes off smelling like a rube. He told us that evolution is "a general condition to which all systems must bow, a curve that all lines must follow" and, sure enough, it appears that the bones of Piltdown Man were manipulated to make them bow to evolution, to make them follow the curveball (or should I say, knuckleball) of evolution, to make them give off the odor of the oft-cited ape-man stage that is required by evolutionists everywhere. It would

> Analysis in the 1950s revealed that "Piltdown Man's" teeth had been whittled down to give them a more human look and that the bones had been treated to make them look amazingly old, and then in the 1980s collagen testing proved that the jaw of "Piltdown Man" was actually that of an orangutan. Thus, old Teilhard de Chardin, Father of the New Age, comes off smelling like a rube. Where Teilhard left off, *Planet of the Apes* continued on, portraying the orangutans as manlike English speakers. Earth to the New Age: Stop trying to make orangutans into men; that's cruelty to animals. Let the orangutans be orangutans. Let our children see them as beautiful orange creatures from God's hand.

109

seem that old Tielhard de Chardin put the boneheaded theory of evolution ahead of critical thought, eager to implant visions of ape-men into the eyes of his contemporaries and desperate to win fame for himself. This acclaimed father of the New Age was intent on a revolution of awareness, but brag as he might about some new plane of enlightenment called the Omega Point, at the end of the day, touting an orangutan bone as evidence for ape-men is just plain dumb.

Norman Vincent Peale is perhaps best known for his book *The Power of Positive Thinking,* but what is less known is that he was a 33rd-degree Mason and that his portrait was hung in the Masonic Temple in Washington, D.C. Perhaps Peale's feel-good strategies belie a hidden goal of taking people's eyes off divisive issues such as doctrine—at least that would seem a sound conclusion based on this warning from Christian author Dave Hunt: "Masonry is an anti-Christian religious cult rooted in paganism. Masonry contains much of the mysticism of Hinduism and Buddhism, and is Luciferian."[11]

The *Changing Image of Man,* a study put out by the Stanford Research Institute in 1974, asserted that "there does indeed appear to be a path, through a profound transformation of society, ... to a situation where our dilemmas are resolvable." Resolvable through a global leader, perhaps? But that would be downright Nimrodian. SRI's societal transformation and dilemma resolution, Hillary's "human reconstruction" and "remolding" of Western society, and the Unitarian/Bahai/U.N. anti-Christian thrust—these all emphasize humanistic solutions rather than repenting of sins and accepting Jesus as Lord and Savior.

Renowned Mason Albert Pike traced Masonry to Hinduism, Buddhism, Zoroastrianism, and other Eastern religions, noting that "like ... alchemy, [Masonry] conceals its secrets from all except the Adepts and Sages, or the Elect, and uses false explanations and misinterpretations of its symbols to mislead those who deserve only to be misled."[12]

Masonry is deceitful and secretive and, beyond that, it is downright satanic. As another authority on Masonry, Palmer Hall noted, "When the Mason ... has learned the mystery of his Craft, the seething energies of Lucifer are in his hands."[13]

What emerges is a picture of an occultic Peale pushing positivity and sugar coating the lie that people are okay by themselves, not in need of God's salvation. Somehow the Peale-inspired New Age goal of fitting in with gobs of positivity contravenes the counsel of Jude in the New Testament, where he says we are to contend for the faith. Those who contend for the faith, Christian doctrine, and the glorious truth of the gospel learn fast that many will give them the cold shoulder.

Peale's feel-good message about endearing oneself to others does in the social realm what ecumenism (ie, interfaithism) does in the realm of faith: it puts the search for short-term good feelings above the search for long-term truth.

While Tielhard de Chardin was busy trying to make people bow to his knuckle-headed general "mental condition" of evolutionary belief, and Peale was worshipping the occult with one hand and meting out grinning handshakes with the other hand, Stanford University couldn't wait to put its own imprimatur on the New Age. No less than Willis Harman, director of policy research at the Stanford Research Institute, lent his approval to the idea that people can evolve to ever higher levels of understanding. The operative word here is evolve. Harman felt that if only more people would be more understanding, then transcendentalism could do its work on society and the result would be something as great as the Protestant Reformation.

In a 1974 study called *The Changing Image of Man,* put out by the Stanford Research Institute and contributed to by Harman, it was claimed that "there does indeed appear to be a path, through a profound transformation of society ... to a situation where our dilemmas are resolvable."[14] If the premise of the Bible is that people are sinners incapable of healing their soul and in need of salvation from the Lord God of Israel, then the premise of these high-sounding New Agers is that people can transform themselves by themselves, transform their understanding by themselves—indeed, perfect themselves—on the way to a post-Protestant, post-Bible society. Notice that Harman and company talk about resolving their dilemmas, not their sins.

Excuse me, but a dilemma is having the runs during a date or spilling juice on the rug and being out of paper towels. But sin is sin, and it won't just go away because a New Ager declares himself to be transformed. After all, Hitler and Goebbels, Mao and Pol Pot, Stalin and Amin were all transformed into monsters. Therefore, transformation cannot be a goal in and of itself. The guiding principles of change are the key, and that's why the US Constitution and Bill of Rights have been so valuable for so long. What the New Agers lack in reason and rigor, they try to make up for in high-sounding, wafty talk that amounts to nothing but mealy mouthed mush. We cannot be saved by good works (Ephesians 2), but we can repent and be saved by the Lord Jesus Christ, the Alpha and the Omega.

New Age Tenets — No Divisions

In the New Age worldview, there are no divisions: hogs are bogs, and rivers are livers! To wit, Alan Watts, in his odd book *Nature, Man, and Woman*, states the following:

> [I]t becomes clearer and clearer that we do not live in a divided world. The harsh divisions of spirit and nature, mind and body, subject and object, controller and controlled are seen more and more to be awkward conventions of language. ... But the important point is that a world of interdependent relationships, where things are intelligible only in terms of each other, is a seamless unity.[15]

Call me old-fashioned, but when I take pictures, I am standing outside the subject of the photo—I don't merge with the subject of the photo. For instance, if a deer walks by and I walk up and take its picture, that's just it. There is nothing awkward about it, no "awkward conventions of language" and no "seamless unity" between me and the deer. There are seams, or divisions, between people and deer.

Another spokesman for the divisionless worldview is the infamous Bhagwan Shree Rajneesh. According to Rajneesh, life is a beautiful, meaningless whole—whatever that means. Here it is in the words of Rajneesh:

Life has no meaning; it simply exists, and exists so beautifully without meaning that there is no need. What is the meaning of a tree existing, or the sun rising every day in the morning, or the moon in the night? What is the meaning when a tree comes to bloom? And what is the meaning when the birds sing in the morning, and the stream goes on flowing, and the waves, tremendous waves of the ocean go on shattering on the rocks again and again and again? What is the meaning?

Meaning is not of the whole. The whole exists so beautifully without meaning. In fact, if there was any meaning the whole would not have been so beautiful. Because with meaning comes calculation, with meaning comes cunningness, with meaning comes reason, with meaning comes division: this is meaningful, that is meaningless, this is more meaningful, that is less meaningful. The whole exists without any distinctions. Everything is absolutely beautiful not because of any meaning, but just by being there. There is no purpose.[16]

Rajneesh would have us think that life has no meaning; there is no purpose; and the whole exists without any distinctions. But that's patently ridiculous: if life had no meaning and there were no distinctions, why did Rajneesh drive around southern Oregon in the 1970s in a huge fleet of Rolls Royces and not in a beat-up Ford Pinto? Why all the Rolls Royces if life has no meaning? Could it be that certain Eastern mystics have come to the United States to prey on Americans who dabble in the devilish realm of nihilism and moral relativism?

> If life had no meaning and there were no distinctions, why did Rajneesh drive around southern Oregon in the 1970s in a huge fleet of Rolls Royces, and not in a single, beat-up Ford Pinto?

Also into the divisionless worldview falls Swami Kriyananda (a.k.a. Donald Walters). Kriyananda founded the Ananda Cooperative Village in 1968 on the outskirts of Nevada City, California, dedicating the village to "plain living and high thinking."[17] He gave the world the following quote: "For in the frenzied pace of big-city life it is as if God were whispering to the soul: 'Dance with bubbles if you like, but when you tire of dancing, and your bubbles begin bursting one by one, look about you at all these other faces. They are your spiritual brothers and sisters, mirrors to your own self! They *are* you. O little wave, transcend your littleness. Be one with all of them. Be one with life!'"[18]

According to Kriyananda, those who watch one dancing with bubbles are themselves the person dancing with bubbles. But that's bogus. The person dancing with bubbles is the person dancing with bubbles, and the people who watch that person are the people who watch that person. The West-rejecting swami intimates that he might have had his little insight from a whisper from God, but if he heard the above message in a whisper it certainly wasn't a whisper from the God of the Bible.

God's Word makes it eminently clear that there are divisions. Take, for example, 1 John 4:1–3, where we read, "Dear friends, do not believe every spirit, but test the spirits to see whether they are from God, because many false prophets have gone out into the world. This is how you can recognize the Spirit of God: Every spirit that acknowledges that Jesus Christ has come in the flesh is from God, but every spirit that does not acknowledge Jesus is not from God. This is the spirit of the antichrist, which you have heard is coming and even now is already in the world" (NIV). Because the swami thought there were no divisions, he was not equipped to distinguish between a godly thought entering his head and a demonic thought entering his head. Therefore he embraced the lie that we live in a divisionless world.

Finally, Marc Allen, author of *Tantra for the West: A Guide to Personal Freedom,* perpetuates the divisionless worldview. "[T]here is no distinction between things," Allen says, "for all things are all the same substance, which is pure energy, at their core. You are one with a blade of grass, a tree, a star. You are the life energy of the Universe. You are endlessly being nourished by this energy ... you are eternally being reborn."[19]

What is it with New Agers and blades of grass? I don't feel one with a blade of grass, and I can roll on a lawn with the best of them. I also walk all over the grass—if I truly were one with the grass then walking on it would be akin to walking on myself, which could hurt. I have met Allen, and I liked him. We had a nice talk about book publishing in the early 1990s; he's sincere, gracious, likeable, and smart. I can say for a fact that he didn't resemble any of the varieties of grass that I've known—and, as I've said, I've seen a blade of grass or two. I've also lived out in the country, where the night was dark and the stars were bright and the trees were tall and stout, and it is with confidence that I can say Allen didn't resemble a tree or a star either.

New Age Tenets — Truth Is Out, Imagination Is In

Bhagwan Shree Rajneesh was not silent on the matter of truth, but his conception of truth was, true to form, alarmingly self-centered: "Truth is not something that you can think about; it is something that you can be. Truth is the experience of oneself being totally alone, without any object. Truth is you in your uttermost purity."[20]

Rajneesh's Hindu lie can be summarized as follows: truth cannot be thought about and, after all, truth is you. But in point of fact, Jesus is the Way, the Truth, and the Life, and people are sinners who need to look to Jesus alone for salvation and truth. One of Satan's evil purposes is to cause people to look inward, and more inward, and more inward still until all they can think about is themselves, thereby steering them away from the God of the Bible and preventing them from being saved. By saying that truth could not be thought about, Rajneesh was trying to diminish his listeners' capacity to think and reason, for true seeking would inexorably bring one to the truth of Jesus Christ.

After taking a swipe at thinking, Rajneesh goes after the function of the mind. "*Ritambhara*," he says, "is a very beautiful word; it is just like Tao. The word truth cannot explain it completely. In the Vedas it is called *rit*. *Rit* means the very foundation of the cosmos. ... [M]ind creates the world and no-mind allows you to know that which is. ... Rather than calling *[rit]* truth, it will be better to call it the very ground of being. Truth seems to be a distant thing, something that exists separate from you. *Rit* is our innermost being.*"*[21]

In short, he's saying that *rit* is simultaneously the foundation of the cosmos as well as a person's innermost being; he's saying that people who create the world with their minds are also the foundation of the cosmos; he's saying that no mind is the way to go, for that allows one to know that which is; and semantics aside, in effect he's saying that the way to truth is to throw away your mind. Rajneesh wants his listeners to check their minds at the door and let him tell them which way is up.

Another New Ager intent on letting the mind take a back seat is Shakti Gawain, author of *Living in the Light: A Guide to Personal and Planetary Transformation:*

> I believe that every being chooses the life path and relationships that will help him or her to grow the fastest. As we continue to evolve, I believe we will gradually stop categorizing ourselves and our relationships with any particular labels such as gay, straight, monogamous, open, and so on. I foresee a time when each person can be a unique entity with his or her free-flowing style of expression. Each relationship will be a unique connection between two beings, taking its individual form and expression. No categories are possible because each one is so different and follows its own flow of energy.[22]

For someone who authored a book called *Living in the Light,* it's amazing how in the dark Gawain is. Her notion that everyone chooses the path for the fastest growth or relationships for the fastest growth is naïve; clearly, many people have passed up potentially good relationships and have fallen into terribly destructive relationships. It would seem very telling that the categories she wants to abandon have to do with sexual proscriptions: many people who run from God are looking for an excuse to justify their sexual lusts.

> The Genesis 19 account of the destruction of Sodom and Gomorrah stands as a powerful reminder that ungodly, licentious sex can lead to the ruin of a man, the ruin of a woman, and the ruin of whole cities.

Out of all the categories she could have singled out for expunging—factory-style dairy farms, big-game hunting, trading with dictators, and high taxes—she chooses to call for the expunging of value-laden sexual morals. As a self-styled guru of "unique and free-flowing personal energy," Gawain envisions a future when homosexuals, adulterers, and fornicators will be one lump of "unique expressions," "unique entities," "unique energy flows," and "free-flowing styles." Rubbish. Attaching the word "unique" to a person doesn't take away that person's sin. "No categories are possible," she says. But, alas, categories are not only possible—they're here and they're here to stay.

On the topic of gays and lesbians, Gawain states that "I do have a strong sense that on a spiritual level, homosexual and bisexual relationships are a powerful step that some beings take to break through old, rigid roles and stereotypes to find their own truth."[23] The idea that homosexuals are, by virtue of their illicit sex, taking powerful steps towards truth is misleading and beguiling. The Genesis 19 account of the destruction of Sodom and Gomorrah stands as a powerful reminder that ungodly, licentious sex can lead to the ruin of a man, the ruin of a woman, and the ruin of whole cities.

"Move to the natural attraction," Rajneesh says. "[T]hen you are one, then you are whole, then you are together. Then you are one piece, not a house divided against itself. And when you move as one piece there is dance in your step and there is nothing which is not divine."[24] Rajneesh describes following one's natural attractions as the way to be whole and even divine. How different this endorsement of self-indulgence is from Paul's endorsement of self-restraint in the book of Romans!

I believe that Hurricane Katrina (August 2005) was clearly punishment on a voodoo-ridden, sodomy-ridden New Orleans, and a wake-up call to San Francisco and America at large. But unfortunately, soon after the physical clean-up, the liberals got back to the dirty business of continuing the hellish Mardi Gras parades and extending homosexual rights. Furthermore, I believe that Katrina, which occurred just days after the forcible evacuation of 9,500 Jews from Gush Katif in Gaza and part of Samaria, was divine retribution for the US-backed action to diminish Jewish Israel. One could say the Katrina event drove home at least two lessons from ancient times: the iniquity of Sodom and Gomorrah brought forth judgment from the LORD in the form of fire and brimstone raining from out of heaven, destroying the cities, their inhabitants, and that which grew on the ground (Gen. 19); and the LORD said unto Abram, "And I will bless them that bless thee, and curse him that curseth thee" (Gen. 12:3a KJV).

According to the New Age gurus, thinking (or using one's mind) is to be scorned, and people are free to express themselves and pursue pleasure without regard for trite categories such as good and bad, homosexual and straight. For the gurus, history would seem to be particularly meddlesome, laden as it is with so many lessons.

Alan Watts was troubled by the past: "Because we are always looking for precedents, for authority from the past for what we are supposed to do now, that gives us the impression the past is all-important and is the determinative factor in our behavior. ... It isn't anything of the kind. The life, the creation, comes out of you now. ... Don't look for the creation of the universe at some very far-distant point in time behind us. The creation of the universe is now in this present instant. This is where it all begins!"[25]

Watts seeks to diminish the importance of history and encourages folks to think that the creation comes out of them. What blasphemy! The reason history had to be excused from the room, so to speak, is that it shows the ridiculousness of Watts' claims.

Marilyn Ferguson says:

> The potential for rescue at this time of crisis is neither luck, coincidence, nor wishful thinking. We are living in [a] time in which we can intentionally align ourselves with nature for rapid remaking of ourselves and our collapsing institutions. ... The paradigm of the Aquarian Conspiracy sees humankind embedded in nature. ... Heirs to evolutionary riches, we are capable of imagination, invention, and experiences we have only glimpsed. ... Human nature is neither good nor bad but open to continuous transformation and transcendence. It has only to discover itself. The new perspective respects the ecology of everything: birth, death, learning, health, family, work, science, spirituality, the arts, the community, relationships, politics.[26]

Ferguson is saying that we can rescue ourselves, remake ourselves, remake our institutions, imagine, and rely on our human natures for transcendence and transformation! Unfortunately for adherents of the New Age, we have a sin nature and can't rescue ourselves by ourselves.

But fortunately for adherents of the New Age, they can repent of their bad ways and give their hearts to Jesus Christ; in that way, they can know the truth, develop their minds, learn from history, study Bible prophecy, and be a good influence on those around them.

Also, Ferguson's use of the word "ecology" is pure gobbledygook. What is "the ecology of work" supposed to mean? This penchant for New Age buzzwords is a tipoff to a rather insipid and unanalytical thought process. But that shouldn't be surprising, since we've already seen that part of the New Age creed is to check one's mind, along with one's hat, at the door.

New Age Tenets — Shades of Consciousness

Pot smokers are seeking something, but altered states of consciousness through illicit drugs can lead to mental fog and an impairment of one's overall faculties. Our minds and faculties of reason are gifts from the Lord our God, enabling us to make sense of the world around us and, most importantly, enabling us to study and appreciate the Word of God. For one thing, it's impossible to learn the intricacies of Bible prophecy when one is strung out on drugs or suffering from delusions of godhood. As far as consciousness is concerned, fearing the Lord and understanding oneself as part of God's creation would be a good place to start.

Swami Kriyananda had other ideas. This American-turned-guru drank of the elixir of the superconscious—and lo and behold, he worked out some Hindu-like notions of the divine self while on a long walk. "And then I came upon excerpts from the Hindu teachings," the swami says, "a few pages only, but what a revelation! Here the emphasis was on cosmic realities. God was described as an Infinite Consciousness; man, as a manifestation of that consciousness. Why, this was the very concept I myself had worked out on that long evening walk in Charleston! Man's highest duty, I read, is to attune himself with that divine consciousness: Again, this was what I had worked out! Man's ultimate goal, according to these writings, is to experience that divine reality *as his true Self.*"[27]

Notice the swami's emphasis on the self, and his own ability to work out the nature of the "infinite consciousness" while walking—in Charleston, South Carolina, no less. The swami-in-the-making read a few pages of Hindu stuff and—wow!—it seemed to confirm what he'd pondered about in Charleston, and he traded the fine Southern tradition of believing in a personal relationship with the God of the Bible for some weird notion of superconsciousness. Bad move.

Another consciousness-tinkerer, Bhagwan Shree Rajneesh had a thing for the unconscious. In my opinion, he just wanted to dumb people down, make them all zoned out, man, so that he could shape them like Silly Putty:

> Listen to your needs whatsoever unconscious is saying. Always remember: unconscious is right, because it has the wisdom of the ages. Millions of lives you have existed. The conscious belongs to this life; it has been trained in the schools and the universities, and the family and this society in which you are born, coincidentally born. But the unconscious carries all the experiences of all your lives. It carries the experience when you were a rock, it carries the experience when you were a tree, it carries the experience when you were animals—it carries all, the whole past. Unconscious is tremendously wise and conscious is tremendously foolish. … Unconscious is eternal wisdom. Listen to it.[28]

The swami-in-the-making read a few pages of Hindu stuff and—wow!—it seemed to confirm what he'd pondered about in Charleston, so he traded the fine Southern tradition of believing in a personal relationship with the God of the Bible for some weird notion of superconsciousness. Bad move.

This guy wanted people to believe in the theory of evolution, conveniently offering no evidence for the idea that we were once rocks, trees, and animals—but nevermind, the guru just expected people to do as he said. The bottom line here is that unconscious (and therefore malleable) people are guru-friendly, whereas conscious and discerning folks have a better chance of seeing through a guru's beguiling words.

Also worth noting is the way he says "Listen to … whatsoever unconscious is saying." It is my sense that Rajneesh adopted a sliver of the older English parlance, specifically that used in the King James Version of the Bible, when he used the word "whatsoever." It's a small point, but such usage would likely make his potential American followers feel more at ease—so able is their guru in using ingratiating language. Rajneesh describes the process of connecting to the "superconscious":

> First become more and more alert in waking hours. That will bring you to a certain degree of heat. It is really a certain degree of inner heat, a certain temperature of your consciousness. That will help you to move into the unconscious. ... Then suddenly one day you will find you are moving upwards; you have become weightless. Now the gravitation doesn't affect you. You are becoming superconscious. ... Superconscious has all the power: it is omnipotent, it is omniscient, it is omnipresent.

> "Those who believe in the possibility of impending social transformation ... trust the transformative process itself.... [T]hey believe that if enough individuals discover new capacities in themselves they will naturally conspire to create a world hospitable to human imagination, growth, and cooperation.... The proven plasticity of the human brain and human awareness offers the possibility that individual evolution may lead to collective evolution."
> —Marilyn Ferguson, New Age Author

Ferguson's "social transformation" and "collective evolution"; Hillary's "human reconstruction" and "remolding" of Western society in tandem with Eastern dictators; Freud and Jung's denigration of Christianity; and Gates' low-bandwidth handshake with Dictator Hu—these all point to a squeezing of Christian America and the amassing of a worldwide Antichrist government.

> Superconscious is everywhere. Superconscious has every power that is possible, and superconscious sees everything…[29]

Of course it's the "inner heat" that brings on the unconscious and then the superconscious—with dreamy and abstruse mechanisms such as inner heat, who could fault the guru? After all, it's too complicated, too ineffable—or so we're to believe. But why believe in this hogwash? Be very wary of the guru.

All the talk about experiments in consciousness is leading up to envisioned global change and human transformation through the accumulation of global mass consciousness. Shakti Gawain explains how she thinks the world will transform by way of an increasingly enlightened mass consciousness: "As each one of us individually surrenders to the power of the universe and allows that power to transform and enlighten us, the group channel is affected accordingly. The mass consciousness becomes more and more enlightened. This is how I see our world being transformed." Even in her workshops, she has opted to "create a group channel and then allow the universe to take over and guide the group as a whole." She says, "[F]ocus on the channel in each person you're with and see that every exchange you have with them is the universe talking to you. As you acknowledge your own true power and that of others the light will grow."[30]

Given that the universe is God's creation, and Gawain wants people to surrender to the universe, in effect, she is advocating a form of pagan worship—that is to say, a worship of the creation. But we know from Romans 1 that we are to worship the Creator, not the creation. It is troubling that Gawain's experiments in group channeling produced the goal of focusing on one's own true power, as if people have the power to transform and redeem themselves—this idea is intended to pull people away from God, so the spirit coming through the group channel process is seen to be an antichrist spirit.

In the same vein, Gawain says that "you can [effect change by asking] your higher self for help in releasing the old and bringing in the new pattern."[31] The higher self? What higher self? This kind of airy talk about latent and transforming inner abilities is very appealing to some people's sense of pride, but pride goes before destruction (Prov. 16:18). Empirically speaking, I've never seen any evidence that anybody I know has some "higher self" hidden away in his sleeve, ready to pop out and transform him and the world at the click of the fingers.

Following along this quest for personal power, Gawain indicates that what one wants one has only to create: "If a person truly and unequivocally wants a committed relationship, he will simply attract another person who wants the same thing. If someone feels completely clear about wanting to explore being with many partners he simply does it. ... Seeing the world as your mirror also gives you wonderful opportunities to receive positive feedback. Think of everything that you like and enjoy about your life right now. You created these things."[32] It is an occultic idea that one can just think his personal world into being; much of our circumstances are dictated by outside factors, indeed by the providence of God.

Perhaps the most articulate explanation of global human transformation through a quantum leap in consciousness comes from Marilyn Ferguson: "Those who believe in the possibility of impending social transformation ... trust the transformative process itself. ... [T]hey believe that if enough individuals discover new capacities in themselves they will naturally conspire to create a world hospitable to human imagination, growth, and cooperation. ... The proven plasticity of the human brain and human awareness offers the possibility that *individual evolution* may lead to *collective evolution*. When one person has unlocked a new capacity its existence is suddenly evident to others, who may then develop the same capacity."[33]

History shows what the human brain and human awareness are capable of, and it proves we are not capable of redeeming ourselves; instead, we need to recognize our sin nature, repent of our sins, and give our hearts to Jesus Christ. Through Him we can attain to the kind of change that heals communities and heals societies, but without Him people are left flailing in the winds of stubborn conceit. Moreover, Ferguson's description of collective evolution is naïve. Evolutionary theory in all its guises is simplistic and devilishly false.

New Age Tenets — Reaching for Godhood

Sometime in the seventies, as near I can tell, there was a wave of satanic deception that swept through our land. The goal of reaching for godhood was gaining momentum in this largely Christian nation. Tal Brooke traced some of the names this reaching for godhood has taken:

> A single thought has danced as a whirling dervish across history, seducing millions in its path. Indeed this very thought seduced the highest created intelligence in the universe. It was also great enough to cause the fall of the entire human race. It has invaded culture after culture, each time captivating the hearts and minds of the people. People find it infinitely desirable and beautiful, its promises irresistible, as it seems to hold such great promise. ... It is the Great Lie. It is the foundation stone of Hinduism, Buddhism, Sufism, Jainism, Sikhism, Taoism ... as well as too many cults to mention. It is the central foundation stone of the New Age movement.
>
> The tenets of the Great Lie have been chanted on the banks of the Ganges since time immemorial. Weather-beaten sages have uttered secret syllables and mantras in caves to invoke its powers. Modern meditators have sought to plumb its secret depths as they have gathered in intimate meetings from MIT to Esalen, from Greenwich Village to Marin County, from the west bank of the Seine to Cambridge, England.
>
> The Great Lie is quite simply the belief that *man is God*... [34]

How audacious that an ordinary man would want to be like unto God, when God is our creator, father, and redeemer! Have people no shame? Have folks lost all sense of proportion? Have they flipped their lids? It boggles the imagination and would be hard to pin down as a real happening were it not for the fact that so many New Agers are all too willing to discuss their goal of godhood.

"It is a rational conclusion," says Bhagwan Shree Rajneesh, "that 'I am part of the whole and the whole is God, so of course I am God.' ... Because sometimes, when you are very quiet and the doors of the senses are clear, this feeling arises of being a god. Listening to music, suddenly you are no more a human being. If your ears are ready and if you have the musical perception, suddenly you are elevated to a different plane. Making love to a woman you love—suddenly, in the peak of the orgasm, you feel you have become a god."[35] Rajneesh is a veritable font of falsehoods.

God created the creation and, as such, He is above and sovereign over the creation, so it's not true that the whole is God; God is above us and His ways are higher than ours. Moreover, one doesn't listen to music or make love and become a god. In the modern vernacular, ecstasy does not a god make.

Not that it's easy being a New Ager. "Being a very evolved spirit in a relatively unevolved form," says Shakti Gawain, "is quite uncomfortable. It accounts for most of the problems we are having. It's as if we are gods and goddesses living in little mud hovels and driving around in clunky, funky, old jalopies. It can be frustrating and demeaning—especially when nobody even recognizes who we are! When we were oblivious of who we were it wasn't so bad; we just accepted it as our lot in life. But now that we remember our true identity, we may feel like we're trapped in an alien world."[36]

Not only is it hard for the would-be gods to endure not being recognized, but it's hard for regular folks to relate to the fake gods as well. I once met a fellow who revealed that he had left Mormondom but still held to the idea that people could become gods—his Mormon training still had a hold on him. I shared my Christian beliefs and that was that. I, too, have enjoyed many Mormons' friendships, but I flatly reject their false prophets, the heretical Book of Mormon, the *Pearl of Great Price*, and *Doctrine and Covenants*.

Not to be outdone, Marc Allen, an advocate of tantric sex, notes that "we are all God-like beings; we all create our own experience—we even create our own bodies, through our deepest mental imagery and affirmations. So when a man admires a woman walking down the street, it is God admiring his own creation. And that woman herself is God enjoying her own creation. ... Sex is ... a deeply sacred act, whether it is part of our deepest relationships, or even whether it is a very casual, impulsive thing with a person we may hardly know."[37]

In this instance, the would-be god apparently created every woman he admires on the street. Call me old-fashioned, but that's just wacky. And since when is casual sex with someone you barely know a deeply sacred act? That kind of claim is a bold attempt to justify and validate fornication because old-fashioned ideals such as eschewing fornication are really a drag for would-be gods. All this open-sex talk from one would-be god after another seems like something of a tip-off: is it possible that one of the attractions of pursuing godhood is nothing more than a desire to make one's own rules and walk in rebellion?

New Age Practices

Why don't the New Agers talk about being one with cow poop? After all, their idea about merging into oneness with nature *is* a bunch of cow poop.

Like Swami Kriyananda, I admire the beauty of raindrops on leaves—but I'll leave it at admiration, thank you very much. But the New Age impulse is to merge with said raindrops, to get inside of them as it were. "I tried consciously," Kriyananda says, "to *feel* the thrill of a raindrop as it quivered on a pine needle; the exquisite freshness of the morning dew; the burst of sunlight through the clouds at sunset. … But now, as I endeavored to intensify my sensitivity, *to enter directly* into the life all around me, I discovered with a pang what an utter prisoner I was, locked in my own ego. I could see; I could not *feel*."[38]

Most raindrops I know of are rather small, so entering directly into them is a bit of a stretch. Of course, I'm not oblivious to the ecstatic sense in which the swami entertained the notion of entering into the life of a raindrop, but really, how are we to relate to the raindrop? The raindrop is the raindrop, and you are you, and there are divisions. Try as they might, the New Agers cannot, and must not, be raindrops—and I say this as someone who is avidly pro-raindrop. The New Agers must be stopped in their quest to become raindrops, for the thought of a whole slew of New Agers hanging all over the leaves after a rain is just too appalling for words.

Let the raindrop be the raindrop. Anyway, why don't the New Agers want to merge with a tornado? That's a part of nature too and also capable of its own brand of forbidding beauty. Why do they always want to merge with a selective few fuzzy parts of nature? If they want to merge, let them merge into the Truckee River, near Lake Tahoe in California, and maybe they'll shed their ecstasy and learn a bit of fear—fear of the Lord! The Truckee River is so cold that it will shut down the New Ager's selective ecstasy in a few short minutes. Indeed, as the Bible says in Rom. 1:20, "For since the creation of the world God's invisible qualities—his eternal power and divine nature—have been clearly seen, being understood from what has been made, so that men are without excuse" (NIV). Ecstatic New Agers should consider the power of nature and fear the one who made the natural world.

Another New Age practice is to bash the West. Fuzzy-headed New Agers decided that the very mindset of Westerners had to change; that while the West counted the trees, it was the East that saw the forest; and that we Westerners must learn to see the forest. New Agers urged one to take "the central door," to borrow a phrase from Aldous Huxley's description of his favored spiritual path, and the central door is just another way of describing a splitting of the difference, which amounts to ecumenism, or interfaithism.

Huxley's central door may sound inoffensive at first, little more than a politic compromise, but it's really a sneaky way of opposing the Christian claim that the Bible offers the only truth and the only true God. So, in spite of the New Agers' hype about harmony and wholeness, the New Age is a direct affront to Christianity and wants no merger with true Christianity. And just as well—true Christianity wants no merger with the New Age conceits either. The difference is that New Age hype promotes the New Age as an agent of wholeness and compromise when it's nothing of the sort, whereas true Christianity advocates just what it is: a singular view of the truth without trying to be everything to everybody.

This New Age practice of throwing away the West's Biblical heritage and embracing any foul thing that flies in from the Far East is quite pervasive. Marilyn Ferguson betrays her bias against the West in the following: "[T]ransforming leaders know that you cannot 'teach' or 'help' others to higher awareness in the same way you might teach them to prepare tax forms. [But] you can seduce people into direct experiences. ... Nor do the most effective leaders take credit for changes they help to elicit. As Lao-Tse said, leadership is best when the people say, 'We did it ourselves.'"[39]

Ferguson is saying that leaders who understand the New Age art of mass transformation know the importance of seduction, experience (as a substitute for rigorous thought, which would be too Western), and sayings by Chinese mystics. Her admission that dutiful, transforming New Age teachers are seducers is very telling. Seduction works when one's faculties have been dulled by dazzling or confusion—but dulled nevertheless. The medieval Latin word *seducere* means "to lead astray," and that is just what the New Age teachers do.

New Agers try to perfect society through networks. In her seminal work *The Aquarian Conspiracy: Personal and Social Transformation in the 1980s,* Ferguson touts networking and coalition building as avenues for societal transformation: apparently Gandhi indicated that a "circle of unities" could envelop the whole world, and Edward Carpenter spoke of using networks upon networks to create a "finished and free society."

How do those networks work anyway? Art historian Jose Arguelles spoke of networks being sort of like the left and right hemispheres of the brain coming together, like the unity of intellect and intuition. Physicist John Platt spoke of bringing about "a kind of local Utopia" by giving to those around us. Ferguson says that once one has seen the power of humans aligned, one "cannot think about the future in old terms." And anthropologist Luther Gerlach believes that networks produce "valuable local mutations" and that "news of successful experiments travels swiftly across the movement linkages, and they are widely adopted."[40]

Lofty-sounding stuff! How heady and daring! Just a few problems: firstly, both hemispheres of the brain are already together inside the cranium, so the push to bring them together is an exercise in redundancy. Secondly, creating utopias locally has been tried and failed; maybe there's a message there. Thirdly, if people could perfect their aligning powers, they would have done so long ago and, contrary to New Age platitudes, the future can be thought of in old terms—in terms of old Bible prophecy to be exact. And fourthly, networking to bring about "valuable local mutations" that will spread widely and globally is to be part of an anthropological fantasy with more than a hint of social Darwinism in it—and social Darwinism was a concept that undergirded Hitler, Stalin, Mao, and Pol Pot's sickening and horrifying dreams of social engineering.

A general New Age practice is to pursue things that seem round or circle-like, such as Taoist symbols with their complementary yin and yang components. Part of the circle appeal is an apparent absence of any necessity to find a clear progression, delineation, or end point, as one would expect in the case of a straight line (especially in the case of the straight-and-narrow way of faith and righteousness spoken of in the Bible). With circles, a la Taoist thought, the goal is to say that every point is somehow interconnected with everything else; much emphasis is put on the purported flow, or interchange, between various conditions represented by the circle of human experience but always without judgment because everything is said to be becoming and merging and never really static and therefore never really judgeable. This creeping Eastern mysticism has lodged in the brains of many impressionable Americans, leaving a disastrous trail of wishy-washy relativistic thinking in American academia.

Gunther Stent, a molecular biologist at the University of California at Berkeley, in his book *The Coming of the Golden Age: A View of the End of Progress,* states that science is already on the decline because young students entering the sciences are no longer convinced that true knowledge is possible. Speaking as a secular observer, Stent feels that since God has been dethroned (in much of American society), there are no longer any clear-cut standards or values. So feeling that correct discriminations are no longer possible with regard to human aspirations and behavior, the pleasure principle becomes the highest value in men's lives.[41]

Taoist moral relativism, as found in the *Yi Ching*, has many Western adherents who wish the Far East to be their own private fantasy. This golden dragon is on the doors of Thian Hock Keng Temple, a Hokkien Chinese temple (Taoist) in Singapore dedicated to the sea goddess Ma Zu. Apostasy is a worldwide problem. This falling away from the true faith and the revealing of the Antichrist will precede the day of the Lord.

"Now we request you, brethren, with regard to the coming of our Lord Jesus Christ and our gathering together to Him, that you not be quickly shaken from your composure or be disturbed either by a spirit or a message or a letter as if from us, to the effect that the day of the Lord has come. Let no one in any way deceive you, for *it will not come* unless the apostasy comes first, and the man of lawlessness is revealed, the son of destruction, who opposes and exalts himself above every so-called god or object of worship, so that he takes his seat in the temple of God, displaying himself as being God" (2 Thess. 2:1–4 NASB).

Speaking of the pleasure principle, check out Marc Allen describing a reshaping period in his life:

> When I started to realize that I was actually creating my life exactly as I wanted it, a lot of changes happened in my life. Sexually, I became more and more open. I saw that I had often dreamed of a great deal of openness, and suddenly I was free to try anything. In my fantasies, I wanted to try group sex, and I wanted to try massage parlors, and prostitutes. These were things which were forbidden, and tantalizing just because they were forbidden—like bars were before I turned 21. So I gave myself permission to do all of these things. I plunged into my fantasies and lived them out. The experiences were invaluable…
>
> Do what you have the energy to do. If you follow your feelings, you'll never go wrong. You may do something extreme, like I did. But you'll find a much greater clarity about yourself afterwards…[42]

Allen describes a spasm of hedonism and fornication and says the experiences were quite valuable, urging others to follow their feelings wherever they may lead. His emphasis on feelings and energy amounts to so much claptrap in my opinion. Without Jesus and without righteousness, these things lead to an all-about-me mentality and little more than a flimsy shell of false integrity. It's just like Gunther Stent indicated—the pleasure principle has come to reign supreme in many Americans' lives.

New Agers are given to self-flattery and absurd self-estimations. Alan Watts shares this:

> Watch your breathing, and become aware that both the voluntary and the involuntary aspects of your experience are all one happening. … You may think … *am I really doing everything that's going along?* If I were, I should be God and that would be very embarrassing because I would be in charge of everything—that would be a terribly responsible position! The truth of the matter is

[that] ... [e]verything is happening to you, and you are doing everything. For example, your eyes are turning the sun into light ... [and] it's your eardrums that are turning vibrations in the air into sound. This is the way in which you are creating the world. ... Don't be selective [or think] 'I should think of this and not that'. ... [T]o have the mind free from discursive, verbal thinking, chanted sound is extremely useful. If you, for example, simply listen to a gong, let that sound be the whole of your experience. ... And then along with that, or alone if you don't have a gong, you can use what in the Sanskrit language is called mantra. Mantras are chanted sounds which are used not for their meaning but for the simple tone, and they go along with slow breathing. One of the basic mantras is, of course, the word spelled OM. That sound is used because it runs from the back of your throat to your lips and contains the whole range of the voice and—it represents the total energy of the universe. This word is called the *pranava,* the name for the Ultimate Reality. ... You will become completely absorbed in the sound and find yourself living in an eternal now in which there is no past and there is no future, and there is not difference between what you are as knower and what you are as the known, between yourself and the world of nature outside you. It all becomes one doing, one happening. ... [Y]ou may find, according to your temperament, it is easier to do a fast-moving [chant]. These have a rhythm that is absorbing. A chant that you may have heard goes *Hari Krishna, Hari Krishna, Krishna Krishna, Hari Hari.* ... And it doesn't matter what it means (actually Krishna and Rama are the names of Hindu divinities). ... But you see, to go out of your mind at least once a day is tremendously important...[43]

Watts has articulated the case for New Age meditation, and it still makes no sense. He cites our ability to see and hear as evidence that we're "creating the world." What madness! Watts would have one throw away "discursive, verbal thinking" (ie, reason), chant mantras about universal energy or Hindu gods, enter into the all-important now, forget the past, forget the future, forget about distinctions or divisions or differences, be part of the one happening, man, and "go out of your mind." In Eastern mysticism, occult notions of god-like grandeur flatter one's senses, and promises of personal power can lead one astray.

In the April 2003 edition of the *Sedona Journal of Emergence,* there is a long list of channelers—people who have opened themselves to familiar spirits, giving rise to some demonic-sounding messages. Channeler Pam Murray acted as a channel for the teachings of the Council of Many Waters in the Luminus Command, and through Murray the Council of Many Waters taught the following:

> [Take] three breaths. This time, while holding your breath, just listen. Focus on your ears. After some practice, you might hear some soft tones or even music. This is the heavenly vibration, the chord of the universe ... If you are disciplined in this little exercise, someday, when you need it most, you will have exactly the right answer or you will attract exactly the right person or money for a want or need. Then you will understand the power of the Now. This is a step toward Eden. That is all. Go in peace.[44]

What is channeled carries the recurrent theme of Satan's lie—a lie which purports that people are god-like and therefore don't need a redeemer, that history and prophecy should be ignored, that people can create a wonderful society, an Eden, on their own without the God of the Bible. I believe channelers are a conduit for the demons, speaking craftily-packaged anti-Christian messages into the world of men.

Once again, we see the present moment being held up and glorified to the exclusion of the past and future (ie, to the exclusion of history and prophecy). We see someone holding his breath, concentrating on his ears, supposedly hearing vibrations of heaven and sounds of the universe, and positioning himself to be able to attract money or people or what not, all as a function of the "power of now" and with some pretensions about moving towards an Edenic society in which people have solved their problems and have ascended to a higher state. What is channeled carries the recurrent theme of Satan's lie—a lie that purports that people are god-like and therefore don't need a redeemer, that history and prophecy should be ignored, that people can create a wonderful society, an Eden, on their own without the God of the Bible. I believe channelers are a conduit for the demons, speaking craftily packaged demonic messages into the world of men.

In another channeling, an entity named Kryon channeled a blatantly anti-Christian message through a man named Lee Carroll. Through Carroll, Kryon taught the following:

> This organization you call the Church is being reevaluated and pruned. And it's not just limited to the Western world, either.
>
> Watch for it worldwide. We told you about this almost three years ago when we said, "The greatest spiritual leaders you have who search for the divine on your planet are coming to a reckoning even as you sit here." Now the energy of what you've created has caught up with them! The result? There will be more integrity within the ranks of those who lead the planet on a spiritual level. ... That's what a vibrational increase does—there are fewer dark places. ... The old energy thinkers will have to change, for if they don't, they'll find themselves in an old consciousness within a new energy. ... Oh, it's true that you're ... seemingly in the dark and you don't understand everything. But we're telling you that during these past years, what has happened is that you've given permission to turn on the light! Much of what is happening now is simply due to that. ...
>
> The gifts of Spirit and self-empowerment lay there, waiting for your discovery in what used to be the darkness. They

represent the new tools of life. They represent what you've called ascension. And what is this ascension? Did you know that this word doesn't mean "leaving the planet?" Ascension means moving to a higher vibration where you stay on the planet in an enhanced form and make a difference![45]

The suggestion that the Christian Church is being reevaluated and pruned is another anti-Christian message, as it is the wish of Satan and the other fallen angels that the Christian Church would be revamped and shrunk down. We read that a "vibrational increase" will lead to fewer dark places in the world, that in effect people can redeem themselves if they'll only empower themselves and discover their hidden potential. It's suggested that "old-energy thinkers" (a sly reference to Christians) will have to change amidst the "new energy" brought about by the channelers and their channeled (New Age) messages. Moreover, it's suggested that people can stay on the planet in an "enhanced form."

In stark contrast, the Bible teaches that we must repent of our sins, not empower ourselves, and that we have the hope of heaven (which will be created anew, after the Millennial Reign of Christ and the subsequent passing away of this planet), not the hope of some super-duper society as the result of self-enhanced hearts. Kryon's denial of a future ascension would seem to be a veiled denial of the coming catching up of the saints (Matthew 24). New Age shopkeepers like to wrap themselves in fuzzy and warm appurtenances such as supposedly power-giving stones and oils and mini cascading waterfalls, and there's often aromatic incense wafting throughout the store. But inside New Age magazines and books are a host of pointedly anti-Christian messages. To the discerning reader, there's nothing fuzzy and warm about those anti-Bible messages.

Yet another anti-Christian message comes to us from Nademus through the channeler Brenda Hill. Hill's channeled message begins with the salutation "Good day, entities," making reference to one's "magnificently creative self," and finally encourages one to be "the god that he or she is." Right off the bat, the message makes it clear that people should be understood as entities and therefore not the creation of the God of the Bible; the emphasis is on the creative power that is inherent in people, going so far as to suggest that people generally are "magnificently creative," and magnificence is assigned to people and not to the God of the Bible. And at length the message gets to its point, that is to say, that people can be gods if they'd only give themselves permission (ie, empower themselves). A key snippet from the message is as follows:

> [I]f you approach confusion with the realization that it is simply a conditioned way to slow down the decision-making process to a manageable pace, then the concept of limitation and inability and lack are not prevalent in your energy field. And when these conditions are not present in your energy field, you begin to recognize that it is your own personal power, as the creator god you are, that is relegating thought to its malleable place. ... Allow yourselves the process of the awakening god. ... Allow yourselves to be the god you are, cloaked in humanity. Indeed, entities, I am Nademus. Adieu.[46]

How strange that confusion is being promoted here as an aid to thought. Obviously, confusion itself is an obstacle, a hurdle to be overcome, and clear thought is achieved by applying reason to an otherwise unwieldy and potentially confusing set of data; confusion is to be avoided, not embraced. One thinks of Pablo Picasso's numerous obscene paintings in which people are depicted as dismembered and stretched and disfigured—his ghoulish and sickening portrayals should act as a warning against an embrace of confusion.

The above message seeks to relegate and demote thought so that one can leave thought behind and embrace one's own supposed godhood. The Bible teaches that if one truly seeks, he will find the Lord (1 Chron. 28:9), but the demons that inspire New Age channelers don't want people to seek with clear-thinking noodles for fear that people might reason their way through Scripture to a saving knowledge of Christ Jesus. Confusion is a tool and a weapon used by the demons to waylay the unwary, seduce the muddle-headed soul away from Holy Scripture and toward the satanic mirage of personal godhood. Hill's channeled message from Nademus has all the earmarks of being demonic.

Thought, in the Bible, is given a place of high importance. "Come now, let us reason together," says the Lord in Is. 1:18–20. "Though your sins are like scarlet, they shall be as white as snow; though they are red as crimson, they shall be like wool. If you are willing and obedient, you will eat the best from the land; but if you resist and rebel, you will be devoured by the sword." Clearly, one's God-given faculty of reason is useful for recognizing the difference between salvation and obedience on the one hand and destruction and rebellion on the other hand. In Prov. 15:2 , we see that "the tongue of the wise commends knowledge, but the mouth of the fool gushes folly" (NIV).

In Prov. 14:15, we see that "a simple man believes anything, but a prudent man gives thought to his steps" (NIV). Careful thought can be used to produce careful and prudent steps, whereas gullible and confused thinking produces confused and errant steps. Certainly, confusion is to be avoided, not embraced. If the messages coming through channelers really represented a realistic and true impulse to achieve global transformation by way of good vibrations and evolutionary advancement, then we would expect to see significant variation from one channeled message to the other. But that's not what we see. We see nearly identical messages coming through the channelers, messages that tout evolution and personal godhood and the prospect of achieving global peace and prosperity by tapping into our own "magnificently creative" selves and raising the collective societal vibrations worldwide. It is precisely the homogeneity and anti-Christian nature of the channeled messages that indicate they stem from a common source—indeed, from the realm of demons.

Through channeler Tom Kenyon comes the message of "the Hathors":

> If you are blocked from your evolutionary advancement by those in power and the religious, social and political structures of your society, your race will be imprisoned in a very real way—not through bars, but through the closing of the doors of perception. Eventually you will free yourselves from this tyranny, but you have in this moment of time an opportunity to tilt the scales in favor of human freedom and to usher in an age of planetary peace and

> renaissance that you have never seen before. ... [Y]ou are nothing less than creator gods and goddesses. Know that you are creating your future now, both individually and collectively. We beseech you to step into your roles as spiritual masters and make the choice to move upward through the evolutionary threshold.[47]

Once again, this channeled screed matches the demonic goals of evolution, personal godhood, and the promise of human-engineered planetary peace. Demons appeal to people's narcissism and pride when they say that people are gods and can effect a renaissance of worldwide peace. But we must remember that pride goes before destruction. By stroking people's pride, the demons are setting them up for destruction. In 1 Thess. 5:2–3, we learn that "the day of the Lord will come like a thief in the night. While people are saying, 'Peace and safety,' destruction will come on them suddenly, as labor pains on a pregnant woman, and they will not escape" (NIV). Therefore we can be assured that the New Agers' boasting of being gods and goddesses and ushering in an age of planetary peace will come to naught. Indeed, New Agers who chant about peace and safety—while entertaining vain notions about leaping to new evolutionary planes and bringing peace to all with their own hands and with their own vibrating minds—will actually be ringing the bell of their own destruction.

In 2 Thess. 2:4, we see that the man of lawlessness, also known as the Antichrist, will set himself up in God's temple and pretend to be God himself. Obviously, the New Agers' obsession with being gods and goddesses themselves is a trend that is paving the way for the emergence of the Antichrist.

New Age Societal Erosion — Western Bad, Eastern Good

When people think of Henry David Thoreau, it seems they often get a little wistful and pine for getting back to nature. In fact, Thoreau ran headlong against the Christian currents that had made America strong. He was a voice in the wilderness, but instead of calling people to repentance and salvation as John the Baptist did, he called people to a mystical blend of pantheism and took pot shots at Christianity from his pond-side seat:

> I wish to meet the facts of life—the vital facts, which are the phenomena or actuality the gods meant to show us—face to face, and so I came down here. Life! [W]ho knows what it is, what it does? … The preacher, instead of vexing the ears of drowsy farmers on their day of rest, at the end of a week—for Sunday always seemed to me like a fit conclusion of an ill-spent week and not the fresh and brave beginning of a new one—with this one other draggletail and postponed affair of a sermon, from thirdly to fifteenthly, should teach them with a thundering voice pause and simplicity.[48]

Thoreau is pushing a pantheistic worldview, referring to "the gods" from whom he aspires to learn the facts of life. In place of the Christian sermon, Thoreau offers "pause and simplicity." That strikes me as overly facile for someone who had few time constraints and was free to snipe at society's shapers from the side of a pond. Pause and simplicity would not have built the railroads or the bridges or the highways or the edifices or even the national park trails that we as Americans hold so dear. Pause and simplicity would not have cleared the daunting white pine forests along America's northern edge, nor would it have established the hectic work schedules of farmers who developed millions of acres of fertile ground to feed a hungry population. Pause and simplicity would not have led Americans to the West Coast even, and Americans would have been hunkered down along the East Coast integrating with the trees and the fishes and doing ecstatic dances in the mist holding their copies of Thoreau's essays—that is, until they got hit by marauding Indians or until they starved for a lack of agricultural engineering, whichever came first.

Thoreau was quick to throw away the merits of the Christian settlers and equally quick to embrace, uncritically, the things of the Indians. In the following passage, Thoreau contemplates Indian hieroglyphs picturing Indian "heroes" amid shaggy trees and carrying bows and arrows and senses that the Western railroad experiment was surely inferior to the simplicity and drama of Indian hieroglyphs on stone:

> How symbolic, significant of I know not what, the pitch pine stands here before my door! Unlike any glyph I have seen sculptured or painted yet, one of Nature's later designs, yet perfect as her Grecian art. There it is, a done tree. Who can mend it? And now where is the generation of heroes whose lives are to pass amid these our northern pines, whose exploits shall appear to posterity pictured amid these strong and shaggy forms? Shall there be only arrows and bows to go with these pines on some pipe-stone quarry at length? There is something more respectable than railroads in these simple relics of the Indian race. What hieroglyphs shall we add to the pipe-stone quarry?[49]

To Thoreau, the Indian fashioners of bows and arrows were heroes, and the white fashioners of trains and railways were suspect at best. But he asked an honest question when he wondered what the Bible-believing settlers should portray in the form of hieroglyphs. Perhaps we Westernized Americans would do well to paint pictures of trains and light bulbs and stethoscopes and penicillin on the rocks. Why not?

Alan Watts clearly squared off against America's Bible-believing culture. "Jesus Christ knew he was God," Watts says. "Wake up and find out eventually who you really are. In our [American] culture, of course, they'll say you're crazy or you're blasphemous, and they'll either put you in jail or in the nut house. ... But if you wake up in India and tell your friends and relations, 'My goodness, I've just discovered that I'm God,' they'll laugh and say, 'Oh, congratulations, at last you found out.'"[50]

Watts reflects the typical New Age mentality in which all things Eastern are good and all things Biblical are suspect. He dismisses American culture and gives a ringing endorsement of India, suggesting that that Hindu, pantheistic nation is a place of wisdom to which all should aspire.

Things Chinese are good in the Watts worldview as well. "Now, you see, living is something spontaneous," Watts says. "In Chinese the word for nature is [*ziran*], which means that which happens of itself, not under any control of an outside entity. And they feel that all the world is happening of itself; it's spontaneous." Watts goes on to say that the secret of life is to be totally absorbed in the here and now, and that the Hindus believe the world to be an illusion anyway.⁵¹ You get the feeling that this Asian studies professor from the San Francisco area might have been taken in by anything Eastern, so woefully ignorant was he of the good and just Christian heritage in the United States.

The here and now has a catchy ring to it, but ultimately it's our relationship with Jesus the Redeemer that matters, and coming to Him in repentance and love entails a recognition of one's past sins as well as the mercy available in the present moment, so clearly the here and now is not all that matters.

An understanding of prophecy is crucial for the mature Christian, taking into account such books as Genesis, Isaiah, Jeremiah, Ezekiel, Daniel, and Revelation (to name just a few); prophetic musings take one well beyond the here and now. Chinese *gong bao* chicken is tasty and Chinese calligraphy is beautiful, but that doesn't make all the Chinese mystical blasphemy right.

Nature was created by God; we learn that in the book of Genesis. Therefore, nature did not arise of itself in spite of Watts' superficially impressive reference to the Chinese word for nature, *ziran*. Nonlinguists like to cherry-pick in a foreign language for some tidbit that supposedly represents those foreign people in a light that just so happens to match the worldview of the cherry picker himself. But if Watts had been a more thorough linguist, he would have noted that the Chinese orthography contains some very remarkable markers of an ancient belief, on the part of Chinese, in the God of the Bible. For instance, the word *zao* ("to create") is written with the character for dirt or clay, the character for mouth, and the walking radical. The upshot of *zao* is that it seems to point to the creation of Adam: Adam, after all, was created from clay, and after he had the breath of life put into his mouth he got up and walked.

We can be pretty sure that Watts' bowing to the particular *ziran*-related concept of nature in China was indeed enmeshed in a larger rejection of the Christian view of nature. It seems he got caught up in the magical atmosphere of Catholic cathedrals, and such was his identification with the multicolored glass and the Mass that when he stepped out of the cathedral and into nature he felt a disconnect. As Watts puts it:

> I can feel like a Christian only when I am indoors. As soon as I get into the open air, I feel entirely out of relation with everything that goes on in a church—including both the worship and the theology. ... I spent much of my boyhood in the precincts of one of Europe's most noble cathedrals, and I have never recovered from its spell. Romanesque and Gothic architecture, Gregorian chant, medieval glass and illuminated manuscripts, the smell of frankincense or of the mere must of ancient stone, and, above all, the ritual of the Mass—these are as magical for me as for the most ardent Catholic romanticist. ...
>
> [T]he Christian world, as we know it, is only a half-world in which the feeling and the symbolically feminine is unassimilated. ... [F]eeling is underestimated or disregarded. ... It has, then, been my impression that there is a deep and quite extraordinary incompatibility between the atmosphere of Christianity and the atmosphere of the natural world. It has seemed well-nigh impossible to relate God the Father, Jesus Christ, the angels, and the saints to the universe in which I actually live. Looking at trees and rocks, at the sky with its clouds or stars, at the sea, or at a naked human body, I find myself in a world where this religion simply does not fit. ... I have found it a basic impossibility to associate the author of the Christian religion with the author of the physical universe. ... [I]t is only to say that they are not by the same hand, and that they do not mix well together.[52]

Watts felt like a Christian only when he was indoors; once outside, he felt out of touch with the doings of a church; he never recovered from the spell of a noble European cathedral; cathedral architecture, Gregorian chant, medieval glass, illuminated manuscripts, the smell of frankincense or musty stones, and the Mass were magical for Watts as they would be for a romanticist. Contained as he was in the Roman Catholic atmosphere, he felt and smelled and chanted, fell under a spell, and got sucked into the allure of magic. He was trying to cultivate his feminine side and feelings in general. Misled as he was by the Catholic misrepresentations of Christianity, Watts was unaware of God's authorship of the nature around him, something that Rom. 1:20 tells us should have been apparent to a clear-sighted individual. Once blinded by unbiblical Roman Catholic teachings, Watts fell into the hands of Eastern mystics.

Watts goes on at length about how Westerners don't understand nature, are too rigid in their views, and aren't particularly moral. And how does he solve the problem? By turning to Chinese mysticism, of course:

> The natural world therefore reveals its content, its fullness of wonder, when respect hinders us from investigating it in such a way as to shatter it to abstractions. If I *must* cross every skyline to find out what is beyond, I shall never appreciate the true depth of sky seen between trees upon the ridge of a hill. If I must map the canyons and count the trees, I shall never enter into the sound of a hidden waterfall. … To the mind which pursues every road to its end, every road leads nowhere. …

> To know nature, the Tao, and the "substance" of things, we must know it as, in the archaic sense, a man "knows" a woman—in the warm vagueness of immediate contact. … [E]ven for Westerners, such formless conceptions as the Tao are to be preferred to the idea of God, with its all too definite associations. … [T]he "pantheistic" and mystical attitude to nature [has the advantage of giving] us a formless background against which the forms of everyday, practical problems may be seen more clearly. When our idea of the background, of God, is highly formal, practical conduct is as tortuous as trying to write upon a printed page. Issues cannot be seen clearly because it is not seen that matters of right and wrong are like the rules of grammar—conventions of communication.

> By grounding right and wrong in the Absolute, in the background, not only do the rules become too rigid, but they are also sanctioned by too weighty an authority. As a

Chinese proverb says, "Do not swat a fly upon your friend's head with a hatchet." By grounding the rules of action in God, the West has not succeeded in fostering any unusual degree of morality. On the contrary, it has invited just those violent ideological revolutions against intolerable authority which are so characteristic of its history. The same would apply to a rigid scientific dogma...[53]

Watts is an articulate purveyor of New Age pseudovalues, and his antipathy toward Western modes of thought could not be more clear in this instance. He suggests that Westerners investigate the natural world to the point of "shattering it to abstractions"; that Westerners have too formal an idea of God, making it impossible for them to see issues clearly; and that the West has not achieved a particularly moral record.

And then in rides pantheism (probably a reference to Buddhism or its progenitor, Hinduism) as well as the ineffable vagueness of Taoism to set the West straight. By implication, pantheism and Taoism are held up as the way to "enter into the sound of a waterfall"; the way to a "formless" background through which issues can be seen clearly; and the way to a looser sense of right and wrong. Perhaps we can all do circular (nonjudgmental) tai chi motions with our hands, click our heels together, and skip when the People's Liberation Army arrives to "liberate" Westerners of their overly rigid worldviews?

Perhaps Watts had trouble seeing issues clearly. How could the "warm vagueness" or "formless conceptions" of Taoism be more weighty than the idea of God? Shouldn't the God over all creation be the weightiest authority? If the Chinese poet Li Bai, famous for his mystical appreciation of nature, is considered a weighty authority on nature poetry, then certainly the Holy Spirit, the inspiration of the Bible, can be rightly understood as the weightiest of all writers and poets! And if pagan Taoists and pantheists strain to "enter into the sound of a waterfall," then shouldn't they honor the God of the Bible, the very creator of that waterfall?

If Westerners, for all their rigid thought and historical dependence on the God of the Bible, can't see issues clearly, then why is it that for so much of the twentieth century the denizens of the East came to the West to pursue higher learning and not the other way around? As for morality, is it possible that Bible believers have done more for charity than pantheists? As for violence, at least the American Revolution produced a Bible-believing republic, while Mao's Cultural Revolution and Pol Pot's killing fields led to more communist tyranny. In India, Hindu mobs have slaughtered huge numbers of Christians, and that's since 2000; and the Chinese Communists treat the Chinese underground church terribly as well. So the dreamy reputations of atheism and pantheism—painstakingly crafted by uncritical, starry-eyed New Agers without regard to real-world evidence—are undeserved.

Watts compares Christianity to, of all things, the natural art of the Far East. "Strangely enough," Watts says, "it is almost impossible to represent the central symbol of Christianity, the Cross or Crucifixion, in the Chinese style of painting. It has been tried many times, but never succeeds, for the symmetrical form of the Cross completely destroys the rhythm of a Chinese painting if it is made the principal image in the picture. ... [W]hen the Chinese artist starts to paint the rigid Cross he finds himself in conflict, for what he really wants to paint is a living tree."[54]

Well, the governing rule in our lives is the Word of God, not esoteric principles of Chinese painting—so the idea that a symbol of Christianity should in any way be subordinated to the rules of Chinese painting is asinine in the extreme. It seems that spending too much time trying to enter into the sound of a waterfall really does impair one's thinking.

Not surprisingly, Bhagwan Shree Rajneesh also has a habit of dismissing Christianity. Meditation, he says, can be centered on any old thing, but he'd prefer that meditation not be centered on Christian things. What a farce it is for a yoga-as-science guru to be spicing up his lectures with anti-Christian rhetoric:

> Says Patanjali, *meditate on anything that appeals to you*— then spontaneously your whole being starts flowing. ... [T]here is nothing special in meditating on the cross; you are simply stupid. What is the need to go and meditate on the cross? ... There is no special quality in a cross. ... When you meditate on something, you give your inner being to it. Suddenly it becomes sacred, holy. Things are not holy; meditation makes them holy. You can meditate

> on a rock, and suddenly the rock becomes the temple. … What is meditation? It is showering the rock with your consciousness. It is moving around the rock, so absorbed, so deep in rapport, that the bridge is there between you and the rock. The gap disappears—you are bridged. In fact, you don't know now who is the observer and who is the observed. … Suddenly, the energies meet and mingle, and there is the temple.[55]

It is telling that of all the objects in the world, Rajneesh singles out a Christian symbol for disqualification as an object of his style of meditation: the meditation he espouses is patently anti-Christian. In fact, Rajneesh's idea of mingling and bonding with a rock is weird. In the mystical lore of Taoism, Zhuang Zi also told of identifying with a butterfly so intensely that he couldn't tell if he was a person dreaming of a butterfly or if it was the other way around. Such gushy nonsense may be appealing to people high on acid or peyote or mescaline, but it doesn't sit well with a lucid person who is in control of his or her faculties.

Rajneesh encourages one to abandon thinking, abandon any judgment of right or wrong, and drink up his every word. "But you can listen to me," Rajneesh says, "without thinking—in deep love, heart-to-heart, not in any way verbalizing what I am saying, right or wrong, no. No valuation—you simply listen in deep love, as if the mind has passed, and the heart listens and beats with joy. Then the unconscious is listening. Then whatsoever I say will go very deep to your roots."[56]

No thinking, no judgment of right or wrong, no valuation, and drinking up the guru's words uncritically: that seems like a description of hypnosis. It's easier to create a following for a false religion when the listeners have been rendered incapacitated and lemming-like. How different this Eastern mind control is from the Biblical teaching that we should use our minds, as we see in the example of the Bereans, in Acts 17, who check out Paul's teachings against Scripture before accepting them. Paul was not the Bereans' standard—the Word of God was.

Marilyn Ferguson, the New Age cataloguer, also applauds the East, throwing in an anti-Christian spin. According to her New Age screed, Eastern mysticism completes the West:

> We turn East for completion. Whitman called it "the voyage of the mind's return. ... Passage to more than India." Hesse spoke of "the eternal strivings of the human spirit toward the East, toward Home." The East does not represent a culture or a religion so much as the methodology for achieving a larger, liberating vision. ...
>
> Formal religion in the West has been shaken to its roots by defections, dissent, rebellions, loss of influence, diminishing financial support. ... If [churches] cannot find new roles in a rapidly changing society, they may go the way of the railroads—without Amtrak.
>
> A Catholic theologian, Anthony Padovano, remarked at a 1976 conference on meditation: "The religious response that has occurred in the Western world—a revolution that has made us more sensitive to the religions of the Orient—is an understanding that whatever answers there are must come from ourselves...[57]

You can sense Ferguson's jubilation as she declares that the Christian churches must change to adapt to an East-moving American society. She tries to soften the specter of a predatory East by claiming that the East is not peddling culture or religion but rather liberation. Are we talking about "liberating visions" from the People's Liberation Army of Communist China? Sort of like the liberating visions that horrible army dealt to the more than seventy million butchered in China in the fifties, sixties, and seventies? Or are we talking about the liberating visions that are the calling card of Communist China's Public Security Bureau, Ministry of State Security, or People's Armed Police? And to think that a radio ad for a shopping mall in Surrey, British Columbia, in January 2012, positively overflowed with excitement about the Chinese Year of the Dragon! Has Canada also forgotten her Judeo-Christian heritage?

Deut. 18:9–12 speaks to the error of astrology clearly enough:

When thou art come into the land which the LORD thy God giveth thee, thou shalt not learn to do after the abominations of those nations. There shall not be found among you any one that maketh his son or his daughter to pass through the fire, or that useth divination, or an observer of times, or an enchanter, or a witch, or a charmer, or a consulter with familiar spirits, or a wizard, or a necromancer. For all that do these things are an abomination unto the LORD; and because of these abominations the LORD thy God doth drive them out from before thee. (KJV)

Our Canadian friends, as Americans, must stand against the insidious demonic and astrological allure surrounding the Chinese Year of the Dragon, the Chinese Year of the Monkey, or any other creature-worshipping mush that floats in on crafty lips.

China, the Vatican, and Satan have all adopted the dragon symbol. This stone dragon is at Yu-yuan Garden in Shanghai. "What profit is the idol when its maker has carved it, *or* an image, a teacher of falsehood? For *its* maker trusts in his *own* handiwork when he fashions speechless idols. Woe to him who says to a *piece of* wood, 'Awake!' To a mute stone, 'Arise!' *And* that is *your* teacher? Behold, it is overlaid with gold and silver, and there is no breath at all inside it. But the Lord is in His holy temple. Let all the earth be silent before Him" (Hab. 2:18–20 NASB). "The manufacturers of idols will go away together in humiliation. … 'They have no knowledge, who carry about their wooden idol and pray to a god who cannot save. … Turn to Me and be saved, all the ends of the earth; for I am God, and there is no other'" (Is. 45:16b, 20b, 22 NASB).

Is the spell of diversity simply too captivating? The dragon is a symbol of Satan, China, and the Vatican. As a linguist, I must demand that the liberating visions be true and sterling, missing that icky element of lying treachery.

In spite of the fantastical notions of self-loathing Americans, the Far East is overflowing with relativistic cultural mores and mystical religions. Therefore, America's embrace of the East has entailed an embrace of false religions. The Catholic meditator has put his finger on something when he notes that Americans, and Westerners in general, have become "more sensitive to the religions of the Orient." But he gives away his pagan motives when he says that "whatever answers there are must come from ourselves."

In fact, whatever answers there are must come from the Word of God. And we don't need the Far East to be complete; we need a saving relationship with Jesus Christ. Hermann Hesse, the German-Swiss poet who authored such novels as *Siddhartha* and *Journey to the East,* displayed a pronounced affection for Indian Buddhism, something that made him popular in the hippie counterculture movement of the sixties. But in spite of Hesse's romantic view of India, the East is not home; rather, a saving relationship with Jesus Christ is a home worth aiming for. Shanghai may be visually stimulating, but it's not that pretty. Mount Fuji may be symmetrical, but it's not the ultimate goal either. A pomegranate stand in Delhi may be beautiful—with pomegranate husks cracked open to bare the glistening handiwork of God's pomegranate seeds—but that's not the ultimate place either. We read about the New Jerusalem in Revelation 21 and 22, and that description is of a home worthy of a Christian's humble aspiration:

> And he carried me away in the Spirit to a mountain great and high, and showed me the Holy City, Jerusalem, coming down out of heaven from God.
>
> It shone with the glory of God, and its brilliance was like that of a very precious jewel, like a jasper, clear as crystal. It had a great, high wall with twelve gates, and with twelve angels at the gates. On the gates were written the names of the twelve tribes of Israel. There were three

gates on the east, three on the north, three on the south and three on the west. The wall of the city had twelve foundations, and on them were the names of the twelve apostles of the Lamb. The angel who talked with me had a measuring rod of gold to measure the city, its gates and its wall. The city was laid out like a square, as long as it was wide. He measured the city with the rod and found it to be 12,000 stadia in length, and as wide and high as it is long. He measured its wall and it was 144 cubits thick, by man's measurement, which the angel was using. The wall was made of jasper, and the city of pure gold, as pure as glass. The foundations of the city walls were decorated with every kind of precious stone. The first foundation was jasper, the second sapphire, the third chalcedony, the fourth emerald, the fifth sardonyx, the sixth carnelian, the seventh chrysolite, the eighth beryl, the ninth topaz, the tenth chrysoprase, the eleventh jacinth, and the twelfth amethyst. The twelve gates were twelve pearls, each gate made of a single pearl. The great street of the city was of pure gold, like transparent glass. I did not see a temple in the city, because the Lord God Almighty and the Lamb are its temple. The city does not need the sun or the moon to shine on it, for the glory of God gives it light, and the Lamb is its lamp. The nations will walk by its light, and the kings of the earth will bring splendor into it. On no day will its gates ever be shut, for there will be no night there. The glory and honor of the nations will be brought into it. Nothing impure will ever enter it, nor will anyone who does what is shameful or deceitful, but only those whose names are written in the Lamb's book of life. Then the angel showed me the river of the water of life, as clear as crystal, flowing from the throne of God and of the Lamb down the middle of the great street of the city. On each side of the river stood the tree of life, bearing twelve crops of fruit, yielding its fruit every month. And the leaves of the tree are for the healing of the nations. No longer will there be any curse. The throne of God and of the Lamb will be in the city, and his servants will serve him. They will see his face, and his name will be on their foreheads. There will be no more night. They will not need the light of a lamp or the light of the sun, for the Lord God will give them light.

And they will reign for ever and ever." (NIV)

For born-again believers in Jesus, the New Jerusalem—and the opportunity it affords to be in the company of God forever—is the ultimate reward.

New Age Societal Erosion — Feelings, Immorality, and Drug-Induced Transformation

Moving through life based on feelings is risky—but don't tell that to the New Agers. "As you learn to live from your intuition," Shakti Gawain says, "you give up making decisions with your head. You act moment by moment on what you feel and allow things to unfold as you go. In this way, you are led in the direction that is right for you. ... Focus on following the energy in the moment and you'll find that [decisions] will all get handled in [their] own time and way."[58]

By ignoring the decision-making head and feeling one's way through the energy of the here and now, the New Ager trusts that whatever will happen is somehow a part of the universal energy, and somehow that's okay. But oftentimes it's really necessary to be guided by one's thinking head. For instance, one time I was descending from the 14,000-foot summit of a mountain and suddenly, without warning, my party was enveloped in a whiteout—clouds everywhere—and where there wasn't a sturdy ridge there might have been a crevasse or a steep slope dropping down out of the air.

It was a tricky situation, and we had to keep our heads and go slowly— very slowly—picking our way carefully and trying to catch whatever glimpses of the mountainside that we could. We wanted to keep moving, if slowly, so as to avoid frittering away too much time inside the cold clouds.

This was not about feelings; it was about keeping our heads and making good decisions.

If a New Ager had been in our party—just doing what he felt and seeing how things unfolded—the day might have taken a tragic turn. Luckily there were four thinkers in the party, and we clambered down ever so gingerly. That whiteout was a very factual situation: nearly zero degrees in the thin atmosphere, and the chance of wind knocking the temperature much lower, was a sobering fact. Feelings were not a big priority. Getting off the mountain alive was front and center in our minds!

Alan Watts makes the extreme case for feelings. "Man is not to be an intellectual porcupine," he says, "meeting his environment with a surface of spikes [ie, with a surface of rigid and spiky thoughts]. ... Hence the importance of opinions, of instruments of the mind, which are vague, misty, and melting rather than clear-cut. ... As Chinese and Japanese painters have so well understood, there are landscapes which are best viewed through half-closed eyes, mountains which are most alluring when partially veiled in mist, and waters which are most profound when the horizon is lost, and they are merged with the sky."[59]

Misty landscapes are fine if one is looking out of a hotel window but if one is forced to think fast in a life-or-death situation, it helps to clear away the romantic mist and see the situation head on. Not all landscapes are forgiving. Even Chinese and Japanese landscapes are not all forgiving—one might have to check with Chinese and Japanese painters to get the final word, but the last time I checked, Yangmingshan (a ridge above Taipei, Taiwan) can be pretty daunting in a typhoon, and the same goes for Keelung, a harbor town north of Taipei.

There are endless angles from which to demonstrate the moral crisis in America. The data in this regard are incontrovertible. In a nutshell, the problem is evil. Many Americans have left the God of the Bible, and they've come to believe that they're inherently great and no longer in need of the Bible or God. Humanistic pride has been the origin of many anti-Christian policies in the schools, in the courts, and all across the land. "What humanism does," Tal Brooke says, "is blur distinctions of good and evil; relativizes them. It says that the old traditional understandings no longer apply, that they don't really matter. Now classrooms in the public sector teach 'values clarification.' Peer groups decide what is okay and what is not. The distinction between good and evil has been powerfully neutralized over [recent] decades."[60]

Values clarification is one of those innocuous-sounding terms of the 1970s that sought to instill a sense of personal empowerment in young kids—the idea was that people would huddle around and jab about some topic, and they'd come up with the best solution in a nonjudgmental way. All answers were okay. Even stupid and immoral ideas were to be given a platform.

I sat through the values clarification curriculum in Davis, California, and was struck by how free-wheeling and directionless the process was. I didn't understand the ramifications at the time, but there was no missing the game: just cock your head and look sincere, and you could say anything and it would get serious consideration. We were free to derive our own baselines for acceptable behavior as long as we copped a serious gaze and stated our wants with feeling.

Entertainment is just one area in which the thirst for the insipid and the debasing is at an all-time high. Reality shows and talk shows on television center on the sensational, disgusting, asinine, and despicable, and the hosts throw knowing winks at the audience, assuring viewers that they're the smart ones and, boy, aren't the show's guests—those buck-toothed twins from the backwoods—amusing? Meanwhile, the entire viewing audience is being dragged into the gutter and possibly dumbed down, as talk show topics run the gamut of dysfunction—sex triangles, swinging couples who swap partners in orgiastic interludes, twelve-year-old girls who go to town in skirts that are hiked up as high as their upper thighs, liars, freaks, pot-smoking kids who are lazy and out of control, etc. The hosts debase and mock their guests, then offer some wispy pseudomoralisms at the end of the staged spectacles.

The blood-splatter and unmitigated evil portrayed in so many of the R-rated movies are nauseating, mortifying, and even downright satanic, and the producers hide behind misconceived mantras about the freedom of expression. Many Americans not only flirt with the dark side, they're addicted to it. "What is really happening is the invasion of evil," Brooke says. "We become more and more curious and knowledgeable about evil."[61]

Brooke is right. Many have become fascinated with violence and sex and lying and all manner of immorality, as the legitimate freedom of expression has been turned into a demented freedom of obsession.

The Fox News Channel once featured an interview with two young women on the topic of so-called freak dancing, a form of dancing in which a man scoots his groin right up behind a woman and, in essence, they simulate coitus on the dance floor *(The O'Reilly Factor,* May 15, 2003). A student at Stanford University actually had the gall to defend this form of dancing, saying that crackdowns on behavior have historically boomeranged to produce even more of the prohibited behavior, and that "there's no scientific study to show there's direct moral corruption [stemming from the freak dancing]."

What unmitigated gall! It's ridiculous to suggest that a scientific study is needed to show that freak dancing, also called grinding, is a form of moral corruption. The host, Bill O'Reilly, soft-handed the whole issue. From the Biblical point of view, such dancing would seem to be unclean. Stanford University is sometimes called "The Farm"; I expect more than animalistic hedonism from Stanford.

In the self-indulgent New Age world of feelings, even sadism and masochism are not rejected but rather are held up as sources of wisdom:

> Perverse and abnormal as they are usually regarded, we should also consider the phenomena of sadism and masochism—better designated by the single term algolagnia, or "lustful pain." Merely to dismiss these phenomena as perverse and unnatural is to say no more than that they do not fit into a preconceived notion of order. The very fact that they are human possibilities shows that they are extensions of ordinary feelings, revealing depths of our nature which are usually left unexplored. Distasteful as they may be, this should not prevent us from trying to discover whether they throw any light on the problem of suffering.[62]

Apparently, rejecting sadism and masochism would be too rigid and divisive for the New Ager. But the activities of sadism and masochism don't throw light on "the problem of suffering" or anything else—instead they throw darkness on all who take part in them. The suggestion that we should study and learn from sadism and masochism is pathetic and proves once again what Brooke says: we're being invaded by evil, and we're becoming "more and more curious and knowledgeable about evil!" Watts tries to rebut the perversion label, which gets applied to sadism and masochism, by stating that the only problem is that sadism and masochism don't fit into a "preconceived notion of order." Watts' perversion speaks for itself.

Sexual immorality is a favorite of New Agers. "We *are* making a leap into the new world," Shakti Gawain says. "I believe that every form of relationship, from the most traditional marriage to open relationships or homosexual or bisexual relationships, represents each being's attempt to find their feminine/masculine balance within."[63]

The New Age dictum is that homosexual behavior is just dandy, an interesting choice, and that sex outside of marriage is just dandy as well. Compare that permissive New Age attitude to the Word of God on the subject. Rom. 1:22–27 lays it down as follows:

> Although they claimed to be wise, they became fools and exchanged the glory of the immortal God for images made to look like mortal man and birds and animals and reptiles. Therefore God gave them over in the sinful desires of their hearts to sexual impurity for the degrading of their bodies with one another.
>
> They exchanged the truth of God for a lie, and worshiped and served created things rather than the Creator—who is forever praised. Amen. Because of this, God gave them over to shameful lusts. Even their women exchanged natural relations for unnatural ones. In the same way the men also abandoned natural relations with women and were inflamed with lust for one another. Men committed indecent acts with other men, and received in themselves the due penalty for their perversion. (NIV)

The Word of God makes it clear that the New Age sex-without-boundaries creed is itself indecent, that the New Agers have "exchanged the truth of God for a lie," and that they will reap a penalty for their perversion. The diseases currently raging through communities of homosexuals and fornicators ought to be a clue. Furthermore, in 1 Cor. 6:18–20 we read this: "Flee from sexual immorality. All other sins a man commits are outside his body, but he who sins sexually sins against his own body. Do you not know that your body is a temple of the Holy Spirit, who is in you, whom you have received from God? You are not your own; you were bought at a price. Therefore honor God with your body" (NIV).

But people are stubborn. Gawain gives an account of an open-sex arrangement that turned sour:

> [A] few years ago I was living with a man and we had an "open relationship"—in other words, we were free to be with other lovers. I had a very strong spiritual ideal that I could love someone deeply and allow him to be free to follow energy he might feel with someone else, while I was free to do likewise. Sometimes I was able to do this, and I had some beautiful moments where I felt an expansive and exhilarating unconditional love, a deep intimacy with my lover; I sometimes even felt a love toward his other lovers! But most of the time I was [racked] with jealousy and emotional pain. I finally realized that I was not emotionally ready to live my ideal at that time. I had enough respect for my feelings to change the situation.
>
> I still feel that I will someday be secure enough in myself to have that balance of depth and freedom in relationships if I want it, but I am allowing myself to move toward that very slowly, at the pace that I can handle emotionally...[64]

For the New Ager, sexual immorality is wrapped in language such as open and free, and the whole immoral pursuit is portrayed as a pursuit of energy (whatever that means). Biblically, such sexual immorality is selfish and wanton, not open and free, and what the participants are following is lust, not some ineffable energy. Unfortunately, I sense the pain that followed this sexual immorality was not even interpreted correctly by Gawain, such was her commitment to self-oriented development. The

Testing the Spirits

lesson should have been that there is a distinction, or a division if you will, between sexual propriety and sexual lasciviousness, and that sexual immorality necessarily results in pain and penalty.

Not to be outdone, Bhagwan Shree Rajneesh is not above some linguistic sleight of hand in order to blur the distinction between morality and immorality. "An immoral man is in many ways innocent," Rajneesh says, "less egoistic. A moral man has all the immorality inside the mind. And new things that he has gathered: those are the moralistic, the puritan, egoistic attitudes. He feels superior. He feels he is the chosen one and everybody else is condemned to hell. Only he is going to heaven. And all the immorality remains inside."[65]

Rajneesh essentially sneers at the moral man, calling him egoistic, supercilious, and inclined toward condemning others. His is a cynical and dishonest description of the person who chooses to cultivate goodness and eschew evil. In fact, Rajneesh's rant against the moral man tells us much about his own values, or lack thereof—perhaps he was just trying to justify his own dissolute lifestyle, wrapped as he was in such a huge and absurd fleet of Rolls Royces at his Oregon commune.

New Agers are drunk on the bogus idea that mystical explorers have the technology. "The transformative technologies offer us passage to creativity, healing, choices," Marilyn Ferguson says. "The gift of insight—of making imaginative new connections—once the specialty of a lucky few, is there for anyone willing to persist, experiment, explore."[66] The problem with the New Age bluster about new-and-delivering personal and social technologies is that mankind has been beset by evil throughout recorded history up until the present. So clearly their social technologies, which have been around since ancient times, are the product of unsupportable hype.

Jean-Paul Sartre underwent a personal transformation in 1935, taking mescaline and exploring his consciousness by way of hallucination. "For several hours," recounts Thomas Riedlinger in the book *Hallucinogens: A Reader,* "Sartre thought himself under attack by giant octopuses, grinning apes, and huge, fat flies. An umbrella appeared to transform itself into a vulture, and a clock tower that he passed upon leaving the hospital seemed to turn into an owl. For months afterward, Sartre suffered flashbacks in which he imagined that he was pursued by giant lobsters."[67] Obviously,

Sartre's experimentation was a disaster, yielding no good for him or his fellow man. It gets even more frightening.

Dennis McKenna, coauthor of *The Invisible Landscape and Psilocybin: The Magic Mushroom Grower's Guide,* says that "psychedelics can be important in individuals' lives in terms of orienting them to a wider vision or [being] an influence in terms of directing people. ... I think that one of the biggest challenges for the next millennium is, how are we going to take our own individualistic psychedelic visions or inspirations and try to diffuse those into a larger society."[68] Let's hope that high-on-mushrooms New Agers won't be directing too many people or diffusing their psychedelic visions into the larger society any time soon!

Rick Strassman, author of the essay "Sitting for Sessions: Dharma & DMT Research," made some interesting observations on the effects of taking drugs. "[I]t seemed as if a big dose of DMT was indeed transformative," Strassman says. "[A] ... number of volunteers had frightening, negative responses that required some care afterward. Other, more subtle adverse effects also crept in (as may happen with Buddhist practice) in the form of increased self-pride."[69]

Subtle and negative pride-related effects coming from Buddhist practice as well as from doses of dimethyl-tryptamine (DMT)—now that there is what I call an astute observation! Strassman continues: "I was impressed by the 'psychedelic' descriptions of intensive meditation practice within some Buddhist traditions. Because their scriptures did not mention drugs, and the states sounded similar to those resulting from psychedelic drug use, I suspected there might be a naturally occurring psychedelic molecule in the brain that was triggered by deep meditation."[70]

The doctor makes an amazing observation in noticing that self-pride and its negative effects are common to both Buddhist practice and drug use: after all, Buddhists believe they can become supremely enlightened and thereby become buddhas, as a result of their own supreme cultivation techniques, and drug users have been known to think they are transcendent and godlike also. But whereas the doctor sees the possibility of a "psychedelic molecule" that responds to meditation as it responds to drugs, I would rather suggest that drug takers and Buddhist meditators go into prideful fits and hallucinations as a result of emptying their minds and opening up a channel for demonic attack.

Roger Walsh, in his essay "Chemical and Contemplative Ecstasy: Similarities and Differences," also addresses the effects of drug use: "[W]ith the advent of psychedelics in the West came a remarkable claim. Noncontemplatives who took these substances reported a vast range of experiences—some high, some low, some ecstatic, some demonic—but also some that seemed remarkably similar to those described by mystics across the centuries. ... Proponents [of 'chemical mysticism'], such as ... Aldous Huxley, Walter Houston Clark, and Huston Smith, argued for the equivalence of chemical and natural mystical experiences."[71]

Again, we see that drug use can produce demonic fits, and that Eastern mysticism produces many of the same reactions that drugs produce. The key is that in both cases—taking drugs and practicing Eastern mystical meditation—the mind has been emptied! Indeed, to hear the Hindu "sage" Ramana Maharshi tell it, "All scriptures without any exception proclaim that for attaining salvation mind should be subdued."[72]

The Hindu gurus advocate emptying, or subduing, the mind. But the Bible encourages Christians to contend for the faith (Jude 3) and to reason one with another (Is. 1:18). Contending and reasoning are acts of the mind and can only be carried out by training the mind, not by subduing it.

CHAPTER FIVE

PSYCHOLOGICAL SELF-ABSORPTION

As with anything in our lives, psychology should be measured against the standards of the Holy Bible. Sigmund Freud is not the standard, nor is Carl Jung. Rollo May, author of *Man's Search for Himself,* is not the standard, nor is Alan Watts, author of *Psychology East & West*. Eastern mysticism is a bad pill, not a multivitamin at all; by contrast, Christianity is the answer for the East and the West. So who are these psychologists and psychiatrists? Who are these self-appointed gurus of thought, mavens

> "The 'redeemer' could be no one else but he who was most guilty, the leader of the brother horde who had overpowered the Father."
> —Sigmund Freud, Beknighted Behavioralist
>
> Freud suffered from Wrong-Opinion Disorder *(opinionus ludicroso)*. The leader of the evil horde was Lucifer (Is. 14, Ez. 28, Rev. 12). Jesus is the Bread of Life that came down out of Heaven (John 6:35, 41), the fulfillment of the unblemished lambs which were sacrificed for sins (Lev. 14). Jesus is the loyal Son, who overturned the money-changers' tables in defense of His Father: "Take these things away; stop making My Father's house a place of business." (John 2:16b, NASB)

of the mental, umpires of understanding, arbiters of the acceptable, and beknighted behavioralists? Do we really want psychologists to be the new linesmen for the thinking realm?

Psychologists Denigrate Christianity

Let's look at the case of Freud. But let's not lie down on his couch; rather, let us put him on the couch and judge his standing as a thinker and propounder. Having fled the German occupation of Austria in 1938, Freud then completed a book called *Moses and Monotheism* while in London; the book was published in 1939, the same year as his death. Let's see what was on the mind of the founder of psychoanalysis just before his death.

Freud positively brims with anti-Christian speculations: "That the Redeemer sacrificed himself as an innocent man was an obviously tendentious distortion, difficult to reconcile with logical thinking. How could a man who was innocent assume the guilt of the murderer by allowing himself to be killed? In historical reality there was no such contradiction. The 'redeemer' could be no one else but he who was most guilty, the leader of the brother horde who had overpowered the Father."[1]

Freud seems to be psychoanalyzing key figures of the Bible. Leave it to a psychoanalyst to view the Bible through the lens of a "brother horde," all the while holding himself up as an example of "logical" thinking! "We can hardly doubt," Freud says, "that in Greek tragedy the hero and the chorus represent this same rebel hero and the brother horde."[2]

Freud seems to have a thing for brother hordes. I've known many families that have many brothers and, in my personal estimation, this brother

> "We understand that primitive man needs a god as creator of the world.... Man in later times ... also remains infantile and needs protection...."
> —Sigmund Freud, Mental Propounder
>
> "For the invisible things of Him from the creation of the world are clearly seen, being understood by the things that are made, even his eternal power and Godhead; so that they are without excuse." (Rom. 1:20, KJV)
>
> "Verily I say unto you, Whosoever shall not receive the kingdom of God as a little child, he shall not enter therein." (Mark 10:15, KJV)

horde business is a charade—the sly concoction of a slinky mind. Moreover, Freud says, "Probably traditions from Oriental and Greek mysteries had exerted their influence on the shaping of this phantasy of salvation. The essence of it seems to be Paul's own contribution."[3]

Freud blithely suggests that Jesus' act of redemption was illogical, historically untrue, a fantasy, and essentially a construction of Paul. Yet such a rejection of Jesus' redemptive grace is itself illogical, a testament to the Austrian's self-absorption and pride. Apparently, Jesus' compassionate act of salvation was not moving to Freud, who was busy protecting a godless theory of brother hordes champing for a chance to push aside fathers. How could one so unable to analyze his own psyche presume to analyze the psyches of others? My ancestors come from the Swiss-German border, but I want nothing to do with the illogical, psychologizing Austrian.

Freud indicates that Oriental and Greek mysteries *probably* brought about the story of Jesus' offer of salvation. The Austrian *didn't even know for sure* that Oriental and Greek mystery religions had led to the story of Jesus' offer of salvation, yet it seems he was willing to bet his very soul on the proposition that they had. And to think that millions of people have reclined on chaise longues and davenports to get a prescription from one of the intellectual heirs of Freud!

Freud implied that God is no more than a hypothesis, and that belief in God is inconsistent with reason and science: "We can only regret it if certain experiences of life and observations of nature have made it impossible to accept the hypothesis of such a Supreme Being. As if the world had not enough problems, we are confronted with the task of finding out how those who have faith in a Divine Being could have acquired it, and whence this belief derives the enormous power that enables it to overwhelm Reason and Science."[4]

For Freud, certain things in nature made it impossible to accept God. But in Rom. 1:20, we learn that nature itself points to the truth of the God of the Bible: "For since the creation of the world God's invisible qualities—his eternal power and divine nature—have been clearly seen, being understood from what has been made, so that men are without excuse" (NIV).

God's eternal power and divine nature can be clearly seen in the power and beauty of God's creation. Thus, God's power and nature can be seen (partly reflected) in the grandeur of a tall mountain, the might of a tall-and-straight Sitka spruce, the beauty of a good heart, the power of a gale-force wind, the serenity of a cat's gaze, the watchfulness of a good shepherd, the delicate gracefulness of a nudibranch, the strength and ferocity of an African lion, and the tenderness of a mother hen.

When Freud wasn't misapprehending the message from the forests and the animals—indeed, from God's creation—he was intimating that Christians are infantile. He suggests that grown-up people should have no need of the protection of God: "We understand that primitive man needs a god as creator of the world, as head of his tribe, and as one who takes care of him. This god takes his place behind the dead fathers of whom tradition still has something to relate. Man in later times—in our time, for instance—behaves similarly. He also remains infantile and needs protection, even when he is fully grown; he feels he cannot relinquish the support of his god."[5]

It's interesting to note that Freud, who wanted to tell people why they behave as they do, didn't want to be bothered by God's proscriptions or Biblical descriptions of man's heart. He wanted to plumb the depths of the soul on his own, unbothered by the very God of the Bible who made man. I believe Freud put

> "My Christian faith had become relative through its encounter with Eastern religions and Greek philosophy.... I was fascinated by the ... controversial skull of Dubois' Pithecanthropus.... As the evolution of the embryonic body repeats its prehistory, so the mind also develops through a series of prehistoric stages."
> —Carl Jung, Besotted Behavioralist

"Be not carried about with divers and strange doctrines." (Heb. 13:9a, KJV) Diversity policy doesn't sound so good anymore! Dubois' "Java Man," even with its Latin name, was nothing more than a gibbon bone, according to Virchow. Leave the gibbons alone! Sabine Schwabenthan's fetoscopy research has shown that fetal development has only human stages, no fish stages: Haeckel's "embryonic recapitulation" has been discredited; there are no "gill slits," only clefts.

people on the couch in an attempt to achieve a semblance of validation—indirectly, of course (through his patients)—for his own godless and humanistic stance.

Similarly, Carl Jung's Christian faith couldn't withstand the onslaught of Eastern mysticism, philosophy, and evolution. To hear him tell it: "My Christian faith had become relative through its encounter with Eastern religions and Greek philosophy. ... I was fascinated by the bones of fossil man, particularly by the much discussed *Neanderthalensis* and the still more controversial skull of Dubois' *Pithecanthropus*. ... As the evolution of the embryonic body repeats its prehistory, so the mind also develops through a series of prehistoric stages. The main task of dreams is to bring back a sort of 'recollection' of the prehistoric, as well as the infantile world, right down to the level of the most primitive instincts."[6]

This is where psychotherapy comes from. Do we really want our sons and daughters to be led to believe that their dreams represent a remembering of some prehistoric alligator phase or a slime phase or a brine phase? Under Jung's influence, psychoanalysts could easily assign a link between a certain dream state and any animal of their choice in the supposed line-up of animals that supposedly led, by a complex trail of slaughter and supposedly beneficial mutations, to man. How weird is that? Who wants to be told theirs is a cow dream, a parrot dream, a brown trout dream, or a brontosaurus dream? Honestly, to think that Americans ate up Jungian this and Freudian that for decades in the build-up to the current spasm of self-help psychobabble! It's amazing, and tragic.

Jung sounds every bit the agnostic: "[S]ince we are dealing with invisible and unknowable things (for God is beyond human understanding, and there is no means of proving immortality), why should we bother about evidence? ... Why, then, should we deprive ourselves of views that would prove helpful in crises and would give a meaning to our existence? ... We are entirely free to choose which point of view to take; it will in any case be ... arbitrary."[7] Jung says why bother with the evidence, that any decision we make about spiritual things will be arbitrary anyway. But that message directly contradicts Rom. 1:20, where we see that God's creation is itself a testimony to God's eternal power and divine nature and, in effect, that the evidence of God's creation should compel people to make a decision for Christ. Jung's message is unbiblical and ungodly. It's no wonder that many psychologists today—as the intellectual heirs to Freud and Jung—routinely tell their patients to go forth and conform to godless lifestyles. With their power of pronouncing people as being normal or abnormal, psychologists herd people inside the boundaries of their value systems. If their value systems are decidedly un-Christian, as Freud's and Jung's were, then they can wield a powerful anti-Christian force in society.

Jung goes so far as to indirectly recommend the sun god of the Pueblo Indians:

> It is the role of religious symbols to give a meaning to the life of man. The Pueblo Indians believe that they are the sons of Father Sun, and this belief endows their life with a perspective (and a goal) that goes far beyond their limited existence. It gives them ample space for the unfolding of personality and permits them a full life as complete persons. Their plight is infinitely more satisfactory than that of a man in our own civilization who knows that he is (and will remain) nothing more than an underdog with no inner meaning to his life.[8]

"The Pueblo Indians believe that they are the sons of Father Sun, and this belief ... gives them ample space for the unfolding of personality and permits them a full life as complete persons."

—Carl Jung, Early Diversity Practitioner

One must worship the Creator, not the created things (Rom. 1). Regarding sun worship: "And beware not to lift up your eyes to heaven and see the sun and the moon and the stars, all the host of heaven, and be drawn away and worship them and serve them, those which the LORD your God has allotted to all the peoples under the whole heaven." (Deut. 4:19, NASB)

Colossians 2 on being a complete person: "Beware lest any man spoil you through philosophy and vain deceit, after the tradition of men, after the rudiments of the world, and not after Christ. For in Him dwelleth all the fulness of the Godhead bodily. And ye are complete in Him, which is the head of all principality and power." (Col. 2:8–10, KJV)

Not indirectly, Jung is saying that Pueblo Indians have infinitely more satisfying lives than Westerners, that the Pueblo Indians are complete persons in contrast to miserable Westerners who have no inner meaning in their lives.

Jung's strange sentiments are distinctly anti-Western, and largely anti-Christian as well.

Alan Watts has also done his part to push Americans away from their puritanical roots:

> Maslow has amassed a most impressive series of quotations from American psychologists, one and all averring the identity of problem-solving, or "coping," and mental health, and to read them thus lumped into a chorus is downright funny: "Western culture generally [writes Maslow] rests on the Judeo-Christian theology. The United States particularly is dominated by the Puritan and pragmatic spirit which stresses work, struggle and striving, soberness and earnestness, and above all, purposefulness. Like any other social institution, science in general and psychology in particular [are] not exempt from those cultural climate and atmosphere effects. American psychology, by participation, is overpragmatic, over-Puritan, and overpurposeful. ... No textbooks have chapters on fun and gaiety, or leisure and meditation, on loafing and puttering, on aimless, useless, and purposeless activity. ... American psychology is busily occupying itself with only half of life to the neglect of the other—and perhaps more important—half."[9]

Abraham Maslow, developer of humanistic psychology and believer in self-actualization, is saying that American psychology is overly Puritan and therefore overly Christian. Maslow wants psychology to break free of Christian moorings and embrace ... other stuff. Watts is amused by, and seemingly in favor of, Maslow's call for a more Christian-free psychology. For Watts, the antidote to be used in supplanting Christian thought is some form of Eastern mysticism. Maslow's call for less Christian thinking and more puttering, loafing, and meditating calls to mind bands of men loafing about beside streams, maybe playing flutes, sleeping, or gazing off into space—the stuff of old Oriental paintings.

Watts says that "our Western and Christian so-called institutions define man in a way that is not only paradoxical but also self-contradictory. Man is seen as an embodied conflict between reason and instinct, spirit and nature, such that to be healthy or to be saved he must always mistrust himself. Jung does not show the contradiction as acutely as Freud."[10]

Watts expressly says that the Christian concept of man is self-contradictory. He's leery of Christian definitions of man and would be happier if he could just define man his way, without any interference from God's Word. His antipathy toward the West is shocking in its condescension: he doesn't even allow that the West has legitimate institutions but only so-called institutions. Call me old-fashioned—nay, a veritable hick—but it's a turn-off when a professor sits in his office in beautiful San Francisco and trashes the West while kowtowing to the East at every opportunity. I, too, enjoy much that is from the East—I've studied three Asian languages (performing at an A+ level in all three) and lived in Taiwan for many years, but that doesn't give me the right to come back to the United States and trash the forefathers.

Watts is given to wild imaginations. "Imagine how the Christian conscience would react," Watts postulates, "to the idea that, behind the scenes, God and the Devil were the closest friends but had taken opposite sides in order to stage a great cosmic game."[11] It is clear that Watts takes particular delight in tweaking Christians with the most blasphemous of notions.

Predictably, Watts is a big fan of evolution. "Nature is boundless lust and rapacity," Watts says, "and man has evolved from it through the ruthless struggle of natural selection. Although it [is] now clear from biology that consciousness [grew] out of the unconscious, the ego from the id, this must be regarded as a natural accident."[12] Watts goes on to call man "nature's accident." Typical of evolutionists, Watts is given to dogmatic, if unsupported, assertions—therefore, he says, it is clear from biology that consciousness grew out of the unconscious and that this must be regarded as a natural accident. As I see it, Watts gives us no reasoning here—just dogma hiding behind the mislaid prestige of errant biology.

In the case of Watts, I think that unconsciousness grew out of the conscious.

In slightly different phraseology, Watts maintains that "consciousness and reason are ... the fragile 'epiphenomena' of the blind and bestial process of physical evolution. They are the freakish products of the famous 'primordial swamp.'"[13] So reason is the freakish product of a primordial swamp? Wow! I'm a little freaked out by the whole idea of Reason Itself crawling out of a swamp, primordial or otherwise. And if Reason Itself did crawl out of a swamp, was it wearing spectacles? Was it smoking a pipe and dressed to the nines? Was it wearing a corduroy suit and cardigan sweater and oozing with academic airs? Perhaps it's clear from biology that reason crawled out of a swamp? But seriously, instead of saying reason was freakish in its origins, why don't evolutionists just admit that their own theory of "swampish" reason and clear-from-biology ids and egos is itself too freaky for words? Perhaps evolutionists should get the swamp gas out of their ears and go back to the story of Genesis.

Watts, the psychotherapist for all time zones (East and West), is friendly to Maslow's call for winnowing psychology of its Christian content. Maslow thinks Western culture, and Christianity in particular, doesn't understand man as well as psychoanalysts Freud and Jung do; he enjoys trying to turn Christianity on its head by postulating that God and Satan could be good friends; and he favors the theory of evolution. Thus it's really not surprising that Watts comes out and recommends the wisdom of the psychotherapist over that of a minister. "[T]he minister," Watts says, "might become an extraordinarily helpful person if he could see through his own religion.

> In spite of Taoist conceits, light and darkness are very different:
>
> "And God saw the light, that it was good: and God divided the light from the darkness." (Gen. 1:4, KJV)
>
> "And the light shineth in darkness; and the darkness comprehended it not." (John 1:5, KJV)
>
> "But ye are a chosen generation, a royal priesthood, an holy nation, a peculiar people; that ye should shew forth the praises of Him who hath called you out of darkness into His marvellous light." (1 Pet. 2:9, KJV)

But his training and his economic situation do not encourage him to do so, and therefore the psychotherapist is in a more advantageous position."[14]

There it is: Watts, a Westerner, put on the Eastern mystic's hat and felt the need to diminish Christianity to justify his new Eastern hat. It's especially condescending for Watts to say that a minister could become helpful if only he could get past his religion. That's like saying a math teacher could be helpful if only he could put aside the math. Of course, Watts portrays the minister as closed-minded, while the psychotherapist is described as having an advantageous position. Watts dances around, but his message is anti-Christian.

Rollo May, author of *A Cry for Myth*, is another psychologist who denigrates Christianity. "It does not matter in the slightest," May says, "whether a man named Adam and a woman named Eve ever actually existed or not; the myth about them in Genesis still presents a picture of the birth and development of human consciousness which is applicable to all people of all ages and religions."[15]

> "Among the modern psychiatrists, Harry Stack Sullivan speaks well of Satan, ... the creature we mistakenly scorn as the Devil."
>
> —Rollo May, California Psychologist
>
> "Then I saw an angel coming down from heaven, holding the key of the abyss and a great chain in his hand. And he laid hold of the dragon, the serpent of old, who is the devil and Satan, and bound him for a thousand years; and he threw him into the abyss, and shut it and sealed it over him, so that he would not deceive the nations any longer, until the thousand years were completed; after these things he must be released for a short time.... And they [Satan and the deceived] came up on the broad plain of the earth and surrounded the camp of the saints and the beloved city, and fire came down from heaven and devoured them. And the devil who deceived them was thrown into the lake of fire and brimstone, where the beast and the false prophet are also; and they will be tormented day and night forever and ever." (Rev. 20:1–3, 9–10, NASB)

May would have people believe that the Adam-and-Eve story is all about consciousness and, by extension, applicable to all religions. Wrong. Adam and Eve are key figures in the Christian account of history, and the veracity of their story *does* matter. Truth matters.

May has tried to strip down the Adam-and-Eve story—a story about creatures of the God of Abraham, Isaac, and Jacob—as if this story were just a psychological tale applicable to Buddhism and Hinduism too. How utterly ridiculous! Earth to Mays: the Adam-and-Eve story ain't no psychological tale, and it derives from, and applies to, the Holy Bible. Many psychologists would probably try to interpret the act of making a sandwich as a tale of consciousness, such is their penchant for psychologizing everything—all the while manifesting their desperate bid to make psychology the new direction-finder in society.

May likens the Old and New Testaments to Freud's Oedipus complex, concluding that the Bible takes on a different meaning for each culture. "Freud used the myth of Oedipus as central in his contemporaneous psychology," May says. "Like most of the ancient Hebrew and Greek myths, this narration of the triangular struggle in the family becomes true in different ways for people of all cultures, since everyone is born of a father and mother and must in some way revolt against them—which is the definition of a classic like Oedipus."[16]

This is another swipe at the belief in one truth, or absolute truth. Just as May says the Adam-and-Eve story is about consciousness that is relevant to all peoples and all religions, here May is saying that the Old and New Testaments (slyly called Hebrew and Greek myths) offer different brands of truth for various cultures. Again, May is desperately trying to loosen the grip that Christianity has on Truth with a capital "T"; seemingly, May wants folks to pick and choose from the Bible, using Bible verses compatible with their culture and rejecting Bible verses that are incompatible with their culture. For May, the Bible is about consciousness and culture, but the Bible emphasizes the importance of establishing a relationship with our Redeemer, the Lord Jesus Christ. The Bible does not teach one to establish a relationship with one's consciousness and tout one's culture, but rather the Bible teaches that people should repent, be saved, and store up treasure in heaven.

May even endorses one who speaks well of Satan. "Among the modern psychiatrists," May says, "Harry Stack Sullivan speaks well of Satan, for very good reason, since Satan emphasizes exactly what we are concerned with in psychotherapy. The late psychologist at Harvard, Henry Murray, has written at length about Satan ... the creature we mistakenly scorn as the Devil. ... If any psychotherapy is to be successful in any deep, lasting way, it must help the patients to relate to such evil and experience again the myth by which human beings make the perilous journey into and through their hell."[17]

May's notion—that the psychiatrist Sullivan has good reason to speak well of Satan—is monumentally disturbing. What blasphemy! May actually says that really successful psychotherapy must help patients relate to evil and go through their hell—the phrase "relating to evil" makes it sound like evil need not be avoided, and the phrase "their hell" makes it sound as if hell is a mental concoction rather than an objective place. May's suggestion that people can go through their hell connotes the sense that the unbelieving dead can come out the other side of hell—a notion that is unbiblical. To sum up, May endorses one who speaks well of Satan; he waters down evil to the point where it represents nothing scarier than a tough psychological stepping stone; and he makes hell sound like a bad blend of coffee that might, at worst, produce some stomach discomfort.

If Christianity is not in favor in psychological circles, what *is* in favor? Care for a little Eastern mysticism, anyone? "For we face monotony in all we do," May says. "[W]e draw in and exhale breath after breath in ceaseless succession through every moment of our lives, which is monotony par excellence. But out of this repetitiveness of breathing the Buddhists and Yoga have formed their religious meditation and a way of achieving the heights of ecstasy."[18]

Hinduism (the source of yoga) and Buddhism are presented in a positive—nay, an ecstatic—light as vehicles that can take one from monotony to delight. Indeed, May, the open-minded psychologist, indirectly pushes false, foreign gods while denigrating Christianity. Truly, May and other psychological brats sponge up the benefits of largely Christian-built societies here in the West, yet they denigrate Christianity with abandon.

Having established himself as a booster of meditation and ecstasy a la Buddhism and yoga, May proffers a secularized version of hell and holds up self-realization as the goal. He says:

> Human beings can reach heaven only through hell. Without suffering—say, as an author struggles to find the right word with which to communicate his meaning—or without a probing of one's fundamental aims, one cannot get to heaven. Even a purely secular heaven has the same requirements. Poincaré, for example, struggles for weeks and months, faces depression and hopelessness, but then struggles again, and finally through hell arrives at a new discovery in mathematics, the 'heaven' of his solution to the problem that he had posed. ... [T]he mordant despair of [Good Friday] is a necessary prelude to the triumphant experience of Easter, the resurrection. The agony, the horror, the sadness, are a necessary prelude to self-realization and self-fulfillment.[19]

May makes it sound like we can reach self-realization and fulfillment on our own after conquering some personal turmoil. French mathematician Henri Poincaré had personal struggles and mathematical breakthroughs, but that does not mean he squeezed out of hell and into heaven by sheer mathematical brilliance. May would cheapen the Biblical resurrection of Christ—the one and only Savior—by implying that people generally can achieve their own triumph (or self-realization) by themselves. May would sully the resurrection by equating it with Ashteroth/Easter, whereas in fact the very pagan Baal/Ashteroth worship is clearly forbidden in the Bible. Jesus' resurrection is about *His* power to give eternal life to the repentant; it's about *His* power to overcome sin and death and offer forgiveness and life.

May speaks of going through a secularized version (ie, a personal version) of hell to get to a personal heaven. Bent on trivializing sacred truth, May suggests that the pain of being unable to solve a math problem may be viewed as a form of hell, while the discovery of a key math solution could be a form of heaven. Obviously, May's descriptions of a secularized hell, resurrection, and heaven are an attempt to portray the Bible as allegorical rather than literal.

Finally, May suggests that each era needs a different myth. "Each myth in human history is interpreted according to the needs of the society which it reflects," May says. "Marlowe's Renaissance needed an opening of hell to represent the audience's own guilt; they would experience the abreaction they so much needed only by Marlowe's bringing literal hell into the picture. But Goethe's Enlightenment needed a quite different abreaction. The people then needed to leave the theater with the feeling that God was on their side in the form of Paradise, that their culture was a great step in advance."[20]

In *The Tragicall History of the Life and Death of Doctor Faustus,* published by English dramatist Christopher Marlowe in the late 1500's, the protagonist is shredded by demons and dragged off, screaming, to hell. In the play *Faust,* published by German playwright Johann Wolfgang von Goethe in 1808, the lovers Faust and Gretchen are saved by a goddess-queen of heaven, reflecting the Marian-worship of Roman Catholicism. May looks on heaven and hell as the constructs of a society that has particular needs at a particular point in history; he views providential blessings as unreal and holds up humanistic self-improvement as the way.

Seemingly nothing is safe from the bulldozer of May's psychologizing ways. "[This] remarkable story," May says, "is actually describing in the primitive way of the early Mesopotamian people what happens in every human being's development some time between the ages of one and three, namely the emergence of self-awareness. Before that time the individual has lived in the Garden of Eden, a symbol of the period of existence in the womb and early infancy when he is entirely taken care of by parents, and his life is warm and comfortable."[21] For May, the Garden of Eden is a symbol—a symbol of the comfort of time in the womb and early infancy. For an unbelieving psychologist, the idea of the Garden of Eden as a geographical place cannot be tolerated.

May is given to providing secular, psychological definitions as replacements for key terms in the Bible. Therefore, he offers secular definitions for "grace" and "conscience," making sure to strain

"For by grace you have been saved through faith; and that not of yourselves, it is the gift of God; not as a result of works, so that no one may boast." (Eph. 2:8–9, NASB)

out the Christian content so as to allow the psychologist to use these lofty terms with abandon:

> The historical term "grace" has a rich meaning at this point, despite the fact that for many people the word has been so much identified with deteriorated forms of the "grace of God" that it is useless. ... Grace is something "given," a new harmony which emerges; and it always "inclines the heart to wonder". ... The approach we are here recommending as the creative use of tradition makes possible a new attitude toward *conscience.* As everyone knows, conscience is generally conceived of as the negative voice of tradition speaking within one—the "thou-shalt-not's" echoing down from Moses on Mount Sinai; the voice of the prohibitions which the society has taught its members for centuries. ... *Conscience, rather, is one's capacity to tap one's own deeper levels of insight, ethical sensitivity and awareness.* [22]

Propelled by arrogance, May denigrates God's grace and pronounces that true grace is a "new harmony which emerges." The key point is that May is not interested in the old grace (that offered by the saving power of Jesus Christ) but rather in new facsimiles of grace and harmony creatively engineered by himself. May is interested in his own insights, sensitivities, and awareness—after all, supposedly May has only to tap his own wondrous profundity.

Psychologists Hold Up Man as the Answer

We've seen that many psychologists have little use for Christianity, and they hold up man's nature and potentialities. And like the New Agers, psychologists often gravitate toward Eastern mysticism. Eastern mysticism is exotic to the Western mind; by allying themselves with Eastern mysticism, psychologists win for themselves a measure of inscrutability.

Western psychologists borrow Eastern notions of personal power and inner potentiality as they instruct patients to look within. "As the Chinese Taoists have seen," Watts says, "there is really no alternative to trusting man's nature. ... The will of the would-be saint can be as corrupt as his passions and the intellect can be as misguided as the instincts. ... Faith in our own nature works if it only works fifty-one percent of the time. The alternative, as Freud saw, is the swelling of guilt 'to a magnitude that individuals can hardly support.'"²³

For Watts, the Chinese Taoists have understood that we must trust man's nature; that the would-be saint can be corrupt; that faith in our own nature can work; and that the alternative of suffering guilt is hardly endurable. Why suffer guilt and repent when you can turn to Taoism and accept yourself? Many psychologists haven't lived in the Far East, and certainly haven't heard of the *Tao Te Ching*, but they do like relativism—so they buy in.

Jack Forem, author of *Transcendental Meditation: Maharishi Mahesh Yogi and the Science of Creative Intelligence,* sells the Eastern mystical idea of untapped potentialities to gullible Westerners:

> [The] new ideal is the self-realized individual: one who uses his powers fully and creatively, who acts with spontaneity and freedom, who radiates love and goodness, accepts himself and others, and is self-expressive and fully alive. ... The quest for self-realization ... is a dominant theme of our age. Is there anyone today who does not want to *be* more, to develop his capabilities and live a fuller life? ... [A]s Maslow said, "the most advanced thinkers and researchers" interested in human development ... are coming to the inevitable conclusion that if we want to make any lasting and profound change in the world we must turn to man himself. ... "Quite clearly the two great things for which we aim," Aldous Huxley said, "are the improvement of intelligence and the deepening and the extension of the feeling of friendliness and love ..." [M]an ... holds [these qualities], potentially, within himself. What he needs is a way to bring them out and become what he really is....

"The first point to agree upon in this enterprise," wrote the great early psychologist William James, "is that as a rule men habitually use a small part of the powers which they actually possess and which they might use under appropriate conditions. ... [T]he human individual ... possesses powers of various sorts which he habitually fails to use. He energizes below his maximum, and he behaves below his optimum. ... We don't come to our own. It is there, but we don't get at it." [S]omewhere in us we all have the capability to function on a much higher (or deeper) level than we ordinarily do, and that self-realization means just that: realizing what we already are. ... Modern psychology is coming to recognize that we all have within us a tremendous, untapped source of creativity, energy and happiness, and that we are all moving toward the goal of tapping that source and living a fulfilled, joyful life. In *Toward a Psychology of Being* and other works Abraham Maslow demonstrated ... that man *is* moving toward this state of fulfillment.[24]

According to Maslow, "the most advanced thinkers and researchers" decided that to change the world, we have to turn to man himself. Psychologists tell you the best thinkers turn to man for answers, then they tell you psychologists are the key to understanding man—in effect, the suggestion is that the best thinkers turn to psychologists for answers. How convenient! James' emphasis on untapped personal potential could lead some to a search for personal power or even godhood. Psychology-inspired self-absorption is consistent with Satan's plot to take people's attention off the Bible and Jesus' offer of forgiveness and salvation.

The rosy premise of TMers, New Agers, and psychology types—that we've now found previously unknown and unutilized wellsprings of creativity, joy, and energy—should raise a red flag for all. Throughout the 1900s, there were wars throughout the world and on a scale previously unheard of. In his 1973 book on transcendental meditation, Forem audaciously claimed that people were moving toward fulfillment—at a time when the slaughter of millions during China's "cultural revolution" should have been fresh in mind! What cloud was Forem on? Was it a cultural revolution (an essentially bogus term) or was it a killing orgy with devilish profiling? Moreover, the carnage of the Vietnam War was still very fresh when Forem made his starry-eyed claims of humanistic fulfillment. TM is proof that meditation on an empty mind leads to dreamy ignorance.

And to think that psychologists, often driven by their own unrealistic claims of starry and unlimited human potential, are placing others on a couch for inspection! Notice the subtitle of Forem's book: a yogi and the science of creative intelligence; it's the same as the packaging job of Rajneesh's book title, *The Science of Yoga*. In each case, we see Eastern mystics putting across starry ideas about humanistic fulfillment and wrapping their religio-psychology in the banner of science. Americans have been in the thrall of science ever since the development of the lightbulb, the railroad, the car, the aeroplane, the helicopter, the atom bomb, the computer, the internet, etc, so the religio-psychologists from India had only to wrap their notions in the word "science" to inculcate and condition their techno-hip American audience.

TM-style meditation was offered as a way to gain access to man's supposedly untapped wellspring of energy, joy, and creativity. As Forem says:

> By expanding the conscious mind ... we can locate, deeper than the deepest aspect of our individual nature, a universal field of life which gives rise to our individual characteristics as effortlessly and profusely as the universal field of the soil gives rise to oak and

> Psychologist Rollo May mocked what he viewed as the "clinging dependency" of Christians, but he must not have finished the Book, because faithful men like Gideon, Barak, Samson, Jephthah, David, Samuel, and the prophets "conquered kingdoms, performed acts of righteousness, obtained promises, shut the mouths of lions, quenched the power of fire, escaped the edge of the sword, from weakness were made strong, became mighty in war, [and] put foreign armies to flight." (Heb. 11) Thus, the face of faithfulness is hardly one of weakness, despite the self-serving insinuations of puffed-up psychologists in posh Marin County, California.

pine, roses and morning glories. … It is a field of Being. … It has been called by many names, in different ages, by great seers of the truth of reality. Buddha called it Nirvana; Jesus called it the Kingdom of Heaven within; Hindus call it Sat-Chit-Ananda (Absolute Bliss Consciousness); Confucius and Lao-tse called it Tao. … The essence of Maharishi's teaching is that in transcendental meditation a systematic technique has been made available by which anyone can incorporate this infinitely rich field of Being within his conscious experience. … The macro-solution? To unfold more of man's latent potential, so that he can display greater creative intelligence and energy in action. … [W]e have entered a new age—an age in which mankind's fondest visions of an ideal world, creative, peaceful and just, can become a reality. …

The science of creative intelligence … has brought self-realization within easy reach, allowing individuals of every age and background to find greater inner resources and *effortlessly* live richer, more meaningful lives. This is the only foundation upon which that ideal world can be built.[25]

According to Forem, TM can cause people to contact their deepest aspect—a "universal field of life" or a "field of being"—and thereby create an ideal world of creativity, peaceableness, and justice. Notice also that Forem's humanistic dogma contains the assertion that Jesus was just one sage among many sages in history—Forem tries to account for Jesus' position in history as if to assure a gullible American readership that Westerners too can use TM in spite of their Christian heritage. The fake "gospel according to TM" is that a "field of being" sent a "systematic technique" of meditating and tapping hidden potential to save people and help them form an ideal world.

Jung was big on acceptance of self. In 1932, he addressed a group of ministers: "Condemnation … oppresses … If a doctor wishes to help a human being he must be able to accept him as he is. And he can do this in reality only when he has already seen and accepted himself as he is. ... [A]cceptance of oneself is the essence of the moral problem and the acid test of one's whole outlook on life."[26]

Many secularists use Jung's idea that condemnation oppresses to oppose the very notion of sin. By implying that belief in sin oppresses, Jung appeals to people's pride in themselves, to the prideful (and unbiblical) feeling that someone need not view himself as a sinner. In fact, the conviction of the conscience and the consequent recognition that one *is* a sinner—these are crucial stepping stones in the road to repentance, veritable bridges on the way to being born again by faith in Jesus the Christ. "Accept yourself" is the mantra of Jung and other psychologists and psychotherapists; "accept Jesus as Lord and Savior" is the message of the Gospel. It's the difference between night and day, darkness and light.

May perpetuates the prideful idea that to stand alone is strong, that to cling to God is weak:

> When one has been able to say "No" to the need that he be "borne up," when, in other words, he is able not to demand he be taken care of, when he has the courage to stand alone, he can then speak as one with authority. ... [S]pinoza gives us a statement which blows like a fresh and cleansing wind through the foggy, morbid swamps of clinging dependency in religion: "Whoso loveth God truly must not expect to be loved by Him in return." Here speaks, in this shattering sentence, the brave man ...
>
> When one is able to relate creatively to the wisdom of his fathers in the ethical and religious tradition, he finds that he discovers anew his capacity for *wonder*. It is self-evident that the capacity for active, responsive wonder has been largely lacking in modern society. ... Those who take a rigid view of religious or scientific truth become more dogmatic and lose the capacity to wonder; those who 'acquire the wisdom of their fathers' without surrendering their own freedom find that wonder adds to their zest and their conviction of meaning in life.[27]

May's suggestion, that the strong man rejects God, is one of the enemy's oldest tricks: it is an appeal to puffed-up personalities that lack shame and have a seared conscience. Dutch philosopher Baruch Spinoza, author of *Ethics* and *Treatise on the Improvement of Understanding,* was known for a pantheistic worldview that had similarities to Kabbalism; his notion that good and evil are relative, not absolute, was unbiblical and drew criticism from his own Portuguese Jewish community.

Psychologists Wild About Feelings

Psychologists are madly in love with feelings. Dr. Martin Rossman, author of *Guided Imagery for Self-Healing: An Essential Resource for Anyone Seeking Wellness,* suggests that any source of information is okay. "Whatever you believe—that [your inner] advisor is a spirit, a guardian angel, a message from God, a hallucination, a communication from your right brain to your left, or a symbolic representation of inner wisdom—is all right," he says.[28] That's some mushy stuff. If I might parody the situation:

"Dr. Quack, I feel like I'm guided by an inner fruitcake."

"*No problemo,* my friend. Flow with your inner fruitcake."

"Well then, Dr. Quack, I feel as if I'm guided by an inner jelly bean. Is that okay?"

"Yes, that's good! Guidance by way of jelly bean is very good and certainly nothing to worry about. However, guidance by way of an inner Swedish Fish can be problematic. Take an aspirin and call me in the morning."

Carl Jung suggested getting closer to nature, intimating that a mountain cave would be a good place for a great demon, and that a snake could be "the embodiment of wisdom." Where are the beavers, porcupines, cougars, and deer in Jung's world? Sadly, it seems the message of nature—that it gives evidence of God's eternal power and Godhead—was woefully lost on Jung (Rom. 1:20). Moreover, it appears that demons and that old serpent, the devil, didn't even register as bad guys for Jung (Gen. 3, Is. 14, Ez. 28, Rev. 12 & 20). Truly, education without the Bible is mischievous.

Not surprisingly, intuition gets the nod from Rollo May. "It is interesting to me," he says, "that Dante identifies intuition as the supreme form of guidance. Therapists who have succumbed to the sin of dogmatic rationalism, if I may be permitted to add it to Dante's hell, might consider the legitimacy of this mental power."[29]

May recommends the mental power of intuition to therapists while flippantly describing dogmatic rationalism as hellish. It seems all too obvious that therapists such as May want to raise the status of intuition and hunches because as intuition goes, so goes the status of the therapist.

At the end of the day, the therapist is unbelievably subjective, a big ball of intuition really; without his sacrosanct intuition, the therapist would be powerless, uncertified, and maybe even jobless.

Psychologists Open Up to the Occultic and the Demonic

Carl Jung says:

> As scientific understanding has grown, so our world has become dehumanized. Man feels himself isolated in the cosmos, because he is no longer involved in nature and has lost his emotional "unconscious identity" with natural phenomena. ... No river contains a spirit, no tree is the life principle of a man, no snake the embodiment of wisdom, no mountain cave the home of a great demon. No voices now speak to man from stones, plants, and animals, nor does he speak to them believing they can hear. His contact with nature has gone, and with it has gone the profound emotional energy that this symbolic connection supplied.[30]

Jung suggests getting closer to nature, but his ideal nature would seem to be one populated by snakes and demons. How eerie is that? Out of all nature, Jung had to choose serpents and demons as selling points in his call to return to nature! Where are the beavers, porcupines, cougars, and deer in Jung's world? His use of the serpent (a symbol of Satan) and the demon to recommend nature is beyond unsettling—it's scary!

"Modern man does not understand how much his 'rationalism' (which has destroyed his capacity to respond to numinous symbols and ideas) has put him at the mercy of the psychic 'underworld…'" Jung says. "His moral and spiritual tradition has disintegrated, and he is now paying the price for this break-up in worldwide disorientation and dissociation."[31] To Jung, rationality is bad; great demons in caves are to be embraced; and snakes are to be revered. Indeed, Jung's lament over moral breakdown and widespread feelings of dissociation rings hollow because it is Jung himself who contributes so mightily to feelings of dissociation and moral decline.

Jung claims that the East's Mother Earth orientation is no worse than the West's Father God orientation: "The masses and their leaders do not realize … that there is no substantial difference between calling the world principle male and a father (spirit), as the West does, or female and a mother (matter), as the Communists do."[32] No substantial difference between Christianity and atheistic, materialistic Communism? In fact, the difference is between the holy worship of God the creator on the one hand and the pagan worship of nature and man on the other hand. How telling that Jung seeks to diminish the Christian West and laud the Communist East: in this sense, he was a revolutionary.

Jung was entranced by the idea of so-called god-men and spirits residing in trees, rivers, etc. "There are no longer any gods whom we can invoke to help us," Jung says. "The great religions of the world suffer from increasing anemia, because the helpful numina have fled from the woods, rivers, and mountains, and from animals, and the god-men have disappeared underground into the unconscious. … Our present lives are dominated by the goddess Reason, who is our greatest and most tragic illusion."[33]

Jung's reference to "helpful numina" makes it abundantly clear that he feels the spirits of the forest are there to help him. We've also seen how serpents and demons are apparently positive aspects of nature for Jung. It doesn't seem to dawn on Jung (in spite of all his intuition) that forest spirits, serpents, and demons might not be friendly or helpful but rather harmful and evil. Certainly the four angels that Revelation 9 indicates will be loosed from the Euphrates River as part of the sixth trumpet judgment to kill a third of mankind—certainly those river spirits are not helpful numina. Satan, referred to in Ephesians 2 as "the ruler of the kingdom of the air," is not a helpful numen! The beast that Revelation 13 indicates will come out of the sea and make war on the saints—that spirit, indeed the antichrist spirit, will not be a helpful numen.

Testing the Spirits

The point is that in spite of Jung—who wants to rush headlong into a world of forest spirits, river spirits, and a mish-mash of god-men—we are called to test the spirits to see whether they are from God or not (1 John 4), not to embrace every foul spirit flitting by (Ephesians 4). And we are to follow Jesus Christ, the one and only God-man, not waste our time searching for false god-men. We should *celebrate* any decline in forest, river, and mountain worship—we should not join Jung in his lament over the decline of such pagan, animist worship (Romans 1).

To the extent that Jung laid much of the groundwork for the modern movement (or religion) of psychology, it matters a lot that he didn't shut the door on forest spirits, cave-dwelling demons, and false god-men. In fact, Jung's openness to false spirits continues on, indirectly at least, in the work of Martin Rossman:

> Talking with an Inner Advisor is not a new idea. Most of our major philosophical, religious, and psychological traditions concern inner guidance in one form or another. Many cultures use rituals that include music, chanting, fasting, dancing, sacrifice, and psychoactive plants to invoke a vision that could inform and guide them at important times. Native Americans would go into the wilderness unarmed, without food or water, build a sweat lodge, and pray for contact with a guiding spirit. From such a visionary experience they would draw their names, their power, and their direction in life. The medicine man in the tribe might make a similar quest in search of healing for an ailing tribe member. ...
>
> A surprising number of people tell me they 'talk' to spouses or other loved ones who have died. In their talks they receive advice and comfort, as people do when they 'talk' with their Inner Advisors. ... Meeting with an Inner Advisor is a way of making this intuitive guidance more available to you.[34]

Rossman's description of inner advisors would seem to be a description of spirit guides. His positive portrayal of spirit guides opens the door to demonic possession, consulting with the dead (prohibited in Deuteronomy 18), and nature worship (prohibited in Romans 1), given that the spirit guides (demons) can pose variously as a bird, a dead relative, etc. In effect, Rossman opens the door to giving one's life over to an intuition-induced spirit guide or whatever might pop up during a drug-induced altered state.

Rossman further paints the inner advisor technique as so much peaches and cream:

> Dr. David Bresler, head of the Bresler Medical Center in Santa Monica, California, frequently uses the Inner Advisor technique with people in chronic pain. … He guides people to relax in an imaginary quiet place, then asks them to get an image for a friendly creature that can act as their advisor. Many of his patients will get animal advisors such as Bambi the deer, or Chuckie the chipmunk. Dr. Bresler and I have compared notes at length and agree that people seem able to receive the same kind of information from the animal figures as from any other inner images. … As I described [to one psychologist] the cute little animal advisors many people created, he laughed and said he could see an image of a lion, looking at him and licking his chops. "Screw all those chipmunks," said the lion. "I'm here, and I'm important." From this image he understood that this inner part of himself was powerful and needed to be approached with respect. … Welcome the advisor that comes and get to know it as it is. One advisor is not better than another, and there is no one way for them to communicate. People have learned profound lessons from gremlins named Jack and rabbits named Thumper… [35]

This whole inner-advisor business would be ridiculous if it weren't so darkly dangerous and demonic. That the two psychologists noted that inner advisors tend to give the same kind of information (ie, advice) is telling: demons and foul spirits are consistent in their attempts to focus people's attention on themselves and take their eyes off the Word of God.

Rossman's statement that one advisor is not better than another shows that Rossman should not be taken seriously at all. If any old advisor will do, then what's the point of getting advice at all? Of course, an advisor must be qualified to give good and sound advice. If you want to dress well for a snowstorm, do you ask advice from a Florida lifeguard or from a member of the Vail ski patrol?

The point is that advice needs to be directed at the specific question posed, and it needs to come from a reliable source. If advice is always the same—that is to say, anti-Christian—and it comes from movie-star deer and chipmunks and any other cockeyed thing, then it's pretty obvious that the advice given is nothing but a demonic tirade engineered to pull people away from Christ and into the clutches of Satan.

CHAPTER SIX

THE UNHOLY PRIDE OF UNITARIANISM

In 2 Peter 2:1–3, we can see that the consequences of false teachings are severe indeed: "But there were also false prophets among the people, just as there will be false teachers among you. They will secretly introduce destructive heresies, even denying the sovereign Lord who bought them—bringing swift destruction on themselves. Many will follow their shameful ways and will bring the way of truth into disrepute. In their greed these teachers will exploit you with stories they have made up. Their condemnation has long been hanging over them, and their destruction has not been sleeping" (NIV).

Unitarianism—like Mormonism and Catholicism—is a works-based religion, denying the fact that Jesus is the only way to salvation and encouraging one to constitute his own potpourri of spiritual beliefs.

Unitarianism — A Vaunted View of One's Own Character-Based Works

A particularly rich source of Unitarian thought is Jack Mendelsohn's book *Why I Am a Unitarian*. Mendelsohn touts Hosea Ballou as a "courageous, scholarly, and extremely persuasive Universalist leader," noting that it was Ballou who added the phrase "salvation by character": "As for the punishment of sin, [Ballou] stated that it was instant, constant and inevitable; but [it] was not everlasting, for the self-evident reason that everlasting punishment makes no sense."[1]

The key here is that Ballou, and Unitarian Universalists in general, believe there is no eternal damnation such as being thrown into hell or the lake of fire. According to Unitarian John Sias, "We believe that human beings should be accountable for their actions and make amends for any harm they may bring to others. But we don't believe that God will punish them."[2]

I would agree that someone who steals a candy bar should not go to prison for life, but who are we to say that a lifetime spent ignoring one's creator and redeemer, Jesus Christ, has no lasting consequences? And if a father can punish a child, why won't the Unitarians recognize that God most certainly can punish wayward and unbelieving people?

Unitarians are hung up on the Christian concepts of sin and salvation by Jesus. Their hang-up over sin is expressed in their wish to have such great character, in and of themselves, that they could save themselves by personal achievements. They think they don't need saving, so they think they have no need of Jesus. Offended by the very concepts of sin and salvation, they become very open to personal blends of religiosity—to everything but Bible-believing Christianity.

Mendelsohn continues in his articulation of the Unitarian ethic:

> For Unitarians, salvation is not an otherworldly journey, flown on wings of dogma. It is ethical striving and moral achievement: respect for the personalities and convictions of others, faith in human dignity and potentiality, aversion to sanctimony and bigotry, hearty enjoyment of life and people. ... [W]e believe in salvation by character. ... [W]e believe salvation *is* character, for we do not mean that character saves a man from the flames of an imaginary hell or for the bliss of an equally imaginary heaven. We do not profess to know the precise dimensions of immortality. But we are sure of this: the inner life, shaped by the power of high and sane ideals, brings to the human soul the finest, most enduring satisfactions, and makes of a man a source of strength, even in the utmost tribulation, to the

> human family of which he is a member. This is what we mean by salvation, and what serves so well in life could not possibly serve less well in afterlife.[3]

Mendelsohn touts moral achievement as though some people are good enough on their own strengths; he touts personalities and potentialities as though people can be all they need to be on their own; he's against dogma and bigotry as though being without doctrine is the way to interpersonal kindness; he's for a hearty enjoyment of life, as though doctrine would somehow prevent that, and as if to suggest that doctrine-centered folks are bores; he's for ridiculing heaven and hell even though he doesn't know the dimensions of the afterlife; and he thinks the inner life, with a concern for unnamed ideals, makes a man strong.

The problem is that many Unitarians hold up self-advancement as their highest ideal, and they often are among the most venal of anti-Christian bigots. In practice, their railing against doctrine means they want everything they have ever done to be totally justified (rationalized), period.

Evil-doer Mao Tse-tung. Calling China's Communist Army the People's Liberation Army cannot undo the stains of the Red Guards' horror. "For this is the message which you have heard from the beginning, that we should love one another; not as Cain, *who* was of the evil one and slew his brother. And for what reason did he slay him? Because his deeds were evil, and his brother's were righteous" (1 John 3:11–12 NASB). "Cain left the presence of the Lord, and settled in the land of Nod, east of Eden" (Gen. 4:16). "But these men revile the things which they do not understand; and the things which they know by instinct, like unreasoning animals, by these things they are destroyed. Woe to them! For they have gone the way of Cain" (Jude 1:10–11a NASB). "He who returns evil for good, evil will not depart from his house" (Prov. 17:13 NASB). "May the Lord repay the evildoer according to his evil" (2 Sam. 3:39b NASB).

History shows that self-reliant men throughout the ages, with all their self-described achievements, have been unable to create righteous societies; leaders such as Nimrod, Nero, Stalin, Hitler, Benito Mussolini, Mao, Pol Pot, and Idi Amin have repeatedly dragged communities and nations into utter ruin; and the inner life of men is often desperate and wicked and hardly a source of strength. Somehow I don't think that Mendelsohn's pie-in-the-sky rhapsodies about the strength of the inner life would be very consoling to the people who were reduced to stacks of bones in the killing fields of the Khmer Rouge or to those Ugandans and Chinese slaughtered under the horrific influence of the inner lives of Amin and Mao.

More than just believers in their own inner lives, Unitarians are big believers in the importance of their work. Mendelsohn says:

> *Why* I exist, nobody on earth is capable of telling me; but, since I do exist, let me strive to give my existence a brightness and glory by setting up for myself the loftiest goals I can reasonably hope to achieve. This is my religious view. ... Interestingly enough, there is nothing new about this view. Since long before the time of Jesus it has been cultivated by some of the Chinese religions. It has been known and cherished by Buddhists for nearly twenty-five hundred years. It is belief in the *immortality of character, of conduct and thought, of influence*. ... But I have something to live and die for: not for a personal survival in which I cannot believe, but a present and lasting immortality of influence in which I can believe.[4]

> "But I have something to live and die for: not for a personal survival in which I cannot believe, but a present and lasting immortality of influence in which I can believe."
> —Jack Mendelsohn, Unitarian
>
> Personal survival is possible, but only through Jesus—the Savior, *El Salvador*. Lasting influence (i.e. legacy) is only possible for those who are saved by Jesus and will put up treasure in Heaven (John 3 & 14).

Instead of serving the God of Abraham, Isaac, and Jacob, Mendelsohn chooses to strive to give his own existence a brightness and glory—unfortunately, that kind of self-absorption and self-exaltation is exactly what led to the fall of Lucifer! Mendelsohn wants to create a name for himself that will outlive him; again, the emphasis is on himself. When Mendelsohn does make reference to Jesus, it is in an off-handed and irreverent manner, framing Jesus as a youngster in the face of the supposedly more ancient and august Buddhists and other Chinese religionists. What sacrilege! Jesus said, "Verily, verily, I say unto you, Before Abraham was, I am" (John 8:58 KJV). Jesus also said, "I am Alpha and Omega, the first and the last" (Rev. 1:11a KJV). In fact, Jesus will break all the corrupt human kingdoms, built as they were on false idols and immorality (Dan. 2:42–45; Rev. 19:13–21).

Mendelsohn says Unitarians think of salvation as "an achievement dependent on deeds rather than creeds."[5] In effect, salvation for the Unitarian is no salvation at all; a person only really needs saving if he is in a bind that he can't get out of by himself, and Unitarians think they can solve their dilemmas by way of their great deeds. (They carefully avoid calling their dilemmas *sins*.) "Unitarianism," Mendelsohn says, "is a religion which cares more about me *as a person*—my potential resources and strengths—than it does about theological explanations or atonements of the dilemmas and failures which beset me."[6]

Again, the emphasis is on Mendelsohn as a person. Well, of course, as a person! Otherwise, as a what? The emphasis is on Mendelsohn's personal resources and strengths, and he eschews the theology of salvation. Notice he talks about atonements in the plural, as if atonement is some garden-variety category the likes of beets, turnips, carrots, or onions. Not only does he avoid the word sin—preferring the more benign and solvable dilemmas and failures—but he also refuses to face the singular importance of the singular atonement accomplished by Jesus Christ at Calvary. Jesus died for our sins, but Unitarians are often too busy admiring their own achievements to have Jesus' offer of the remission of sins explained to them.

At the social level, the Unitarian Service Committee aims to "[demonstrate] that good deeds lead the way to One World, One Humanity."[7] Unitarians are trying to bring about world peace and harmony by dint of their own amazing achievements, whatever those may be. In fact, all of history screams that people have not achieved world peace and cannot do so by themselves. So why should anyone suddenly believe the Unitarian claim that good deeds lead to one world and one humanity? Could there be a more antihistorical claim? In fact, on hearing such Unitarian boasting, true Christians should be more vigilant than ever. In 1 Thess. 5:2–3 , we learn the following: "[F]or you know very well that the day of the Lord will come like a thief in the night. While people are saying, 'Peace and safety', destruction will come on them suddenly, as labor pains on a pregnant woman, and they will not escape" (NIV).

In the end times, people will be deluded into thinking that a one-world government, headed by the Antichrist, can deliver peace to the world—but this delusion will lead to ruination as the Antichrist reveals his real motives of killing Christians and Jews and people in general. Just as the chant of "peace and safety" will lead to the Antichrist raining down destruction, so too the Unitarian's chant of "one world and one humanity through good deeds" is paving the way for the Antichrist's ultimate deception.

Instead of deluding ourselves that we can achieve world peace, we should look up and be instilled with the hope of the catching up of the saints. In 1 Thess. 4:14, 16–18, we learn this:

> We believe that Jesus died and rose again and so we believe that God will bring with Jesus those who have fallen asleep in him. ... For the Lord himself will come down from heaven, with a loud command, with the voice of the archangel and with the trumpet call of God, and the dead in Christ will rise first. After that, we who are still alive and are left will be caught up together with them in the clouds to meet the Lord in the air. And so we will be with the Lord forever. Therefore encourage each other with these words. (NIV)

Instead of looking for one-world government and globalistic harmony, we should be looking up, reading the doctrines of the Holy Bible, repenting, praying for souls, and praising Jesus Christ!

Unitarianism — Where Doctrine Is Not Welcome

If there is no unifying thought in a worship group, then how can it really be called anything at all? Yet Unitarians are very dogmatic when it comes to the importance of personal whim, even if that emphasis leads to a nonunified group. "A church is expected to require assent to certain concrete theological beliefs," Mendelsohn says. "Not so among Unitarians. Whether the subject is immortality, God or science, there may be as many ideas as there are Unitarians present, yet there will be one unifying principle; namely, the right of every person to make his own decision about what he believes."[8]

But how can the unifying principle be that people can believe anything they want? What if I were to believe that *Star Trek*'s Captain Kirk is the way to truth? Would that decision be okay in Unitarian circles? Yep. What if I were to believe that rainbow trout are going to evolve their way out of the water and lead people to the truth? Would that be okay in Unitarian circles? Yep—that would be just another wrinkle in the idolatrous Unitarian decision-making process.

Mendelsohn gives praise to the atmosphere created by Unitarian minister John Haynes Holmes, saying that he "created a temple of the human spirit just by his being and his speaking. ... The service was religious—deeply religious—yet there were no divisive, mind-splitting, doctrinal elements."[9] Mendelsohn was impressed by the home that Holmes gave to the human spirit. Nevertheless, the Bible teaches that people are enlivened and saved by the touch of the Holy Spirit, and that left to themselves people's hearts are full of wickedness (Jeremiah 17, Matthew 15). "For out of the heart proceed evil thoughts, murders, adulteries, fornications, thefts, false witness, blasphemies: These are the things which defile a man" (Matt. 15:19–20a KJV).

Worshipping the human spirit is a staple of humanism, but this amounts to pride and sin. What people need is the Holy Spirit, not more of the human spirit. Indeed, in 1 Cor. 6:19–20 we learn that in the body of a believer resides the Holy Spirit: "Do you not know that your body is a temple of the Holy Spirit, who is in you, whom you have received from God? You are not your own; you were bought at a price. Therefore honor God with your body" (NIV).

Mendelsohn, an articulate Unitarian, refers to doctrinal elements as "divisive and mind-splitting." In Unitarian speak, the word doctrine can't even rear its head without being smashed down vengefully, lest doctrine should get loose and devour free-thinking Unitarians. And why would doctrine be mind-splitting? That's strategic fear-mongering designed to keep people in the habit of devising their own systems of thought and belief. There need not be anything mind-splitting about doctrine unless someone fails to use his mind to differentiate between good and true doctrine on the one hand and bad and false doctrine on the other hand. In the case of false doctrine, that not only can split one's mind, but it can also split one's very soul and run one straight into hell.

"For the present, at least," Mendelsohn says, "the proper study of man is man. Let religion throw its entire and undistracted strength into the struggle to extricate man from his present failings and dilemmas. Someday we may know enough to make responsible statements about God. At present it is not possible."[10]

"Religion to the rescue!" the Unitarian says. "Study man!" Religion and man contain life's answers, according to Unitarianism. But how naïve is that? In the history of man, there's been no shortage of men and religiosity, and look where it has gotten us. Clearly, the answers to life are to be found in God's Word and not in man's self-devised notions. Moreover, the incessant reference to failings and dilemmas among Unitarians really reeks of dishonesty. What were the Nazi or Communist slaughterhouses? Were those failings or dilemmas? Or were those expressions of unbridled satanic evil?

A Unitarian's refusal to call evil and sin what they are makes him susceptible to tyrannical deceptions—seemingly all a dictator would have to do is mention a utopian potentiality, and the Unitarian might just fall for the ploy. Unitarianism and other forms of idolatry are actually bad for America's national security because idolatrous thinking makes people unknowledgeable and undiscerning, easily deceived by lying dictators, and ungrateful for God's hand of protection.

How could there be monsters like Mao, Stalin, Pol Pot, Hitler, Amin, and Caligula? Methinks the activities of monsters have something to do with this: "And even as they did not like to retain God in their knowledge, God gave them over to a reprobate mind, to do those things which are not convenient; being filled with all unrighteousness, fornication, wickedness, covetousness, maliciousness; full of envy, murder, debate, deceit, malignity; whisperers, backbiters, haters of God, despiteful, proud, boasters, inventors of evil things, disobedient to parents, without understanding, covenant-breakers, without natural affection, implacable, unmerciful: Who, knowing the judgment of God, that they which commit such things are worthy of death, not only do the same, but have pleasure in them that do them" (Rom. 1:28–32 KJV). It seems those who do not retain God in their knowledge are given over to reprobate minds and are given reprobate leaders.

Mendelsohn says, "[T]he need in our world community… is for an understanding of man himself. … It must also be an understanding frank enough to accept man as part of a naturalistic order, a creature who first emerged from the animal world as a caprice of nature."[11] For leading Unitarians, a truly frank understanding of man must include a belief in evolution—sounds like a doctrinal requirement to me! The articulate Unitarian is a hypocrite, and his arguments fall down under the weight of their own inconsistency and naïveté.

> "[The world needs] an understanding of man himself.... It must ... be an understanding frank enough to accept man as part of a naturalistic order, a creature who first emerged from the animal world as a caprice of nature...."
> —Jack Mendelsohn, Unitarian

Though ostensibly against "divisive, mind-splitting doctrinal elements," Mendelsohn nevertheless indicated that the anthropological view the world needs must be evolution-based. He postured as being against limiting doctrines, but actually insisted on his own personal blend of views. The self-centered, anti-Christian nature of Unitarianism always lurks just below the surface.

"To me, the important thing about Jesus is not that he was *just* human, but that the human race is capable of producing him," Mendelsohn says. "And not him alone, but others like him. And not only in ancient times, but now."[12] Mendelsohn doesn't want Jesus to be the one and only God-man because then he'd have to accept the

Bible; he would rather that Jesus was just a provider of nice sayings—and enlightened sayings at that—but essentially no different from Isaiah or Paul. He and like-minded Unitarians expose children to many religions and encourage them on the path of developing a religion of one's own. Religious truth for Mendelsohn is to be confirmed by experience and not by referring to Jesus, the Bible, or doctrine.[13] Thus we have the Unitarian end game: "Don't mind the utopia-gone-bad slaughterhouse, just enjoy the undoctrinal experience!" Interfaith utopians of all brands walk away from the God of Israel and into the hands of tyrants.

Unitarianism — Much To-Do About Ethics and No Trepidation Over Sin

Unitarians gloss over the matter of sin. Marjorie Newlin Leaming says that "God forgives our imperfections because we were created that way. It's all right to be human."[14] In the same vein, Chworowsky and Raible say that "Unitarian Universalists reject the traditional Christian idea that the original sin of disobedience of Adam is inherited by all."[15]

When I told a Unitarian he was a sinner, he got up from the table and walked away. It is my fervent and constant prayer that that man will be saved and his entire family (Acts 16:31)! In point of fact, sin is something that none of us can deal with on our own; that is precisely why Jesus' gift of redemption to those who believe in Him is so wonderful!

The Unitarian creed that it's all right to be human is about as vacuous as it gets. People are human. But even if one feels okay about his general character traits and his capabilities, that doesn't mean he should whitewash his bad traits. Bad traits should be faced, and when we realize that we can't undo our bad tendencies and our bad acts and our selfish motives by our own strength, we should then repent of our sins and receive Jesus as our Lord and Savior.

Matt. 7:7–8 teaches us this: "Ask and it will be given to you; seek and you will find; knock and the door will be opened to you. For everyone who asks receives; he who seeks finds; and to him who knocks, the door will be opened." Recognition of one's own sin should stimulate one's conscience, propel one into a state of repentance, and throw one into a search for God's mercy and truth. Yes, we're human, and no, it's not all right to make friends with one's sinful nature. God has made a provision for men to come back to Him in spite of their wretchedness, and that's the key! Jesus Christ is there—believe in Him and accept His saving grace. "That if thou shalt confess with thy mouth the Lord Jesus, and shalt believe in thine heart that God hath raised him from the dead, thou shalt be saved" (Rom. 10:9 KJV).

The Unitarian desperately wants people to think that ethics (the system of practicing a veneer of good while whitewashing one's sins) are not only valid as a way of life but more productive than the Christian mindset. "[W]e believe that our religious concept of ethical responsibility is much more in tune with reality, and much more productive of good," Mendelsohn says, "than the traditional doctrine of man's inherent depravity through 'original sin.'"[16]

> "[W]e believe that our religious concept of ethical responsibility is much more in tune with reality, and much more productive of good, than the traditional doctrine of man's inherent depravity through 'original sin.'"
> —Jack Mendelsohn, Unitarian
>
> "Do not be amazed that I said to you, 'You must be born again.'"
>
> "Enter through the narrow gate; for the gate is wide and the way is broad that leads to destruction, and there are many who enter through it."
> —Yeshua, The Alpha and The Omega (John 3:7; Matt. 7:13, NASB)

Excuse me, but the United States was built more by Puritans and other Protestants than it was by puffed-up Unitarians. It was Protestantism that formed the backdrop for the Declaration of Independence (1776), the Constitution (1787), and the Bill of Rights (1789).[17] In Ben Franklin's time, the Bible and *The Pilgrim's Progress,* a Puritan classic, were the two most commonly owned and read books.[18] Indeed, it was the Protestant work ethic that ran through the heartwood of America's founding timbers, not idolatrous notions of Unitarian ethics. If the Unitarians can point to a Unitarian nation that is more productive than the Protestant-inspired United States, let them do it.

In fact, American Unitarians, trumpeting their allegedly superior productivity and realism, are like deluded children admiring all the

Unitarian handiwork of a whittled stick while rolling through the American landscape in a Protestant-built train. Albert Schweitzer spoke of an ethical will that welled up inside of him as an expression of God. "The advantage of such genuinely felt [ethical] mysticism is its universality," Mendelsohn says. "It is not a denominational or sectarian experience. The Hindu, Buddhist, Jewish, Moslem, Roman Catholic and Unitarian ethical mystics stand on common ground."[19]

Ah, can't you just feel the "universality" of Mendelsohn's Unitarian Universalism? Can't you just feel the warm "universal" hug from Mendelsohn's multipronged ethical will? Notice that Mendelsohn doesn't miss a chance to trivialize Protestantism by suggesting it offers a mere denominational or otherwise divisive experience; by implication, Unitarianism supposedly offers an inclusive super-umbrella that will protect from the oppression of divisive rains. The picture here is of Hindus, Buddhists, Jews, Muslims, Roman Catholics, and Unitarians holding hands and swaying in unison to the music of their ethical wills; meanwhile, Protestants are supposed to be off somewhere ranting about sins and squabbling over doctrine and generally being divisive. Could this articulate Unitarian be any more disingenuous? Could his analysis be any more preposterous?

Mendelsohn describes how he came to reject the Bible. "It was not about meek acceptance and a cringing sense of sin that I wished to hear. … [Yet] I was backed into a corner and implored to surrender my soul to the Lord and Savior. … I have sought a spiritual life that offers not surrender and salvation but 'love of life in spite of life.' I have striven to accept the flaws and to find things to live for that transcend and conquer them."[20]

> "[Yet] I was backed into a corner and implored to surrender my soul to the Lord and Savior.... I have sought a spiritual life that offers not surrender and salvation but 'love of life in spite of life.'"
> —Jack Mendelsohn, Unitarian
>
> "Everyone who is proud in heart is an abomination to the LORD; assuredly, he will not be unpunished."
>
> "Pride goes before destruction, and a haughty spirit before stumbling."
> (Prov. 16:5, 18, NASB)

Mendelsohn is mightily offended at being cornered and made to cringe by the specter of sin, and he flippantly tosses aside the need for salvation; so offended is he that he doesn't even want salvation. Even a cursory look at his own words shows how proud and haughty is his stance. How could the Lord over Creation reprove him! Acceptance of the God of Abraham, Isaac, and Jacob is portrayed as being meek and weak, the implication being that forging a self-styled religion is a strong thing to do. Never mind that self-styled Unitarian religion is just self-centered religion all dressed up in pretty terminology.

Mendelsohn basically refuses to cringe or repent, and rather than talking directly about sin, he talks about flaws. What he overlooks is that far from wanting all men to cringe forever, the Lord wants men to partake of His saving grace and, ultimately, the gift of Heaven. In Matthew, we read this: "Which of you, if his son asks for bread, will give him a stone? Or if he asks for a fish, will give him a snake? If you, then, though you are evil, know how to give good gifts to your children, how much more will your Father in heaven give good gifts to those who ask him! So in everything, do to others what you would have them do to you, for this sums up the Law and the Prophets" (Matt. 7:9–12 NIV).

Repenting is not the final goal; rather, it's a step in the process laid out by God the Father to draw people to Him. If a father on earth can rightfully expect to have his children come and recognize him, it's clearly even more crucial that people come and give their hearts to the God that created them!

CHAPTER SEVEN

TOWARD A GLOBAL FALSE RELIGION

In Revelation 17, the Holy Spirit gives us a picture of a terrible woman who goes by the name of Mystery, Babylon the Great, the Mother of Prostitutes, and of the Abominations of the Earth. She is dressed in purple and scarlet and glitters with gold, precious stones, and pearls. In her hand is a golden cup that brims with abominations and the filth of her adulteries. She is drunk with the blood of the true saints who testified of Jesus. She sits on many waters, which signify many peoples, throngs, nations, and languages. She sits on a scarlet beast that is covered with blasphemous names and has seven heads and ten horns; the seven heads signify seven hills and seven kings, and the ten horns signify ten kings who will receive their kingly authority for one hour along with the beast. The ten kings will give the beast the power to rule, and the ten kings and the beast will hate the woman who rides the beast and eventually wreak ruination on her. Finally, this terrible woman is a powerful city that rules over the kings of the earth; indeed, she commits adultery with the kings of the earth, and her magic spell leads all the nations astray.

Rome is a city on seven hills. Roman Catholicism's top clergy are dressed in purple and scarlet. The Roman church is overflowing with glittering treasures that were plundered in the course of the Crusades, the Inquisition, etc. Rome and Vatican City make a pretense of carrying on the Christian faith, yet really Roman Catholicism has pandered to false religions and world leaders since the time of Constantine, thus the filth of Rome's spiritual adulteries have made Rome fit for the titles "Mother of Prostitutes" and "Mother of the Abominations of the Earth." Rome has long ruled over world leaders, leading nations astray with the magic of her spell.

The identification of Rome as the Great Whore of Babylon, pictured in Revelation 17, is quite compelling. It is important to notice that the Great Whore of Babylon is pictured as sitting astride the beast, or riding the beast, before the beast turns on the woman and gobbles her up. Therefore, we should expect a significant period of collusion between the forces of the great spiritual adulterer, the Roman Catholic Church, and the beast, who is the Antichrist and builder of a bestial one-world government. In this vein, it is interesting that the Roman Catholic Church is currently engaged in an aggressive campaign to bring the world's religions together. In sum, the picture in Revelation of a terrible woman building a false one-world religion juxtaposed against a terrible man, a beast, building a brutal one-world government needs to have the attention of true Christians everywhere.

By staying close to their Bibles, Protestants can avoid getting bamboozled by the enticing words of Roman Catholics who prattle on about tolerance and the Roman Catholic tradition and the Roman Catholic canon. The Protestant heritage of *Sola Scriptura* (Scripture only) is good and needs to be maintained.

The Catholic Push for Interfaithism

In Tokyo in 1981, Pope John Paul II praised Shintoism and Buddhism, saying that both of those religions inspire folks to see a divine presence inside each person. In Togo in 1985, he prayed together with animists; in the same year in Brussels, he implied that the Muslims' Koran is a holy book. In Africa in 1993, John Paul II sought common ground with voodoo practitioners—he said the Second Vatican Council recognizes that the various and diverse religions possess "something true and good, the seeds of the Word."[1] Clearly, recent popes have fawned over false teachers routinely and with zeal.

Before large Hindu audiences in 1986, John Paul II praised Hinduism, saying that India's great contribution to the world was its spiritual vision and that the world ought to pay attention to such ancient wisdom. Moreover, he is not alone on this score. Pope Paul VI told a Hindu leader that "the Hindu life and the Christian life shall go together. Your message and my message are the same." Influential Hindu Sri Chinmoy, who at one time held twice-weekly meditations for United Nations staff, was greeted by John Paul II with these words: "Special blessings to you ... [and] to your members. We shall continue together."[2] "Catholicism," according to Dave Hunt, "has become the ecumenical leader in a move to unite not only the 'separated brethren' of Protestantism but all of the world's religions in a new world church." To wit, in 1986, John Paul II convened one hundred thirty leaders of the world's twelve major religions in Assisi, Italy, for the ostensible purpose of praying for peace.

This stone-scape of Buddhist iconography is found in Borobudur, Java, Indonesia. There is more than a whiff of Baal-Ashteroth worship in the air at Borobudur. It should be remembered that Gideon, son of Joash, tore down the altar of Baal and cut down the Asherah that was beside it (Judges 6). Moreover, Gideon keeps good company: "For time will fail me if I tell of Gideon, Barak, Samson, Jephtah, of David and Samuel and the prophets, who by faith conquered kingdoms, performed acts of righteousness, obtained promises, shut the mouths of lions, quenched the power of fire, escaped the edge of the sword, from weakness were made strong, became mighty in war, put foreign armies to flight" (Heb. 11:32b–34 NASB). If Gideon was so brave and faithful, could American Christians not rally and demand that anti-Christian idols be taken down (safely) as well? If Americans don't learn from Gideon in this matter, it could well be said of them that, "My people are destroyed for lack of knowledge. … For a spirit of harlotry has led them astray, and they have played the harlot, departing from their God" (Hosea 4:6a, 12b NASB).

Testing the Spirits

In attendance were snake worshippers, fire worshippers, African animists, North American witch doctors, Buddhists, Hindus, Muslims, spiritists, Catholics, and professing Christians. The pope actually declared that all in attendance were praying to the same God, and he let his friend the Dalai Lama replace the cross with the Buddha (on the altar of Assisi's St. Peter's Church) and conduct a Buddhist worship right there.[3]

In 1987, the World Congress on Illumination brought together 2,500 "light workers" in Honolulu, Hawaii, ostensibly to focus on unity and oneness with nature. But promotional literature associated with this event bore a striking relationship to the Revelation 17 description of the Great Whore of Babylon: a New Age newsletter favorable to the event noted that "Light Workers from all over the world can come together to meet each other and form a unified cup. This activity will be held with the force-field of Peace and Harmony that pulsates at Diamond Head in Hawaii."

One of the workshops was called "Workshop and Guided Visualization to Energize Our Unified Chalice of Service."[5] Gary Kah astutely observes that such language is reminiscent of the last-days false religion described in Rev. 17:4. To wit, "The woman was dressed in purple and scarlet, and was glittering with gold, precious stones and pearls. She held a golden cup in her hand, filled with abominable things and the filth of her adulteries."[4]

Why did the light workers meet and form a unified cup? And why was the workshop aimed at sparking a unified chalice of service? What kind of workers meet and form a cup? The language is so weird that it sounds forced. If it was forced, it would seem that it was likely created by the same dark forces that will pull the religions of the world into the Roman Catholic fold and into an unholy one-world religion.

Also, what on earth is a unified chalice of service? This latter usage is even stranger, if only because the word "chalice" is so uncommon in America's crude and coarse pop culture, which favors tumblers and glasses over something so grandiose as a chalice! It's almost as if this New Age event was paying homage to the inevitable leader of the emerging one-world religion, the Roman Catholic Church. The language sounds like a direct reference to the golden, abomination-filled cup held in the hand of the Great Whore of Babylon.

If the connection between the 1987 World Congress and Revelation 17's Great Whore of Babylon weren't already clear enough, then it should be clear after reading what Harmonic Convergence, a New Age organization in Boulder, Colorado, had to say about the event. Harmonic Convergence personnel said that on August 16, 1987, the first day of the World Congress on Illumination, 144,000 people would gather at sacred sites worldwide, joining at the Earth's acupuncture points to create a link between "universal energies" and the Earth.[5] For Christians versed in the matter of the 144,000 Jews whom the Bible says will witness for the Lord Jesus during the tribulation period, alarm bells should be going off. The combination of the cup, the chalice, and the 144,000 people joining to invoke universal energies along the Earth's acupuncture points is too much to ignore.

The 1987 World Congress definitely had the signature of anti-Christian demonic forces all over it—thus the eerie use of a cup and a chalice, of all things, to symbolize the work of the light workers in attendance; the misappropriation of the number 144,000 in an apparent mockery of the Jews who will be so wonderful in witnessing for the Lord in the Tribulation period (doing work that will be directly opposed to Satan and his dark antichrist forces); and even the term "light workers," which superficially would seem to have a good connotation but which, in the hands of antichrist forces, would be a mockery of the good, in keeping with the aims of Satan who, according to 2 Cor. 11:14, himself masquerades as an angel of light. As Kah puts it, "[T]he people who sponsored this event are familiar with the Book of Revelation but have distorted its meaning and are trying to make it conform with their own theology. Their choosing of 144,000 people (Revelation 7:4) and their reference to a unified 'cup' (Revelation 17:4) leave little doubt of their intent."[6]

In 1993, the Parliament of the World's Religions was held in Chicago. It was attended by some 6,000 representatives of the world's major faiths and featured the awarding of the Templeton Prize for Progress in Religion, an ecumenical prize, to Chuck Colson. The prize was to Colson for his work in promoting a recognition of the benefits of each of the major religions. Roman Catholic theologian Hans Kung was at the meeting, as was the main drafter of the Global Ethic, a framework of ideas about interreligious common ground in the realm of ethics. During the meeting, Wiccan witches reportedly conducted a full-moon ritual.[7]

Pagan Catholicism

Christian author Dave Hunt has pointed out some New Age and occult tendencies of the Catholic Church, citing from a publication called *Spirituality of the Catholic Educator*. For instance, a philosophy professor at the College of Saint Mary in Omaha, Nebraska, promotes Hindu and Buddhist techniques as part of a Catholic curriculum. At some Catholic schools in New York and New Jersey, sisters teach something called "energetics for living," which they describe as curriculum enhancement for "peace education." Their energetics for living, which supposedly imbue the rest of their courses with a twist of peacefulness, stress visualization and interconnectedness with all living creatures. They even employ a Hindu greeting—*namaste*—which means "the god in me greets the god in you."[8] Such Roman Catholic teachings are really just a lot of New Age and pagan jive, in my opinion, and underscore the extent to which Catholic education is divorced from and removed from basic Biblical precepts.

A Franciscan meditation center in Willard, Wisconsin, teaches techniques for reaching one's own so-called Christ consciousness. Such consciousness is, in my opinion, unholy and wholly unbiblical and is akin to the Buddhist concept that everyone can attain to godhood by activating the bodhisattva god within. A leading Franciscan sister has justified such teaching by saying that Catholics can recognize the "mystical truth in all religions."

The marriage between the Roman Catholic Church and Eastern mysticism is further demonstrated by the fact that the Dalai Lama, a Tibetan Buddhist, was celebrated at New York's St. Patrick's Cathedral in 1979. While at the cathedral, the Dalai Lama declared that the major religions are pretty much the same—needless to say, his interfaith message earned him a standing ovation from the paganistic Roman Catholic crowd. Cardinal Terence Cooke said the Spirit was dramatically in evidence at the event.⁹ Cooke's assessment is naïve, in my estimation, and blasphemous to the true Holy Spirit of the Bible.

New Orleans is a center for the synthesis of Catholicism and voodoo. Slaves from Africa and the French colonies of Guadeloupe, Martinique, and Santo Domingo brought their voodoo to New Orleans long ago. In time, these voodoo-bearing slaves disguised their practices by changing the names of African gods to the names of Catholic saints, and today many voodoo practitioners are also Catholics. Voodoo practitioners in New Orleans use voodoo dolls and special potions to invoke revenge, and they also use snakes and skeletons in their rituals.¹⁰

Dharma wheel at Jokhang Temple in Lhasa, Tibet. If one was not convinced that the specter of a one-world, anti-Christian religion is glowering like a red coal, one need only observe the amazing movements of the Dharma wheel. One could understand the Dharma wheel being in Lhasa, the center of Tibetan Buddhism, but what is the Dharma wheel doing at the Vatican, center of Roman Catholicism, and at the house of the late TV magnate Aaron Spelling? An old Buddhist symbol, the Dharma wheel represents the eight-fold path—right view, right intention, right speech, right action, right livelihood, right effort, right mindfulness, and right concentration. Dharma sounds like a works-based religion, and while the eight-fold way may sound impressive, actually there's only one way: "I am the way, the truth, and the life," Jesus said. "No one comes to the Father but through Me" (John 14:6 NASB). Paul later developed the point: "For by grace you have been saved through faith; and that not of yourselves, *it is* the gift of God; not as a result of works, so that no one may boast" (Eph. 2:8 NASB).

Indeed, Catholicism is a broad net that venerates all manner of pagan beliefs. Catholicism is well suited to spearhead the emerging one-world pagan religion.

Spot-On Cautionary Tales From Britain

Michael de Semlyen, author of *All Roads Lead to Rome?: The Ecumenical Movement,* points out the danger of falling for Rome's lie. "The danger today," de Semlyen says, "is that in opting for a man-made unity based on compromise, and abandoning the Protestant Reformation and the truths of the Scriptures that were sealed in the blood of the martyrs, we are heading back to whence we came."[11]

De Semlyen laments that in Britain there is a "love Gospel" that confines itself to the positive and is opposed to confronting doctrinal error. "The Gospel, the light which has illuminated Western civilization, has gone into hiding," de Semlyen says, "as God's truth has been devalued. The leadership of the national Church [in Britain] has spoken of other faiths as 'many pathways to God' and 'many mansions of the same Holy Spirit.' The Commonwealth Day Service attended by Her Majesty the Queen is no longer recognizably Christian, and army chaplains serving the Allied forces ... in the Gulf War disguised themselves as 'Welfare Officers' in order not to offend the indigenous Muslims."[12]

The queen of England, according to de Semlyen, took a solemn oath to do her best to uphold the statutes and laws of Scripture as well as the Protestant Reformed religion. Yet during the decades of her reign, the queen has given her assent to divorce-facilitating legislation, legalized abortion and homosexuality, and liberalized adultery and pornography. Princess Diana, enamored as she was with her Irish Roman Catholic psychic Betty Palko as well as Roman Catholic Mother Teresa, was reported to have shown an interest in converting to Catholicism at a secret Oxford address.[13]

George Ashdown, secretary of the Protestant Alliance, provides a crucial reminder to any who might be sleeping or otherwise in a spiritual haze. "The Reformers," Ashdown says, "saw the whole Catholic system as anti-Christian. Luther and Calvin went so far as to identify the Papacy with the Antichrist and they—like Wycliffe, Tyndale, Matthew Henry, Spurgeon, Lloyd-Jones and many others—saw the Roman Catholic

Institution as Mystery Babylon, the Mother of Harlots, vividly described in Revelation chapter 17."[14]

Back in the 1880s, Dr. H. Grattan Guinness veritably sounded an alarm over the danger posed by the Roman Catholic Church:

I see the great Apostacy, I see the desolation of Christendom, I see the smoking ruins, I see the reign of monsters; I see those vice-gods, that Gregory VII, that Innocent III, that Boniface VIII, that Alexander VI, that Gregory XIII, that Pius IX, I see their long succession, I hear their insufferable blasphemies, I see their abominable lives; I see them worshipped by blinded generations, bestowing hollow benedictions, bartering lying indulgences, creating a paganized Christianity; I see their liveried slaves, their shaven priests, their celibate confessors; I see the infamous confessional, the ruined women, the murdered innocents; I hear the lying mass; I hear the anathemas, the curses, the thunders of interdicts; I see the racks, the dungeons, the stakes; I see that inhuman Inquisition, those fires of Smithfield, those butcheries of St. Bartholomew, that Spanish Armada, those unspeakable dragonnades, that endless train of wars, that dreadful multitude of massacres. I see it all, and in the name of the ruin it has brought in the Church and in the world, in the name of the truth

> "The danger today is that in opting for a man-made unity based on compromise, and abandoning the Protestant Reformation and the truths of the Scriptures that were sealed in the blood of the martyrs, we are heading back to whence we came. . . . The Gospel, the light which has illuminated Western civilization, has gone into hiding, as God's truth has been devalued. The leadership of the national Church [in Britain] has spoken of other faiths as 'many pathways to God. . . .'"
>
> —Michael de Semlyen, Christian Author

it has denied, the temple it has defiled, the God it has blasphemed, the souls it has destroyed; in the name of the millions it has deluded; the millions it has slaughtered, the millions it has damned; [together] with holy confessors, with noble reformers, with innumerable martyrs, with the saints of ages, I denounce it as the masterpiece of Satan, as the body and soul and essence of antichrist.[15]

Another 19th-century preacher, Charles Haddon Spurgeon, sounded a similar alarm over the dangers of Roman Catholicism:

It is the bounden duty of every Christian to pray against Anti-Christ, and as to what Anti-Christ is no sane man ought to raise a question. If it be not the Popery in the Church of Rome there is nothing in the world that can be called by that name ... because it wounds Christ, because it robs Christ of His glory, because it puts sacramental efficacy in the place of His atonement, and lifts a piece of bread in the place of the Saviour, and a few drops of water in place of the Holy Ghost, and puts a fallible man like ourselves up as the Vicar of Christ on earth; if we pray against it, because it is against Him, we shall love the persons though we hate their errors; we shall love their souls though we loathe and detest their dogmas, and so the breath of our prayers will be sweetened, because we turn our faces towards Christ when we pray.[16]

At Westminster Chapel, Martin Lloyd-Jones also warned people about the dangers posed by the Roman Catholic Church:

I remind you that the Protestant Reformers were not just bigoted zealots or fools. Their eyes were opened by the Holy Spirit; Luther, Calvin, Knox, all of them. They saw this horrible monstrosity depicted in the Bible and the warning against it. At the risk of even losing their lives they stood up and protested. They confronted Rome. ... The Roman Catholic Church is a counterfeit, a sham, it represents prostitution of the worst and most diabolical kind. It is indeed a form of the antichrist; it is to be rejected and denounced, but, above all, it is to be countered. And there is only one thing that can counter it and that is a Biblical, doctrinal Christianity. ... People who hold evangelistic campaigns and say, "Are you Roman Catholics? Go back to your church," are denying New Testament teaching. We must warn them.[17]

De Semlyen gives convincing evidence that renowned evangelist Billy Graham compromised in his dealings with the Catholic church. In 1981, Graham called the Pope the "greatest moral leader of the world and the world's greatest evangelist." Graham accepted an honorary doctorate from a Jesuit seminary and, in 1972, he received the Catholic International Franciscan Award for his contributions to ecumenism.

In a 1988 interview with the magazine *US News and World Report,* Graham indicated that he had become an ecumenical being as a result of much world travel and many meetings with the clergy of all denominations; moreover, he noted that theological differences were of no concern to him anymore. Dr. Charles Woodbridge, an American Bible teacher, warned Graham this way: "If you persist in making common cause with those that deny the Word of God, and thus in minimizing the sharp line of distinction between those that are loyal and those who are disloyal to the Scriptures, it is my strong opinion that you will be known as the great divider of the church of Christ [in] the 20th century."

As an ecumenist and erstwhile interfaith advocate, Graham has consistently sought to please the powerful: when asked about Nancy Reagan's consultation of an astrologer on a BBC radio program, Graham said that "astrology is all right as long as it is not taken too seriously."[18] In fact, the Bible is very clear about the dangers of astrology. Is. 47:13–14 lays it down: "Let your astrologers come forward, those stargazers who make predictions month by month, let them save you from what is coming upon you. Surely they are like stubble; the fire will burn them up. They cannot even save themselves from the power of the flame" (NIV).

Before Graham's July 1989 mission to Hungary, three Protestant pastors issued a letter calling on Graham to repent for having collaborated with oppressive Eastern European dictatorships. The pastors opined that Graham had been "manipulated by dark powers" during his 1985 trip to Romania. Graham said the Ceausescu regime had resolved all nationality problems and guaranteed total religious freedom—this at a time when Ceausescu was known to be raining down incalculable suffering on Romanians and brutally flouting their human rights. The pastors rightly chastised Graham, noting that "the task of the faithful is not to protect the oppressor, but to express unambiguously solidarity with the oppressed. The preaching of the gospel of Christ is incompatible with political falsehood."[19]

In response to Graham's visit to England in the late 1980s, Rev. Donald MacLean of the Free Presbyterian Church of Scotland's Clerk to the Synod sent this scathing letter to the press:

> The Ecumenical movement which you praise is the greatest disaster to affect the Christian church this century. It has reduced the professing churches of this country to a collection of bloodless, spineless and boneless organisations, which can hardly raise a whimper on the side of Christ and His Truth. Small wonder that evil progresses as it does, and spiritual darkness becomes more intense as the years go by. You appear to regard a body of professing Christians, of sober conduct, and deep spirituality of mind, as fanatical and bigoted. If this be so then the eminent men of God, such as John Knox in Scotland, John Calvin and Martin Luther on the Continent, and Archbishop Cranmer in England were bigots in their contests with the errors of Popery. We are glad to be in such company.[20]

The Big Picture of Apostasy and Interfaithism

Left to his own pride, man will plunge into false beliefs and worship. Eve believed the lying serpent in the Garden of Eden—the lie being that she could eat of the Tree of the Knowledge of Good and Evil, be like God, and not die (Genesis 3). In the days of Noah, men's hearts were evil all the time (Genesis 6). On a plain in Shinar after the Flood, Noah's sons' descendants rebelled against God's command that they scatter over the whole earth; instead, they chose to build a city with a tower reaching to the heavens in an effort to make a name for themselves (Genesis 11). The residents of Sodom and Gomorrah gave their minds over to homosexual lusts (Genesis 19). Rebellions such as these constituted a form of apostasy.

In Egypt, Pharaoh's sorcerers and magicians used secret arts to make their staffs become snakes, but when their staffs were swallowed up by Aaron's staff, Pharaoh nevertheless remained unmoved (Exodus 7). Pharaoh's inclination toward the secret arts of magic and sorcery caused him to be unmoved in spite of the miracles performed by Aaron. Full of pride in Egyptian sorcery and magic, Pharaoh refused Moses' exhortation to let the Israelites go, and in so doing, Pharaoh prevented the Israelites from being able to freely worship the Lord.

In the Song of Moses, the people of Jeshurun (a name for Israel) are described as having angered God with their foreign gods, detestable idols, and practice of sacrificing to demons (Deuteronomy 32). The Philistines had a temple devoted to a false god named Dagon, the god of grain, and Samson was led by God to bring the false temple crashing down upon the unbelieving Philistines (Judges 16).

Is. 44:9 gives a stinging indictment against idol worship: "All who make idols are nothing, and the things they treasure are worthless. Those who would speak up for them are blind; they are ignorant, to their own shame" (NIV). Rom. 1:21–25 gives a similarly stinging rebuke to humanistic apostasy:

> For although they knew God, they neither glorified him as God nor gave thanks to him, but their thinking became futile and their foolish hearts were darkened. Although they claimed to be wise, they became fools and exchanged the glory of the immortal God for images made to look like mortal man and birds and animals and reptiles. Therefore God gave them over in the sinful desires of their hearts to sexual impurity for the degrading of their bodies with one another. They exchanged the truth of God for a lie, and worshipped and served created things rather than the Creator—who is forever praised. Amen. (NIV)

St. Peter's Square. Notice the Buddhist Dharma wheel here in this most Roman Catholic of spots—akin to other Buddhist Dharma wheels, such as that at the Jokhang Temple in Lhasa, Tibet, and that at the mansion of late TV mogul Aaron Spelling. It seems the enemy has put his ghoulish stamp on the Vatican, Hollywood, and much of the Far East. In Revelation 17, John describes a great harlot who committed acts of immorality with the kings of the earth, made men drunk with the wine of her immorality, was dressed in purple and scarlet (the colors of Roman Catholic bishops and cardinals), was the mother of harlots and of the abominations of the earth, and was drunk on the blood of the saints. Could there be a dark side to the white-clad Pope, perhaps even a black-clad Pope along the lines of the anti-Protestant Ignatius Loyola and his Jesuits?

"Pantheism, with its earth (or Gaia) worship, has inevitably had the effect of enslaving man," Gary Kah says. "Whether it was the version presented by the Pharaohs of Egypt, the Brahmins of India, or the Caesars of Rome, the result of earth-centered religion was always the same—the enslavement of man under a ruthless, occultic system."[21]

The Council of Nicea, in 325 AD, was the first ecumenical council, and its presider, Constantine, was the first ecumenist. Constantine presided in much the same way that Charlemagne would preside over the Council of Chalon some 500 years later. Constantine made a show of having become a Christian, but his real interest was in political unity, not the gospel truth. This is evidenced by the fact that after his supposed conversion to Christianity, Constantine continued in his role as the leader of the pagan priesthood, under the pagan title of Pontifex Maximus. As a professing Christian, Constantine called himself *Vicarius Cristi*, which translates as "Vicar of Christ" or "another Christ." *Vicarius Cristi* also translates to the word "antichrist" in Greek; therefore we know that Constantine was a prototype of the antichrist of the end times that is prophesied about in the book of Revelation.[22]

"Over the course of a thousand years," Christian author Grant Jeffrey says, "the medieval Church perverted its doctrine, lost sight of the Bible, and compromised with the kings of the earth. Later, it persecuted and martyred tens of millions of believers in Christ who rejected her false Babylonian religious practices."[23]

The false interfaith system under Constantine and others was laying the groundwork for the great apostasy in the end times—indeed, for the great apostasy of our time. In 2 Thess. 2:3, we see that the great apostasy and the revealing of the antichrist will precede the coming of the Lord Jesus Christ (and the gathering of the saints to meet Him); therefore, the current apostasy inherent in interfaith and ecumenical gatherings should be most disturbing to discerning Christians.[24]

In the one-world, interfaith-based, and false religion that will pave the way for the Antichrist, Christian terms and modes will be incorporated so as to disarm undiscerning Christians and hide this new worldwide religion's virulently anti-Christian designs. In short, the new interfaith-based, antichrist-introducing religion will be paganism disguised inside a shell of Christian terms and modes (2 Cor. 11:13–15). This is one reason why it is so important for true Christians to take the Word, and sound doctrine, seriously (Eph. 4:14).

During the Reformation, Protestant reformers drew a bright, shiny line between sound Protestant doctrine and false Roman Catholic teachings. Then, in 1893, at the Parliament of the World's Religions held in Chicago, the spirit of apostasy spread as Protestants prayed together with Roman Catholics, Hindus, Buddhists, Muslims, and followers of other faiths for more than two weeks.

> "John Paul [II] actively rejects Marxism and Capitalism as models for the emerging New World Order. His goal is to create a new spiritual-political model for Europe and Russia based on a Catholic-socialism."
>
> —Grant Jeffrey, Prophecy Scholar (citing information in Malachi Martin's *The Keys of This Blood*)

In 1948, the pro–United Nations World Council of Churches was formed to be part of a new world order and bring different Protestant denominations closer together—the council's first meeting, in Amsterdam, was an attempt to bring Protestantism more into line with the trend of worldwide religious blending. A huge step toward interfaithism occurred in 1962, when the Second Vatican Council got under way. It is famous for having issued a call to Christians to promote what is good in other religions, such as Hinduism and Buddhism.[25]

According to Grant Jeffrey, Malachi Martin's book *The Keys of This Blood* "provides evidence that Pope John Paul II and the Catholic Church are actively campaigning to establish the primacy of their church over the emerging ecumenical worldwide church. Their goal is to obtain the spiritual leadership of the New World Order. John Paul actively rejects Marxism and Capitalism as models for the emerging New World Order. His goal is to create a new spiritual-political model for Europe and Russia based on a Catholic-socialism."[26]

The State of the World Forum, held in 1995 in San Francisco, demands our attention. The event was presided over by Mikhail Gorbachev and cosponsored by the Gandhi Foundation, which is a Hindu organization. Religious leaders invited to the event included Thich Nhat Hanh, a Vietnamese monk who has maintained an altar devoted to the Buddha and Christ; has written a book called *Living Buddha, Living Christ;* and generally seeks the merger of Buddhism and Christianity. Also at the event were Isabel Allende, author of *House of Spirits;* Richard Baker, an abbot at the Crestone Mountain Zen Center; and Akio Matsumura, founder of the Global Forum of Spiritual and Parliamentary Leaders. Gorbachev called for a new global synthesis that would blend Buddhist and Christian values, together with a sense of oneness with nature.[27]

Indeed, Gorbachev called the environmental crisis the cornerstone for a New World Order.[28] Gorbachev's organization, Green Cross International, is ostensibly about environmentalism, but in light of Gorbachev's penchant for global syncretism and considering the personal sting Gorbachev must have felt when the Berlin Wall came down in 1989, it would seem likely that the Green Cross is actually using the environmental craze to spur a broad-based and massively ambitious political power grab. Kah addresses Gorbachev's real intentions:

> He is literally seeking to replace Christianity with a new religious order in which humanism (the central teaching of Communism) and pantheism (the basis for Eastern mysticism) are combined. To make this new religion more acceptable, he is lacing it with Christian terminology. In using this tactic, he is simply following the lead of [Teilhard de] Chardin, Jung, Hanh, and other mystics who have done the same. In reality, Gorbachev's religion is anti-Christian to the core.[29]

"Professing to be wise, they became fools, and exchanged the glory of the incorruptible God for an image in the form of corruptible man and of birds and four-footed animals and crawling creatures. Therefore God gave them over in the lusts of their hearts to impurity, so that their bodies would be dishonored among them. For they exchanged the truth of God for a lie, and worshiped and served the creature rather than the Creator, who is blessed forever. Amen." (Rom. 1:22–25, NASB)

The ingredients for an end-times, apostate, and interfaith-based religion wouldn't be complete if a sprinkling of earth worship were not thrown into the pot. Of course, not all the earth worshippers are going to come right out and say they're earth worshippers—that would smack of paganism. But environmentalism—now there's a word the earth worshippers can rally around without arousing too much alarm too soon.

To this end, the Earth Summit, officially known as the United Nations Conference on Environment and Development (UNCED) was held in 1992 in Rio de Janeiro, Brazil. UNCED Secretary-General Maurice Strong was immodest when describing the influence envisioned for his environmental networking:

> UNCED also holds a broader significance. The environmental issue was set up as a global issue in need [of] global action. There were demands to strengthen international law, which could make nations tow the line. Non-government organizations (NGOs) had been forming global networks and were working on global campaigns. These efforts at the global level directly contributed to building a sense of *global identity*, or *global citizenship* which would be *the first step towards global governance*. Such global governance would *further distance power from the people while giving unlimited access to governments and multinationals.*[30] (italics mine)

Strong's language is quite eerie. The environmental issue was set up as a global issue! We've been set up! There it is: the environmental issue and the networks and conventions that it spawns are envisioned as taking power away from the people and giving UN-based enviro-organizations control over governments and big business. That's how I read it. Therefore, this is no ordinary earth worship; rather, it is using the earth as leverage to gain power over mankind. That should be of concern to all Americans and all people worldwide.

Similarly, UN Secretary-General Boutros Boutros-Gali made it clear that this environmentalism thing would be offered as taking precedence over man's relationship with God:

> Over and above the moral contract with God, over and above the social contract concluded with men, we must

Testing the Spirits

now conclude an ethical and political contract with nature, with this Earth to which we owe our very existence and which gives us life. ... To the ancients, the Nile was a god to be venerated, as was the Rhine ... or the Amazonian forest, the mother of forests. Throughout the world, nature was the abode of divinities that gave the forest, the desert or the mountains a personality which commanded worship and respect. The Earth had a soul. To find that soul again, to give it new life, that is the essence of Rio.[31]

Boutros-Gali appeals to ethics as he talks of the need to make a compact with nature—this notion of ethics is also what Unitarian Universalists and some humanists hold so dear as they seek to valuate the facets of their lives in the absence of a godly respect and love for the Holy Bible, as they run from God's determination that men need to repent of their sins and receive Jesus the Redeemer. Boutros-Gali maintains that the need

> "Hallelujah! Salvation and glory and power belong to our God; BECAUSE HIS JUDGMENTS ARE TRUE AND RIGHTEOUS; for He has judged the great harlot who was corrupting the earth with her immorality, and HE HAS AVENGED THE BLOOD OF HIS BOND-SERVANTS ON HER." (Rev. 19:1b–2, NASB)

for a contract with nature—indeed the need for a return to nature worship—is over and above a person's moral contract with God. What blasphemy! The misguided UN Secretary-General pushes for a return to pagan nature worship on a vast scale and, as such, he is part of the growing apostasy.

Almost five years after the original Earth Summit, a follow-up summit of sorts was held in 1997 in Rio, this time going by the rubric Rio+5. At this summit, Gorbachev introduced the Earth Charter, and in so doing, he further articulated the dimensions of the growing anti-Christian, one-world religion. "In its essence," Gorbachev said, "the Earth Charter shifts the focus to people on the Earth, their responsibilities, their morals and spirituality, their way of consumption. To save humankind and all future generations, we must save the Earth. By saving the Earth, humankind saves himself; it is that easy to understand."[32]

Notice the slippery language employed by this anti-Christian zealot. Gorbachev indicates that people can save themselves by saving the Earth and focusing on their own responsibilities, morals, spirituality, and modes of consumption! This is totally antithetical to the teachings of the Bible, which hold that far from being able to save themselves, people need to repent of their sins and embrace their loving Lord and Redeemer, Jesus. Gorbachev speaks of spirituality and morals and floats the lie that people can save themselves, but he contradicts the central Biblical teaching that people are sinful by themselves and in need of saving by Jesus Christ. Moreover, Gorbachev refers to morals and consumption without mentioning the God of Israel—however, man-made morals and dictatorial consumption patterns are not worth lauding, and the former Soviet leader remains a very cunning, yet unpersuasive, communicator.

CHAPTER EIGHT

TOWARD A GLOBAL ANTICHRIST GOVERNMENT

[T]he sons of God saw that the daughters of men were beautiful; and they took wives for themselves, whomever they chose. Then the L<small>ORD</small> *said, "My Spirit shall not strive with man forever. ..." The Nephilim were on the earth in those days, and also afterward, when the sons of God came in to the daughters of men, and they bore children to them. Those were the mighty men who were of old, men of renown. Then the* L<small>ORD</small> *saw that the wickedness of man was great on the earth, and that every intent of the thoughts of his heart was only evil continually. ... God looked on the earth, and behold, it was corrupt; for all flesh had corrupted their way upon the earth. Then God said to Noah, "The end of all flesh has come before Me; for the earth is filled with violence because of them; and behold, I am about to destroy them with the earth. Make for yourself an ark. ..." Then the LORD said to Noah, "Enter the ark, you and all your household, for you alone I have seen to be righteous before Me in this time." (Gen. 6:2–3a, 4–5, 12–14a; 7:1 NASB)*

Now Cush became the father of Nimrod; he became a mighty one on the earth. He was a mighty hunter before the L<small>ORD</small>*;*

therefore it is said, "Like Nimrod a mighty hunter before the Lord." The beginning of his kingdom was Babel and Erech and Accad and Calneh, in the land of Shinar. From that land he went forth into Assyria, and built Nineveh and Rehoboth-Ir and Calah, and Resen between Nineveh and Calah; that is the great city. …

[T]hey found a plain in the land of Shinar and settled there. They said to one another, "Come, let us make bricks and burn them thoroughly." And they used brick for stone, and they used tar for mortar. They said, "Come, let us build for ourselves a city, and a tower whose top will reach into heaven, and let us make for ourselves a name, otherwise we will be scattered abroad over the face of the whole earth." The Lord came down to see the city and the tower which the sons of men had built. The Lord said, "Behold, they are one people, and they all have the same language. And this is what they began to do, and now nothing which they purpose to do will be impossible for them. Come, let Us go down and there confuse their language, so that they will not understand one another's speech." So the Lord scattered them abroad from there over the face of the whole earth; and they stopped building the city. Therefore its name was called Babel, because there the Lord confused the language of the whole earth; and from there the Lord scattered them abroad over the face of the whole earth. (Gen. 10:8–12; 11:2b–9 NASB)

Pharaoh and his servants had a change of heart toward the people, and they said "What is this we have done, that we have let Israel go from serving us? So he made his chariot ready and took his people with him; and he took six hundred select chariots, and all the other *chariots of Egypt with officers over all of them. The Lord hardened the heart of Pharaoh, king of Egypt, and he chased after the sons of Israel as the sons of Israel were going out boldly. Then the Egyptians chased after them* with *all the horses* and *chariots of Pharaoh, his horsemen and his army, and they overtook them camping by the sea, beside Pi-hahiroth, in front of Baal-zephon. …*

Then Moses stretched out his hand over the sea; and the LORD swept the sea back by a strong east wind all night and turned the sea into dry land, so the waters were divided. The sons of Israel went through the midst of the sea on the dry land, and the waters were like a wall to them on their right hand and on their left. Then the Egyptians took up the pursuit, and all Pharaoh's horses, his chariots and his horsemen went in after them into the midst of the sea. At the morning watch, the LORD looked down on the army of the Egyptians through the pillar of fire and cloud and brought the army of the Egyptians into confusion. He caused their chariot wheels to swerve, and He made them drive with difficulty; so the Egyptians said, "Let us flee from Israel, for the LORD is fighting for them against the Egyptians."

Then the LORD said to Moses, "Stretch out your hand over the sea so that the waters may come back over the Egyptians, over their chariots and their horsemen." So Moses stretched out his hand over the sea, and the sea returned to its normal state at daybreak, while the Egyptians were fleeing right into it; then the LORD overthrew the Egyptians in the midst of the sea…

Your right hand, O LORD, shatters the enemy. And in the greatness of Your excellence You overthrow those who rise up against You. (Ex. 14:5b–9, 21–27; 15:6b–7a NASB)

Mighty ones such as the Nephilim, Nimrod, and the Egyptian pharaoh all tried to arrogate importance to themselves without regard for the Lord God of Israel. Truly, we see the importance of Prov. 16:18, "Pride *goes* before destruction, and a haughty spirit before stumbling" (NASB). Human history is littered with examples of rulers and people who have ignored the lesson of the judgments against the Nephilim, Nimrod, and the Egyptian pharaoh.

In Revelation 17, we see that the Great Whore of Babylon is seated atop a beast—a scarlet-colored beast that is full of blasphemous names and has seven heads and ten horns. The beast's seven heads represent seven mountains, and his ten horns represent ten kings that will receive kingly power for one hour with the beast. The ten kings will act with one mind, and they'll cede their power to the beast, waging war with the beast against the Lamb. These ten kings will even hate the whore and make her desolate and naked, eating her flesh and burning her with fire. It was God who put it in the ten kings' hearts to cede their power to the beast that God's will and His words would be fulfilled. The beast and the kings of the earth will fight against the Lord Jesus, and lose; the beast will be thrown into the lake of fire along with the false prophet. (Of course, the Lamb—being Lord of lords and King of kings—will overcome the bestial government!)

Indeed, the son of perdition, or man of sin, will be revealed amidst a spiritual falling away (apostasy) before the day of Christ (2 Thessalonians 2). The beast (son of perdition, man of sin) will be powered by Satan himself, oppose God and exalt himself above all that is called God, and sit in the temple of God pretending to be God. Interestingly, the beast suffers from the same delusions as Satan, who as the rebellious Lucifer, listed the five blasphemous "I will's" in Is. 14:13: "I will ascend into heaven; I will exalt my throne above the stars of God; I will sit also upon the mount of the congregation, in the sides of the north; I will ascend above the heights of the clouds; I will be like the most High" (KJV). When the restrainer is taken out of the way, then that wicked will be revealed, whose coming is after the working of Satan with power and signs and lying wonders (2 Thessalonians 2).

The Chinese character for dragon, or *long*. That old serpent, the dragon (Revelation 20), has long striven for supremacy—whether through the big, bad Nephilim, Nimrod, the Egyptian pharaoh, Chinese emperors, Antiochus Epiphanes, Communist tyrants, evil popes or, finally, the beast. Revelation 13 notes the dragon's cultivation of the beast power:

"Then I saw a beast coming up out of the sea, having ten horns and seven heads, and on his horns *were* ten diadems, and on his heads *were* blasphemous names. ... And the dragon gave him his power and his throne and great authority. ... There was given to him a mouth speaking arrogant words and blasphemies, and authority to act for forty-two months was given to him. And he opened his mouth in blasphemies against God, to blaspheme His name and His tabernacle, *that is*, those who dwell in heaven. It was also given to him to make war with the saints and to overcome them, and authority over every tribe and people and tongue and nation was given to him. All who dwell on the earth will worship him, *everyone* whose name has not been written from the foundation of the world in the book of life of the Lamb who has been slain. ... Here is the perseverance of the saints." (Rev. 13:1, 2b, 5–8, 10b NASB)

As the hellish antichrist government is being set up, it is crucial that people everywhere turn to the Lord Jesus, repenting of their sins and receiving Jesus as their glorious Savior: this is where the rubber meets the road at the level of the individual. Those who have not received a love of the truth (that they might be saved) will be sent a strong delusion (by God), so that those who did not believe the truth and took pleasure in unrighteousness would be damned (2 Thessalonians 2). We see a similar warning in Romans 1:

> For since the creation of the world His invisible attributes, His eternal power and divine nature, have been clearly seen, being understood through what has been made, so that they are without excuse. For even though they knew God, they did not honor Him as God or give thanks, but they became futile in their speculations, and their foolish heart was darkened. Professing to be wise, they became fools, and exchanged the glory of the incorruptible God for an image in the form of corruptible man and of birds and four-footed animals and crawling creatures.
>
> Therefore God gave them over in the lusts of their hearts to impurity, so that their bodies would be dishonored among them. For they exchanged the truth of God for a lie, and worshiped and served the creature rather than the Creator, who is blessed forever. Amen.
>
> For this reason God gave them over to degrading passions; for their women exchanged the natural function for that which is unnatural, and in the same way also the men abandoned the natural function of the woman and burned in their desire toward one another, men with men committing indecent acts and receiving in their own persons the due penalty of their error.
>
> And just as they did not see fit to acknowledge God any longer, God gave them over to a depraved mind, to do

those things which are not proper, being filled with all unrighteousness, wickedness, greed, evil; full of envy, murder, strife, deceit, malice; *they are* gossips, slanderers, haters of God, insolent, arrogant, boastful, inventors of evil, disobedient to parents, without understanding, untrustworthy, unloving, unmerciful; and although they know the ordinance of God, that those who practice such things are worthy of death, they not only do the same, but also give hearty approval to those who practice them. (Rom. 1:20–32 NASB)

In Revelation 13, we see that the sea beast has seven heads and ten horns—in other words, the same as the beast of Revelation 17. The dragon, or Satan, gives his power, seat, and great authority to the beast. (Is the church of Pergamos the place where Satan's seat is? Compare Rev. 2:12–13.) One of the beast's seven heads will sustain a deadly wound but will then heal up, causing the world to wonder after the beast and worship both the dragon and the beast. Many will wonder who could possibly make war against the beast. (2 Thess. 2:8 tells us that the Lord Jesus will consume the beast with the spirit of His mouth, destroying that wicked with the brightness of His coming!)

In Revelation 13, we also see an earth beast that has two horns like a lamb and speaks as a dragon. He causes people to worship the first beast, whose deadly wound was healed. He will give life to the image of the beast, causing it to speak, and he will kill those who refuse to worship the image of the beast. Furthermore, he will force people to take a mark on their right hand or forehead, such that only those with the mark, the name of the beast, or the number of his name (666) will be allowed to buy or sell. In effect, the earth beast will implement satanically conceived "economic sanctions."

In Daniel 2, Daniel retells Nebuchadnezzar's dream and interprets it, showing the unfolding of kingdoms throughout human history. In the depiction of the fourth kingdom, the ten toes were partly iron and partly clay—that is to say, partly strong and partly broken. The ten toes will mingle themselves with the seed of men but will not adhere together because iron is not mixed with clay. In the days of these (ten?) kings,

God shall set up a kingdom that shall never be destroyed and which will break in pieces the merely human kingdoms depicted in Nebuchadnezzar's dream (Dan. 2:44).

In Daniel 7, the same story is told through different imagery:

> After this I saw in the night visions, and behold a fourth beast, dreadful and terrible, and strong exceedingly; and it had great iron teeth: it devoured and brake in pieces, and stamped the residue with the feet of it: and it *was* diverse from all the beasts that *were* before it; and it had ten horns. I considered the horns, and, behold, there came up among them another little horn, before whom there were three of the first horns plucked up by the roots: and, behold, in this horn *were* eyes like the eyes of man, and a mouth speaking great things. ...

> Then I would know the truth of the fourth beast, which was diverse from all the others, exceeding dreadful, whose teeth *were of* iron, and his nails *of* brass; *which* devoured, brake in pieces, and stamped the residue with his feet; and of the ten horns that *were* in his head, and *of* the other which came up, and before whom three fell; even *of* that horn that had eyes, and a mouth that spake very great things, whose look *was* more stout than his fellows. I beheld, and the same horn made war with the saints, and prevailed against them; until the Ancient of days came, and judgment was given to [ie, in favor of] the saints of the most High; and the time came that the saints possessed the kingdom.

> Thus he said, The fourth beast shall be the fourth kingdom upon earth, which shall be diverse from all kingdoms, and shall devour the whole earth, and shall tread it down, and break it in pieces. And the ten horns out of this kingdom *are* ten kings *that* shall arise: and another shall rise after them; and he shall be diverse from the first, and he shall subdue

> three kings. And he shall speak *great* words against the most High, and shall wear out the saints of the most High, and think to change times and laws; and they shall be given into his hand until a time and times and the dividing of time. But the judgment shall sit, and they shall take away his dominion, to consume and to destroy *it* unto the end. (Dan. 7:7–8, 19–26 KJV)

> I beheld till the thrones were cast down, and the Ancient of days did sit. ... The judgment was set, and the books were opened. I beheld then, because of the voice of the great words which the horn spake: I beheld *even* till the beast was slain, and his body destroyed, and given to the burning flame. As concerning the rest of the beasts, they had their dominion taken away: yet their lives were prolonged for a season and time. I saw in the night visions, and, behold, *one* like the son of man came with the clouds of heaven, and came to the Ancient of days, and they brought him near before him. And there was given him dominion, and glory, and a kingdom, that all people, nations, and languages, should serve him: his dominion *is* an everlasting dominion, which shall not pass away and his kingdom *that* which shall not be destroyed. (Dan. 7:9a, 10b–14 KJV)

In Daniel 8, more light is shed on the antichrist government and its dark characteristics:

> And out of one of them came forth a little horn, which waxed exceeding great, toward the south, and toward the east, and toward the pleasant *land*. And it waxed great, *even* to the host of heaven; and it cast down *some* of the host and of the stars to the ground, and stamped upon them. Yea, he magnified *himself* even to the prince of the host, and by him the daily *sacrifice* was taken away, and the place of his sanctuary was cast down. And a host was given *him* against the daily *sacrifice* by reason of

transgression, and it cast down the truth to the ground; and it practised, and prospered …

Now that being broken, whereas four stood up for it, four kingdoms shall stand up out of the nation, but not in his power. And in the latter time of their kingdom, when the transgressors are come to the full, a king of fierce countenance, and understanding dark sentences, shall stand up. And his power shall be mighty, but not by his own power: and he shall destroy wonderfully, and shall prosper, and practise, and shall destroy the mighty and the holy people. And through his policy also he shall cause craft to prosper in his hand; and he shall magnify himself in his heart, and by peace shall destroy many: he shall also stand up against the Prince of princes; but he shall be broken without hand. (Dan. 8:9–12, 22–25 KJV)

Stone dragon on bridge in Slovenia. The sea beast, invested with the power of the dragon, will speak arrogant words and blasphemies against God, and he will have authority to act for forty-two months. He will war against the saints and overcome them; the saints will have to persevere (Revelation 13). In the long run, at the completion of the Millennial Reign of Christ, the devil will be thrown into the lake of fire and brimstone, where the beast and false prophet will be also (Revelation 20).

In Daniel 9, we see the prophecy on the seventy weeks and, moreover, a description of the seventieth week in particular:

> Seventy weeks have been decreed for your people and your holy city, to finish the transgression, to make an end of sin, to make atonement for iniquity, to bring in everlasting righteousness, to seal up vision and prophecy and to anoint the most holy *place.* So you are to know and discern *that* from the issuing of a decree to restore and rebuild Jerusalem until Messiah the Prince *there will be* seven weeks and sixty-two weeks; it will be built again, with plaza and moat, even in times of distress. Then after the sixty-two weeks the Messiah will be cut off and have nothing, and the people of the prince who is to come will destroy the city and the sanctuary. And its end *will come* with a flood; even to the end there will be war; desolations are determined. And he will make a firm covenant with the many for one week, but in the middle of the week he will put a stop to sacrifice and grain offering; and on the wing of abominations *will come* one who makes desolate, even until a complete destruction, one that is decreed, is poured out on the one who makes desolate." (Dan. 9:24–27 NASB)

In Daniel 11, we read this:

> And after the league *made* with [the prince of the covenant] he shall work deceitfully: for he shall come up, and shall become strong with a small people. He shall enter peaceably even upon the fattest places of the province; and he shall do *that* which his fathers have not done, nor his fathers' fathers; he shall scatter among them the prey, and spoil, and riches: *yea,* and he shall forecast his devices against the strong holds, even for a time …
>
> [B]ut the people that do know their God shall be strong, and do *exploits.* And they that understand among the

people shall instruct many: yet they shall fall by the sword, and by flame, by captivity, and by spoil, *many days*. Now when they shall fall, they shall be holpen with a little help: but many shall cleave to them with flatteries. And *some* of them of understanding shall, to try them, and to purge, and to make *them* white, *even* to the time of the end: because *it is* yet for a time appointed. (Dan. 11:23–24, 32b–35 KJV)

Then the king will do as he pleases, and he will exalt and magnify himself above every god and will speak monstrous things against the God of gods; and he will prosper until the indignation is finished, for that which is decreed will be done. He will show no regard for the gods of his fathers or for the desire of women, nor will he show regard for any *other* god; for he will magnify himself above *them* all. But instead he will honor a god of fortresses, a god whom his fathers did not know; he will honor *him* with gold, silver, costly stones and treasures.

He will take action against the strongest of fortresses with *the help of* a foreign god; he will give great honor to those who acknowledge *him* and will cause them to rule over the many, and will parcel out land for a price. ... But rumors from the East and from the North will disturb him, and he will go forth with great wrath to destroy and annihilate many. He will pitch the tents of his royal pavilion between the seas and the beautiful Holy Mountain; yet he will come to his end, and no one will help him. (Dan. 11:36–39, 44–45 NASB)

In Daniel 12, we're told there will be a time of distress such as never was since there was a nation, and that this period will last for a

"If you confess with your mouth Jesus as Lord, and believe in your heart that God raised Him from the dead, you will be saved." (Rom. 10:9, NASB)

time, times, and half a time—that is, three-and-a-half years or forty-two months or 1,260 days. The antichrist coalition will shatter the power of God's holy people during this unprecedented time of wickedness called the Great Tribulation, and at this time God's people (those whose names are written in the book) also will be rescued. Praise be to the God of Israel! Many of those who understand will be purged, purified, and refined, but the wicked will, without understanding, continue to do wickedly. From the abolishing of the regular sacrifice and the setting up of the abomination of desolation, there will be 1,290 days, and some will wait till 1,335 days. Therefore, after the 1,260-day tribulation, there will be a thirty-day period and a forty-five-day period after that.

Immediately after the tribulation, the powers of the heavens will be shaken, and then the sign of the Son of Man will appear in the sky—they will see the Son of Man coming on the clouds with power and great glory. He will send His angels with a great trumpet, and they will gather His elect from the four winds, from one end of the sky to the other. This coming of the Son of Man will be as in the days of Noah: people will be eating and drinking, marrying and giving in marriage right up until His coming (Matthew 24).

If people today ask how all the suffering in the world could be allowed to happen, then so much the more it will be a question for people of conscience during the tribulation. I struggle with these things personally, as do many, and one thing I come back to is the concept—and reality—that God is higher than we are, and His ways are higher than ours. As such, the level of sin in the world is palpable to a believer, especially if he or she is in prayer and in the Word regularly. But do we really appreciate the difference between His holiness and our conduct? It's a question. When one ponders the magnificence of a California redwood or a Sitka spruce, one should also marvel at the very obvious greatness of the one who made those great trees! When one ponders the excellent conduct of a loving missionary who shares the gospel in distant lands, one ought to be in awe of the love of a gracious God that imbued that believer with the capacity for love and mercy! When one considers the coarseness of modern society

> "Whoever confesses that Jesus is the Son of God, God abides in him, and he in God." (1 John 4:15, NASB)

in many parts of the world, one knows that our holy God will act to be true to His Word and His ways, and it is we who must accord to His holiness, not the other way around. Perhaps, then, if we were really honest about just how humanistic and at times despicable our cultures have become around the world, then just possibly we might understand that something like the tribulation-period antichrist government could be an instrument for purifying believers and giving the wicked over to their devices.

We remember Rom. 1:28–32:

> And just as they did not see fit to acknowledge God any longer, God gave them over to a depraved mind, to do those things which are not proper, being filled with all unrighteousness, wickedness, greed, evil; full of envy, murder, strife, deceit, malice; *they are* gossips, slanderers, haters of God, insolent, arrogant, boastful, inventors of evil, disobedient to parents, without understanding, untrustworthy, unloving, unmerciful; and although they know the ordinance of God, that those who practice such things are worthy of death, they not only do the same, but also give hearty approval to those who practice them. (NASB)

We remember Deut. 18:9–12:

> When you enter the land which the Lord your God gives you, you shall not learn to imitate the detestable things of those nations. There shall not be found among you anyone who makes his son or his daughter pass through the fire, one who uses divination, one who practices witchcraft, or one who interprets omens, or a sorcerer, or one who casts a spell, or a medium, or a spiritist, or one who calls up the dead. For whoever does these things is detestable to the Lord; and because of these detestable things the Lord your God will drive them out before you. You shall be blameless before the Lord your God. For those nations, which you shall dispossess, listen to those who practice

> witchcraft and to diviners, but as for you, the LORD your God has not allowed you *to do* so. (NASB)

This list of abominable behavior in Deuteronomy 18 is pretty much a description of the so-called New Age that has decimated so much of Western culture for fifty years or more. Did we really think the modern fascination with evil would go unpunished?

The United States of America has been a blessed country—blessed for its people's adherence to God's ways. But what is the shape of American society today? We would do well to remember the fullness of the famous message in 2 Chronicles 7. There are two conditions given, and two very different results—a blessing will follow godly ways, and punishment will follow ungodly ways:

> If I shut up the heavens so that there is no rain, or if I command the locust to devour the land, or if I send pestilence among My people, and My people who are called by My name humble themselves and pray and seek My face and turn from their wicked ways, then I will hear from heaven, will forgive their sin and will heal their land. … But if you turn away and forsake My statutes and My commandments which I have set before you, and go and serve other gods and worship them, then I will uproot you from My land which I have given you, and this house which I have consecrated for My name I will cast out of My sight and I will make it a proverb and a byword among all peoples. As for this house, which was exalted, everyone who passes by it will be astonished and say, "Why has the Lord done thus to this land and to this house?" And they will say, "Because they forsook the Lord, the God of their fathers who brought them from the land of Egypt, and they adopted other gods and worshiped them and served them; therefore He has brought all this adversity on them." (2 Chron. 7:13–14, 19–22 NASB)

Believers need to be very interested in these standards, which were set out before King Solomon. Americans did not learn the lesson of Hurricane

Testing the Spirits

Katrina. What was meant as a wake-up call and a call to repentance was instead taken by many in New Orleans as a mere act of nature and a reason to embrace the very abominable Mardi Gras debauchery all the more.

And Americans have not learned the lesson of the 9-11 attacks. What was meant as a chastisement and a punishment was taken as mere international intrigue, as an excuse to flex American military muscle and rebuild more ostentatious and humanistic skyscrapers. Those towers reeked of Nimrod-esque excess (reminiscent of the Tower of Babel), and while the loss of life was truly lamentable, the American people cannot routinely miss the chance to repent and expect constant blessings from the holy God of Israel. What did American leaders do in response to 9-11? They resolved to rebuild defiantly when they should have repented of their collective hubris and called on the denizens of New York City to dedicate themselves to the worship of the God of Israel.

Isaiah 9 and 10 tell the story of Israelites who proudly rebuilt when they should have accepted their losses and moved forward by repenting and drawing closer to God:

> The LORD sends a message against Jacob, and it falls on Israel. And all the people know *it, that is,* Ephraim and the inhabitants of Samaria, asserting in pride and in arrogance of heart: "The bricks have fallen down, but we will rebuild with smooth stones; the sycamores have been cut down, but we will replace *them* with cedars." Therefore the LORD raises against them adversaries from Rezin and spurs their enemies on ... and they devour Israel with gaping jaws. ... Yet the people do not turn back to Him who struck them, nor do they seek the LORD of hosts. ... For those who guide this people are leading *them* astray; and those who are guided by them are brought to confusion. ... For every one of them is godless and an evildoer, and every mouth is speaking foolishness. ... Manasseh *devours* Ephraim, and Ephraim Manasseh, *and* together they are against Judah. ... I send [Assyria] against a godless nation and commission it against the people of my fury to capture

booty and to seize plunder, and to trample them down like mud in the streets. …

"O My people who dwell in Zion, do not fear the Assyrian who strikes you with the rod and lifts up his staff against you, the way Egypt did. For in a very little while My indignation against you will be spent and My anger will be directed to their destruction." The LORD of hosts will arouse a scourge against him like the slaughter of Midian at the rock of Oreb; and His staff will be over the sea and He will lift it up the way He did in Egypt. (Is. 9:8–11, 12a, 13, 17b, 21a; 10:6, 24b–26 NASB)

Washington, D.C., is teeming with pagan symbols, laid out in the street design and set in stone by anti-Christian saboteurs. Baal and Ashteroth worship are forbidden in the Old Testament, but here those horrendous practices are given prominence in bestial architecture. What secret-society saboteurs constructed this 555-foot-tall Egyptian obelisk, an abomination cunningly dubbed the Washington Monument, in this largely Christian land?

God's anger over Israel's arrogance would seem to be applicable today. If Israelites did not get the message that the Lord had judged them, it could be argued that Americans also have not gotten the message that God has judged America. Jerry Falwell warned his countrymen that the 9-11 attacks were a judgment against his beloved country, and did his countrymen thank him for his insight? No, instead he was pilloried in the media to the point that he apologized for his comment. I think that Falwell was a good watchman on the wall for sharing his excellent insight—but rather than apologize to his biblically illiterate detractors, he would have done well to expand on his original cry that the sin in the land had brought divine judgment against America. Because of many Americans' refusal to learn from God's chastisement, America can now expect to have its enemies rally against it (indeed spurred on by the Lord!) and devour this land with gaping jaws.

Too many in this land do not seek the Lord God of Israel; they do not repent to the living God who chastised them; they elect bad leaders who lead them astray with sleight of hand and confusion; godless evildoers roam the land; and the land is divided against itself: So will God send a powerful enemy against America to trample Americans down like mud in the streets? If so, we should not fear the enemy because once God's indignation against America passes, the scalpel He used to judge us will also be destroyed (Is. 10).

Isn't it interesting that Is. 9:11 says, "Therefore the Lord raises against them adversaries from Rezin and spurs their enemies on" (NASB), and on 9-11 the enemies of America were in the skies bringing destruction to the land? And isn't it interesting that the most famous example of misguided building is Nimrod's building of the Tower of Babel in Genesis 11? That arrogant project was put down with the confusion of tongues and scattering. Genesis 11, Is. 9:11, and 9-11-2001—that's a whole lot of elevens, all of which have to do with misguided and arrogant building projects, unbelief, and divine punishment.

What can Americans expect? The choices may be few: "Now what will you do in the day of punishment, and in the devastation which will come from afar? To whom will you flee for help? And where will you leave your wealth? Nothing *remains* but to crouch among the captives or fall among the slain. ... Only a remnant within them will return; a destruction is determined, overflowing with righteousness" (Is. 10:3–4a, 22b NASB).

Isaiah 2 furthers the case against prideful and boastful building projects:

> For the LORD of hosts will have a day *of reckoning* against everyone who is proud and lofty and against everyone who is lifted up, that he may be abased. And *it will be* against all the cedars of Lebanon that are lofty and lifted up, against all the oaks of Bashan, against all the lofty mountains, against all the hills that are lifted up, against every high tower, against every fortified wall, against all the ships of Tarshish and against all the beautiful craft. The pride of man will be humbled and the loftiness of men will be abased; and the LORD alone will be exalted in that day, but the idols will completely vanish. ... Stop regarding man, whose breath *of life* is in his nostrils; for why should he be esteemed? (Is. 2:12–18, 22 NASB)

If the Lord will have His day of reckoning against every high tower, then the immense World Trade Center buildings would seem to have been prime candidates for destruction. Could it be that the American love affair with skyscrapers has been a fiasco? I personally don't like tall buildings and don't think they're safe. If our people knew Scripture better, as our forefathers did, they would feel compelled to stop putting up tall buildings—this out of a due reverence for the Lord God of Israel.

Again, Hosea shows the consequences of dallying in false teachings and leaving the God of our fathers:

> My people are destroyed for lack of knowledge. Because you have rejected knowledge, I also will reject you from being My priest. Since you have forgotten the law of your God, I also will forget your children. ... For a spirit of harlotry has led *them* astray, and they have played the harlot, *departing* from their God. ... Ephraim is joined to idols; let him alone. Their liquor gone, they play the harlot continually; their rulers dearly love shame. The wind wraps them in its wings, and they will be ashamed because of their sacrifices. ...

The revolters have gone deep in depravity, but I will chastise all of them. … They have dealt treacherously against the Lord, for they have borne illegitimate children. Now the new moon will devour them with their land. … The princes of Judah have become like those who move a boundary; on them I will pour out My wrath like water. … When Ephraim saw his sickness, and Judah his wound, then Ephraim went to Assyria and sent to King Jareb. But he is unable to heal you, or to cure you of your wound. For I *will be* like a lion to Ephraim and like a young lion to the house of Judah. … I will go away *and* return to My place until they acknowledge their guilt and seek My face; in their affliction they will earnestly seek Me.

Therefore I have hewn *them* in pieces by the prophets; I have slain them by the words of My mouth; and the judgments on you are *like* the light that goes forth. For I delight in loyalty rather than sacrifice, and in the knowledge of God rather than burnt offerings. But like Adam they have transgressed the covenant; there they have dealt treacherously against Me. …

Ephraim mixes himself with the nations; Ephraim has become a cake not turned. Strangers devour his strength, yet he does not know *it;* gray hairs also are sprinkled on him, yet he does not know *it.* … So Ephraim has become like a silly dove, without sense; they call to Egypt, they go to Assyria. When they go, I will spread My net over them; I will bring them down like the birds of the sky. I will chastise them in accordance with the proclamation to their assembly. Woe to them, for they have strayed from Me! Destruction is theirs, for they have rebelled against Me! I would redeem them, *but they* speak lies against Me. And they do not cry to Me from their heart when they wail on their beds; for the sake of grain and new wine they assemble themselves, they turn away from Me. They turn, *but* not upward, they are like a deceitful bow. …

Israel has rejected the good; the enemy will pursue him. They have set up kings, but not by Me; they have appointed princes, but I did not know *it*. With their silver and gold they have made idols for themselves, that they might be cut off. ... How long will they be incapable of innocence? ... For they sow the wind and they reap the whirlwind. ... Israel is swallowed up; they are now among the nations like a vessel in which no one delights. For they have gone up to Assyria, *like* a wild donkey all alone; Ephraim has hired lovers. Even though they hire *allies* among the nations, now I will gather them up; and they will begin to diminish because of the burden of the king of princes. ... Though I wrote for [Ephraim] ten thousand *precepts* of My law, they are regarded as a strange thing. ... Now He will remember their iniquity, and punish *them* for their sins; they will return to Egypt. For Israel has forgotten his Maker and built palaces; and Judah has multiplied fortified cities, but I will send a fire on its cities that it may consume its palatial dwellings.

For you have played the harlot, forsaking your God. You have loved *harlots'* earnings on every threshing floor. Threshing floor and wine press will not feed them, and the new wine will fail them. They will not remain in the LORD's land, but Ephraim will return to Egypt, and in Assyria they will eat unclean *food*. ... I found Israel like grapes in the wilderness; I saw your forefathers as the earliest fruit on the fig tree in its first *season. But* they came to Baal-peor and devoted themselves to shame, and they became as detestable as that which they loved. ... All their evil is at Gilgal; indeed, I came to hate them there! Because of the wickedness of their deeds I will drive them out of My house!

You have plowed wickedness, you have reaped injustice, you have eaten the fruit of lies. Because you have trusted in your way, in your numerous warriors, therefore a tumult will arise among your people, and all your fortresses will be destroyed.

But Assyria—he will be their king because they refused to return *to Me*. The sword will whirl against their cities, and will demolish their gate bars and consume *them* because of their counsels. So My people are bent on turning from Me.

Yet I *have* been the Lord your God since the land of Egypt; and you were not to know any god except Me, for there is no savior besides Me. I cared for you in the wilderness, in the land of drought. As *they had* their pasture, they became satisfied, and being satisfied, their heart became proud; therefore they forgot Me. So I will be like a lion to them. …

Return, O Israel, to the Lord your God, for you have stumbled because of your iniquity. … Say to Him, "Take away all iniquity and receive *us* graciously. … Nor will we say again, 'Our god,' to the work of our hands; for in You the orphan finds mercy." I will heal their apostasy, I will love them freely, for My anger has turned away from them. I will be like the dew to Israel; he will blossom like the lily, and he will take root like *the cedars of* Lebanon…

Whoever is wise, let him understand these things; *Whoever* is discerning, let him know them. (Hosea 4:6, 12b, 17–19; 5:2b, 7, 10, 13–14a, 15; 6:5–7; 7:8–9, 11–16a; 8:3–4, 5b, 7a, 8–10, 12, 13b–14; 9:1b–3, 10, 15a; 10:13–14a; 11:5b–7a; 13:4–7a; 14:1, 2b, 3b–5, 9a NASB)

To a large extent, the book of Hosea stands as a warning of the consequences of unbelief. We are encouraged to use discernment to understand Hosea. The ways in which Israel strayed in the time of Hosea are eerily like the ways in which America has strayed in recent decades.

Therefore the question arises: does America have a date with national disaster in much the same way that Israel met ruination at the hands of the Assyrians in 722 BC? If so, who would be America's overthrowers? I sense that our overthrowers would come from among the "hired lovers" and "hired allies" that we have curried favor with in recent decades—false allies who pose as friends while conspiring against Americans behind their backs: the Vatican that is drunk on the blood of the saints; Russia and China and their merciless, slaughtering hordes; the Federal Reserve and other cruel central banks; and Saudi Arabia, the Muslim brotherhood, and other anti-Jewish forces (including the so-called United Nations) definitely come to mind.

If the four horses of Revelation 6 and Zechariah 6 represent the subtle instigator, the Roman Catholic Church (white), the bloodthirsty Communist warmonger (red), the economic wrecker (black), and the Mohammedan death cult (pale or green), then it would seem that all four horses are running at a full gallop.

The Roman anti-Protestant armies of Loyola and the Jesuits have spawned conflicts far and wide, even if they don't ride out in full Jesuit regalia as in the Middle Ages; the so-called Counter-Reformation sounds innocuous enough until one realizes that its motivation is the amalgamation of Roman power and the stunting of true Christian revival. The Reformation-minded John Knox of Scotland preached about the dangers of the little horn of Daniel 7—that is to say, popery and the Antichrist—and Knox was a good influence.

Centuries later, the misinformation and propaganda in the West have made many dull and oblivious to the anti-Christian treacheries of the Vatican. We remember Jesus' words: "Take heed that no man deceive you. For many shall come in my name, saying, I am Christ; and shall deceive many" (Matt. 24:4b–5 KJV). Roman Catholic pretensions about having the Vicar of Christ are dangerous indeed, for there is only one Jesus the Christ who died for man's sins, was buried, and was resurrected (praise God!), and any Roman Catholics who presume to have a substitute for Christ are false teachers. There is no substitute for Jesus Christ, and we remember Jesus' words: "I am the way, the truth, and the life: no man cometh unto the Father, but by Me" (John 14:6 KJV). The pope, Hindu idols, Masonic idols, Mormon idols, Buddhist idols, Baal-Ashteroth idols,

Molech idols, Taoist mystics Lao-tzu and Zhuang-tzu, and all manner of interfaith amalgamators, are not the way.

Did Stalin's killing machines and his horrible gulags not offend Americans? Did Mao's maniacal Red Guards and work-to-death camps not offend Americans? Did Pol Pot's Cambodian Reds (Khmer Rouge) not kill enough people with glasses to offend Americans? Did Pol Pot have only to stack the skulls of his victims neatly to get a pass in public opinion? Did Mao have only to call his spasm of bloodletting cotton candy and peaches and cream—or better yet, the Great Leap Forward and the Cultural Revolution—to get a pass? Is first-grade linguistic trickery all that is needed to get the West to embrace Communist treachery? I know, let's call Chinese Communism "Socialism with Chinese Characteristics."

And what about that two hundred-million-man army from Revelation 9 (sixth trumpet judgment) that will kill one-third of mankind with fire, smoke, and brimstone (aided by the four angels loosed from the Euphrates)? Where is that army going to come from? Will the anti-people, non-liberation army (cleverly called the People's Liberation Army) be involved in that horrible specter? Why not just call all Communist armies something in French or something about cotton candy? There could be the Chinese-UN Cotton Candy Fake-Peacekeeping Force, the Russian-UN Cotton Candy Invasion Force, and the North Korean Nonvolunteer Army.

For that matter, is there a communist-sympathizing propaganda element in American political circles? In American business and industry? In the mainstream American media? In Western academia? In the Western intelligence agencies? Could such an element fool Americans in between such highly-intellectual programming as *The Simpsons* or *Lost?* Could the heirs of the Pilgrims' Judeo-Christian heritage be programmed by globalist, anti-Christian programming? If American schools would stop teaching Malcolm X and the *Communist Manifesto* and start teaching Knox and the Holy Bible, then maybe we could lay claim to the blessings of 2 Chron. 7:14 : "If my people, which are called by my name, shall humble themselves, and pray, and seek my face, and turn from their wicked ways; then will I hear from heaven, and will forgive their sin, and will heal their land" (KJV).

Feudal lords used to ride around Europe checking on the condition of their fiefs, assessing the strength of their fiefdoms; vassals could use their lord's land provided they showed loyalty to him. In capitalism, there can be a middle class, but the size of it can be influenced by central bankers who control the money supply and loan policies. Therefore, in theory, the central bankers could shrink the middle class and create an economic disparity of rich and poor and not much in between, something very much out of the feudalistic handbook.

James was very aware of the habit of the rich to abuse the poor: "Go to now, *ye* rich men, weep and howl for your miseries that shall come upon *you*. Behold, the hire of the labourers who have reaped down your fields, which is of you kept back by fraud, crieth: and the cries of them which have reaped are entered into the ears of the Lord of sabaoth. Ye have lived in pleasure on the earth, and been wanton; ye have nourished your hearts as in a day of slaughter. Ye have condemned *and* killed the just" (James 5:1, 4–6a KJV).

In spite of the crushing materialism in society today, as believers we need to move away from the black heart of greediness and towards a knowledge of the Lord: "Let not the wise *man* glory in his wisdom, neither let the mighty *man* glory in his might, let not the rich *man* glory in his riches: But let him that glorieth glory in this, that he understandeth and knoweth me, that I *am* the LORD which exercise lovingkindness, judgment, and righteousness, in the earth: for in these *things* I delight, saith the LORD" (Jer. 9:23–24 KJV).

CHAPTER NINE

RECEIVING JESUS, GUARDING ONE'S HEART, AND KEEPING ONE EYE ON ISRAEL

But if some of the branches were broken off, and you, being a wild olive, were grafted in among them and became partaker with them of the rich root of the olive tree, do not be arrogant toward the branches; but if you are arrogant, remember that it is not you who supports the root, but the root supports *you (Rom. 11:17–18 NASB).*

Therefore, take up the full armor of God, so that you will be able to resist in the evil day, and having done everything, to stand firm. Stand firm therefore, HAVING GIRDED YOUR LOINS WITH TRUTH and HAVING PUT ON THE BREASTPLATE OF RIGHTEOUSNESS, and having shod YOUR FEET WITH THE PREPARATION OF THE GOSPEL OF PEACE; in addition to all, taking up the shield of faith with which you will be able to extinguish all the flaming arrows of the evil one. And take THE HELMET OF SALVATION, and the sword of the Spirit, which is the word of God. (Eph. 6:13–17 NASB)

For You shall break the yoke of their burden and the staff on their shoulders, the rod of their oppressor, as at the battle of Midian. For every boot of the booted warrior in the battle tumult, and cloak rolled in blood, will be for burning, fuel for the fire. For a child will be born to us, a son will be given to us; and the government will rest on His shoulders; and His name will be called Wonderful Counselor, Mighty God, Eternal Father, Prince of Peace. There will be no end to the increase of His government or of peace, on the throne of David and over his kingdom... (Is. 9:4–7a NASB)

I was born again at the age of twenty-two at the end of my junior year at the University of California at Berkeley. It was on the South Side, south of the UC Berkeley campus, where I was approached by a couple of Christian brothers, evangelized, and saved: that area is teeming with intellectuals, pseudo-intellectuals, pot smokers, flower power die-hards, tarot card occultists, quasi-Communist social activists, rock-and-roll groupies, and heritage-crushing humanists. The brothers told me about the Gospel of Jesus Christ, sin, and the need to accept the Lord Jesus as one's personal Lord and Savior. Praise God! I had been primed for that moment. I'd had many conversations about God over the years—with classmates, family, and friends—and instinctively knew that the timing was right.

I grew up in the town of Mount Shasta, California, and there was lovingly bundled up on Sundays, along with my brothers, to make the nine-mile drive down Interstate 5 to Dunsmuir, where we would attend the Episcopalian church. My mother had a sense of the sacred, and in the mid-sixties, when the Hippie movement was in full swing, she carefully took her three boys to church; for this I am very grateful because the idea that God is there and we are to worship Him was planted in my brothers and me from an early age.

My father, a hardworking general practitioner, took good care of his family, attending at the local clinic during the day and often going out at night, in all weather, on house calls. Many of our friends in Mount Shasta were Christians, and the culture was much more conservative in those days, the Hippie movement notwithstanding. Patriotism was a given,

Fourth of July festivities were a big thing, and the movies—*The Sound of Music, Swiss Family Robinson,* etc.—had not yet disintegrated into sacrilege and blasphemy.

When we lived in Davis, California, in the early- and mid-seventies, my family drifted spiritually. The Hippie movement had gone mainstream, and the "do-your-own-thing-man" hipster vibrations even infected an otherwise conservative family like mine, causing my parents to flirt with the cancer of Unitarianism.

At Bellevue High School in Washington, I excelled academically and played varsity singles on a state championship tennis team but did not feel satisfied (few people watch tennis). At UC Berkeley, I studied Chinese language and literature and ran in the Berkeley hills, but did not feel satisfied. I went on a few dates, attended some stupid parties, socialized with some marijuana smokers, walked all around Berkeley, studied a lot, and still felt unsatisfied.

The men who evangelized me in Berkeley gave me the gift of their testimonies; they were believers in the Lord Jesus Christ, and they wanted me to be their brother in Christ. I believed, was baptized in water, and met with the brothers and sisters of the Local Church, an outgrowth of Watchman Nee's and Witness Li's ministries. It is ironic that, as a Chinese major, I should have been saved through a congregation that is so heavily populated by Chinese. But there it is. A few weeks after my conversion to Christ, I made my first trip to Taiwan.

The Lord of the whole earth (Zechariah 4), who walks among the seven golden candlesticks (Revelation 2), rebukes and chastens those whom He loves, so we best be zealous and repent (Revelation 3). Learning from the Lord Jesus' review of the seven churches, we know the following: we must remember from whence we have fallen, repent, and do the deeds we did at first (Ephesus); we must be faithful in tribulation, even unto death (Smyrna); we must avoid the false teachings of Balaam and the Nicolaitans, thereby avoiding immorality and not causing the sons of Israel to stumble (Pergamum); we must not tolerate the false prophetess Jezebel, who leads God's people astray (Thyatira); we must wake up and strengthen the things that were about to die, keeping what we have received and heard, for we have work to do for the Lord God of Israel (Sardis); we must not be lukewarm, acting rich when we're actually wretched, miserable, poor, blind, and naked, and we ought to buy from God gold refined by fire (Laodicea); and finally, those in the Church who have kept the word of God's perseverance will be kept from the hour of testing that is about to come upon the whole world (Philadelphia) (Revelation 2–3).

One time I went to Ruifang, a railroad town north of Taipei, with some Chinese brothers. We went to evangelize the locals there, and though I was not practiced in evangelism, I went over to several young Chinese men who were staring at me and laughing. I spoke to them in Chinese (Mandarin), and they got more serious. When my fellow evangelists came over, the young guys really got engaged with the topic. A seed was planted, developed, and I hope there were some conversions that day. I think the lesson is that we might be unpracticed, facing some cultural barriers or the like, but the Holy Spirit makes conversions happen.

Another experience from Taiwan that I hold dear is meeting a tiny, hunched Chinese man after an evangelical meeting in Taipei. He was a *waisheng-ren,* a Mainlander who came to Taiwan in 1947 (or thereabouts) after the Nationalists (Kuomintang, or KMT) under Chiang Kai-shek were routed by Mao's Communist forces. He was old and far from whatever strength he had wielded in his prime, but his eyes were bright with hope and possibilities: he held out his prayer list, and it was like no other prayer list I had ever seen. It was huge—a massive collection of names all scrawled in his own hand, with fervency and passion, extending many pages and embodying the very core of his evangelical mission. The pages were not prim and perfect; rather they were somewhat crumpled—working papers in the service of the Lord Jesus. He was a prayer warrior, hunched and withered, slipping through the dark alleys of Taipei with a less-than-perfect gait but armed with a brilliancy of spirit. He was not long for this world, but he was going to be with the Lord Jesus, and he wanted to bring others with him! He was so hunched that he could barely look up to speak with another, but he was one of the most beautiful souls I have ever met.

Testimonies are important. We remember Paul's letter to Timothy: "Therefore do not be ashamed of the testimony of our Lord or of me His prisoner, but join with *me* in suffering for the gospel according to the power of God, who has saved us and called us with a holy calling, not according to our works, but according to His own purpose and grace which was granted us in Christ Jesus from all eternity, but now has been revealed by the appearing of our Savior Christ Jesus, who abolished death and brought life and immortality to light through the gospel" (2 Tim. 1:8–10 NASB).

Receiving Jesus

It is of the uttermost importance that one receive the Lord Jesus Christ as one's Lord and Savior, immediately, forthwith, and as soon as possible:

> For God so loved the world, that he gave his only begotten Son, that whosoever believeth in him should not perish, but have everlasting life. ... He that believeth on him is not condemned: but he that believeth not is condemned already, because he hath not believed in the name of the only begotten Son of God. And this is the condemnation, that light is come into the world, and men loved darkness rather than light, because their deeds were evil. For every one that doeth evil hateth the light, neither cometh to the light, lest his deeds should be reproved. But he that doeth truth cometh to the light, that his deeds may be made manifest, that they are wrought in God. ... He that believeth on the Son hath everlasting life: and he that believeth not the Son shall not see life; but the wrath of God abideth on him. (John 3:16, 18–21, 36 KJV)

"He was in the world, and the world was made by him, and the world knew him not. He came unto his own, and his own received him not. But as many as received him, to them gave he power to become the sons of God, *even* to them that believe on his name" (John 1:10–12 KJV).

"My sheep hear my voice, and I know them, and they follow me: And I give unto them life; and they shall never perish, neither shall any *man* pluck them out of my hand. My Father, which gave *them* me, is greater than all; and no *man* is able to pluck *them* out of my Father's hand. I and *my* Father are one" (John 10:27–30 KJV).

"Yet a little while is the light with you. Walk while ye have the light, lest darkness come upon you: for he that walketh in darkness knoweth not wither he goeth. While ye have light, believe in the light, that ye may be the children of light" (John 12:35–36a KJV).

"Let not your heart be troubled: ye believe in God, believe also in me. In my Father's house are many mansions: if it were not so, I would have told you. I go to prepare a place for you. And if I go and prepare a place for you, I will come again, and receive you unto myself; that where I am, there ye may be also" (John 14:1–3 KJV).

By believing in the Lord Jesus Christ (by receiving Him), one can have everlasting life; become a son of God; be in Jesus' hand and in the Father's hand; have the indwelling of the Holy Spirit; be a child of light; and have a place in the Father's house, where Jesus will be. These are wonderful advantages for the Christian.

The Lion of Judah will defend His own. God's eternal power and Godhead are clearly seen in His lions (Rom. 1:20).

Guarding One's Heart

The world can be a frightening place. With the rise of the antichrist government, the enemies of Christians and Jews are on the march. We, as Christians, have assurances from God's Word that can assuage our groaning hearts in times of hurt or trouble. No matter what the world may throw at us, it is nice to be on the side of the good, standing in the light, and worshipping the Messiah, Yeshua, our very present Lord and Savior:

> And you *hath he quickened,* who were dead in trespasses and sins; wherein in time past ye walked according to the course of this world, according to the prince of the power of the air, the spirit that now worketh in the children of disobedience: Among whom also we all had our conversation in times past in the lusts of our flesh, fulfilling the desires of the flesh and of the mind; and were by nature the children of wrath, even as others. But God, who is rich in mercy, for his great love wherewith he loved us, even when we were dead in sins, hath quickened us together with Christ, (by grace ye are saved;) and hath raised *us* up together, and made *us* sit together in heavenly *places* in Christ Jesus. ... That at that time ye were without Christ, being aliens from the commonwealth of Israel, and strangers from the covenants of promise, having no hope, and without God in the world: But now, in Christ Jesus, ye who sometimes were far off are made nigh by the blood of Christ (Eph. 2:1–6, 12–13 KJV).

"Behold, God *is* my salvation; I will trust, and not be afraid: for the LORD JEHOVAH *is* my strength and *my* song; he also is become my salvation. And in that day shall ye say, Praise the LORD, call upon his name, declare his doings among the people, make mention that his name is exalted. Sing unto the LORD; for he hath done excellent things: this *is* known in all the earth" (Is. 12:2–5 KJV).

"*It is of* the LORD's mercies that we are not consumed, because his compassions fail not. *They are* new every morning: great *is* thy faithfulness.

The Lord *is* my portion, saith my soul; therefore will I hope in him. The Lord *is* good unto them that wait for him, to the soul *that* seeketh him. *It is* good that *a man* should both hope and quietly wait for the salvation of the Lord" (Lam. 3:22–26 KJV).

"For ye are all the children of God by faith in Christ Jesus. For as many of you as have been baptized into Christ have put on Christ. … And if ye *be* Christ's, then are ye Abraham's seed, and heirs according to the promise" (Gal. 3:26–27, 29 KJV).

"Giving thanks unto the Father, which hath made us meet to be partakers of the inheritance of the saints in light: Who hath delivered us from the power of darkness, and hath translated *us* into the kingdom of his dear Son: In whom we have redemption through his blood, *even* the forgiveness of sins" (Col 1:12–14 KJV).

"[Y]e were … redeemed … with the precious blood of Christ, as of a lamb without blemish and without spot: Who verily was foreordained before the foundation of the world, but was manifest in these last times for you. … Seeing ye have purified your souls in obeying the truth through the Spirit unto unfeigned love of the brethren, *see that ye* love one another with a pure heart fervently: Being born again, not of corruptible seed, but of incorruptible, by the word of God, which liveth and abideth for ever" (1 Peter 1:18a, 19–20, 22–23 KJV).

"[T]he Father sent the Son *to be* the Saviour of the world. Whosoever shall confess that Jesus is the Son of God, God dwelleth in him, and he in God. … God is love; and he that dwelleth in love dwelleth in God, and God in him" (1 John 4:14b–15, 16b KJV).

There is something inspiring about an athlete at his best. I used to watch the epic matches between tennis players Jimmy Connors, John McEnroe, and Bjorn Borg. But even those great athletes reached a time when they could no longer play at their best. We are subject to physical decay and then death—this the result of the Fall and the resultant curse of death (Genesis 3). We are in earthly houses, tents, or tabernacles, if you will; we are pilgrims on a journey, groaning in our ailing bodies and hoping for comfort and rest. We're like pots in a pottery shop, and eventually something or someone will knock us down and we'll break: We must admit that we're weak and give all praise to the Potter—our Lord, Creator, and Savior, Jesus the Messiah. We are weak, but He is strong:

> For we know that, if our earthly house of *this* tabernacle were dissolved, we have a building of God, an house not made with hands, eternal in the heavens. For in this we groan, earnestly desiring to be clothed upon with our house which is from heaven. ... For we that are in *this* tabernacle do groan, being burdened: not for that we would be unclothed, but clothed upon, that mortality might be swallowed up of life. Now he that hath wrought us for the self-same thing *is* God, who also hath given unto us the earnest of the Spirit. ... We are confident, *I say*, and willing rather to be absent from the body, and to be present with the Lord. (2 Cor. 5:1–2, 4–5, 8 KJV)

"[The Lord] raiseth up the poor out of the dust, *and* lifteth up the beggar from the dunghill, to set *them* among princes, and to make them inherit the throne of glory: for the pillars of the earth *are* the Lord's, and he hath set the world upon them. He will keep the feet of his saints, and the wicked shall be silent in darkness; for by strength shall no man prevail" (1 Sam. 2:8–9 KJV).

As for me, I came to the Lord Jesus because my esteemed mother took me to church in Dunsmuir, California, in the sixties, planting a seed; and later, a couple of good brothers witnessed for their faith amidst the crooked and perverse city of Berkeley, California, in 1984, reaping a harvest. Praise be to God for His elect who choose to stand in faith, drawing others to the God of Israel with the sweet fragrance of a truthful voice.

We can walk with the Word in our minds, letting it instruct our feet where to go. We are born again with a purpose. We are to bring glory to our God and Father, Yeshua, standing out as lights amid a crooked and perverse society. We should not shrink away from a chance to contend for the faith; rather we should let any godly knowledge, wisdom, understanding, or discretion that we may possess shine on the crooked and perverse thinking that is all around. As for me, I came to the Lord Jesus when I did because my esteemed mother took me to church in Dunsmuir, California, in the sixties, planting a seed; and later, a couple of good brothers witnessed for their faith amidst the crooked and perverse city of Berkeley, California, in 1984, reaping a harvest. Praise be to God for His elect who choose to stand in faith, drawing others to the God of Israel with the sweet fragrance of a truthful voice:

"[W]ork out your own salvation with fear and trembling. For it is God which worketh in you both to will and to do of *his* good pleasure. Do all things without murmurings and disputings: That ye may be blameless and harmless, the sons of God, without rebuke, in the midst of a crooked and perverse nation, among whom ye shine as lights in the world" (Phil. 2:12b–15 KJV).

"[Y]e should earnestly contend for the faith which was once delivered unto the saints" (Jude 3b KJV).

We know from the Beatitudes in Matt. 5:7 that mercy is one of the godly traits: "Blessed *are* the merciful: for they shall obtain mercy" (KJV). One time I popped out of my bindings while skiing on Mount Shasta in a whiteout; when my brother side-stepped his way back up the hill to help me back into my skis, that was mercy. One time it was cold at my other brother's house, and my brother put a blanket over me before he was fully dressed himself; that was mercy. My esteemed father and mother have shown great mercy to my brothers and I—sheltering us, instructing us, loving us, and encouraging us to chart decent paths. If we can show mercy, then how much more is the mercy of the living God of Israel! We have a God who cares, and that is a very good thing:

"Seeing then that we have a great high priest, that is passed into the heavens, Jesus the son of God, let us hold fast *our* profession. For we have not an high priest which cannot be touched with the feeling of our infirmities; but was in all points tempted like as *we are, yet* without sin. Let us therefore come boldly unto the throne of grace, that we may obtain mercy, and find grace to help in time of need" (Heb. 4:14–16 KJV).

Keeping One Eye on Israel

Jerusalem and all of Israel are important. Jerusalem, or Zion, is the apple of God's eye (Zechariah 2). Israel, properly speaking, is much larger than most realize, in spite of her current reduced form; and the descendants of Abraham, Isaac, and Jacob (Israel) are a wellspring of blessing for all the families of the earth:

> For I, saith the Lord, will be unto [Jerusalem] a wall of fire round about, and will be the glory in the midst of her. Ho, ho, *come forth,* and flee from the land of the north, saith the Lord: for I have spread you abroad as the four winds of the heaven, saith the Lord. Deliver thyself, O Zion, that dwellest *with* the daughter of Babylon. For thus saith the Lord of hosts; After the glory hath he sent me unto the nations which spoiled you: for he that toucheth you toucheth the apple of his eye. For, behold, I will shake mine hand upon them, and they shall be a spoil to their servants: and ye shall know that the Lord of hosts hath sent me. Sing and rejoice, O daughter of Zion: for, lo, I come, and I will dwell in the midst of thee, saith the Lord. And many nations shall be joined to the Lord in that day, and shall be my people: and I will dwell in the midst of thee, and thou shalt know that the Lord of hosts hath sent me unto thee. And the Lord shall inherit Judah his portion in the holy land, and shall choose Jerusalem again. (Zech. 2:5–12 KJV)

"Now the Lord had said unto Abram, Get thee out of thy country … unto a land that I will shew thee: And I will make of thee a great nation, and I will bless thee, and make thy name great; and thou shalt be a blessing: And I will bless them that bless thee, and curse him that curseth thee: and in thee shall all families of the earth be blessed" (Gen. 12:1a, 1c–3 KJV).

"[T]he LORD made a covenant with Abram, saying, Unto thy seed have I given this land, from the river of Egypt unto the great river, the river Euphrates: The Kenites, and the Kenizzites, and the Kadmonites, and the Hittites, and the Perizzites, and the Rephaims, and the Amorites, and the Canaanites, and the Girgashites, and the Jebusites" (Gen. 15:18b–21 KJV).

Many have not taken God's words about the Jews seriously. For example, in the book of Esther, we learn of one Haman the Agagite, an enemy of all Jews. Haman had devised a plan to kill the Jews, but Mordecai the Jew and Queen Esther acted as good watchmen, exposing Haman's evil plot before King Ahasuerus. Like Haman's ten sons, the ten kings of the earth that fight (with the beast) against the God of Jacob will be cursed (becoming food for birds):

> Then the king Ahasuerus said unto Esther the queen and to Mordecai the Jew, Behold, I have given Esther the house of Haman, and him they have hanged upon the gallows, because he laid his hand upon the Jews. ... Then said Esther, If it please the king, let it be granted to the Jews which *are* in Shushan to do to morrow also according unto this day's decree, and let Haman's ten sons be hanged upon the gallows. And the king commanded it so to be done: and the decree was given at Shushan; and they hanged Haman's ten sons. ... Because Haman the son of Hammedatha, the Agagite, the enemy of all the Jews, had devised against the Jews to destroy them, and had cast Pur, that *is,* the lot, to consume them, and to destroy them; but when *Esther* came before the king, he commanded by letters that his wicked device, which he devised against the Jews, should return upon his own head, and that he and his sons should be hanged on the gallows. Wherefore they called these days Purim after the name of Pur. (Est. 8:7, 13–14, 24–26a KJV)

The demise of Haman and his ten sons is clearly a fulfillment of Gen. 12:3, where the Lord tells Abram, "And I will bless them that bless thee, and curse him that curseth thee: and in thee shall all families of the earth be blessed" (KJV). Haman cursed the descendants of Abraham, Isaac, and Jacob, therefore Haman was cursed by God.

In a similar vein, the fourth kingdom, with ten toes partly of iron and partly of clay (partly strong and partly broken), will be broken into pieces and consumed by the Kingdom of the God of Heaven, which shall stand forever and never be destroyed (Daniel 2): "And the ten horns which thou sawest are ten kings, which have received no kingdom as yet; but receive power as kings one hour with the beast. These have one mind, and shall give their power and strength unto the beast. These shall make war with the Lamb, and the Lamb shall overcome them: for he is Lord of lords, and King of kings: and they that are with him *are* called, and chosen, and faithful" (Rev. 17:12–14 KJV):

> And the armies *which were* in heaven followed [The Word of God] upon white horses, clothed in fine linen, white and clean. And out of his mouth goeth a sharp sword, that with it he should smite the nations: and he shall rule them with a rod of iron. … And I saw the beast, and the kings of the earth, and their armies, gathered together to make war against him that sat on the horse, and against his army. And the beast was taken, and with him the false prophet that wrought miracles before him, with which he deceived them that had received the mark of the beast, and them that worshipped his image. These both were cast alive into a lake of fire burning with brimstone. And the remnant were slain with the sword of him that sat upon the horse, which *sword* proceeded out of his mouth: and all the fowls were filled with their flesh. (Rev. 19:14–15a, 19–21 KJV)

Jerusalem, Israel

In the one case, the anti-Jewish ten sons were destroyed, and later the anti-Jewish ten toes/ten horns of the fourth kingdom will be destroyed. In both cases, Gen. 12:3 will have been fulfilled. Be it Genesis 12, Daniel 2, Revelation 17, or Revelation 19, the Word of God is true and not to be mocked. We know that the Lord will fight for Jerusalem:

> The burden of the word of the Lord for Israel, saith the Lord, which stretcheth forth the heavens, and layeth the foundation of the earth, and formeth the spirit of man within him. Behold, I will make Jerusalem a cup of trembling unto all the people round about, when they shall be in the siege both against Judah *and* against Jerusalem. And in that day will I make Jerusalem a burdensome stone for all people: all that burden themselves with it shall be cut in pieces, though all the people of the earth be gathered together against it. … In that day will I make the governors of Judah like an hearth of fire among the wood, and like a torch of fire in a sheaf; and they shall devour all the people round about, on the right hand and on the left: and Jerusalem shall be inhabited again in her own place, *even* in Jerusalem. … In that day shall the Lord defend the inhabitants of Jerusalem; and he that is feeble among them at that day shall be as David; and the house of David *shall be* as God, as the angel of the Lord before them. And it shall come to pass in that day, *that* I will seek to destroy all the nations that come against Jerusalem. And I will pour upon the house of David, and upon the inhabitants of Jerusalem, the spirit of grace and of supplications: and they shall look upon me whom they have pierced, and they shall mourn for him, as one mourneth for *his* only *son,* and shall be in bitterness for him, as one that is in bitterness for *his* firstborn. …
>
> And it shall come to pass, *that* in all the land, saith the Lord, two parts therein shall be cut off *and* die; but the third shall be left therein. And I will bring the third part through the fire, and will refine them as silver is refined, and will try them as gold is tried: they shall call on my name, and I will hear them: I will say, It *is* my people: and they shall say, The Lord *is* my God.

> For I will gather all nations against Jerusalem to battle; and the city shall be taken, and the houses rifled, and the women ravished; and half of the city shall go forth into captivity, and the residue of the people shall not be cut off from the city. Then shall the LORD go forth, and fight against those nations, as when he fought in the day of battle. And his feet shall stand in that day upon the mount of Olives, which *is* before Jerusalem on the east, and the mount of Olives shall cleave in the midst thereof toward the east and toward the west, *and there shall be* a very great valley; and half of the mountain shall remove toward the north, and half of it toward the south. ... And the LORD shall be king over all the earth: in that day shall there be one LORD, and his name one. ... And this shall be the plague wherewith the LORD will smite all the people that have fought against Jerusalem; Their flesh shall consume away while they stand upon their feet, and their eyes shall consume away in their holes, and their tongue shall consume away in their mouth. ... And it shall come to pass, *that* every one that is left of all the nations which came against Jerusalem shall even go up from year to year to worship the King, the LORD of hosts, and to keep the feast of tabernacles. (Zech. 12:1–3, 6, 8–10; 13:8–9; 14:2–4, 9, 12, 16 KJV)

"[H]e shall smite the earth with the rod of his mouth, and with the breath of his lips shall he slay the wicked. And righteousness shall be the girdle of his loins, and faithfulness the girdle of his reins. The wolf also shall dwell with the lamb" (Is. 11:4b–6a KJV).

Jerusalem is the apple of God's eye (Zechariah 2): He has disciplined her, but He will fight for her also. Those who trifle with Jerusalem (Zechariah 12, Isaiah 11) or with Israel at large (Genesis 12) make a big mistake. Sure, the Assyrians were used as a corrective agent against Israel in 722 BC, but where are the Assyrians now? The Babylonians were used as a corrective agent against Judah in 586 BC, but where are the Babylonians now? The Medes, Persians, and Romans likewise took their turns at glory at the expense of the Holy Land, and where are they now? Even now the four horses are running: the Roman Catholic church (dressing in white in a display of feigned purity), the Russian and Chinese Communists (red for slaughter), the greedy Capitalists (black for cruel heart), and the Jew-hating, Christian-hating Islamic jihadists (green for Ishmael-like and Esau-like envy) already plot against Israel and Jerusalem, and they too will be destroyed. It is unwise to pick a fight with the King of kings and Lord of lords.

There will be a sweet transformation from the current groaning in our fallen bodies to a healthier, more convivial state during the Millennial Reign of Christ: "For we know that the whole creation groaneth and travaileth in pain together until now. And not only *they*, but ourselves also, which have the firstfruits of the Spirit, even we ourselves groan within ourselves, waiting for the adoption, *to wit,* the redemption of our body. … Likewise the Spirit also helpeth our infirmities: for we know not what we should pray for as we ought: but the Spirit itself maketh intercession for us with groanings which cannot be uttered" (Rom. 8:22–23, 26 KJV).

"Behold, I shew you a mystery; We shall not all sleep, but we shall all be changed, in a moment, in the twinkling of an eye, at the last trump: for the trumpet shall sound, and the dead shall be raised incorruptible, and we shall be changed. For this corruptible must put on incorruption, and this mortal *must* put on immortality. … [Y]e know that your labour is not in vain in the Lord" (1 Cor. 15:51–53, 58b KJV).

> But with righteousness shall he judge the poor, and reprove with equity for the meek of the earth: and he shall smite the earth with the rod of his mouth, and with the breath of his lips shall he slay the wicked. And righteousness shall be the girdle of his loins, and faithfulness the girdle of his reins. The wolf also shall dwell with the lamb, and the leopard shall lie down with the kid; and the calf and the young lion and the fatling together; and a little child shall lead them. And the cow and the bear shall feed; their young ones shall lie down together: and the lion shall eat straw like the ox. And the sucking child shall play on the hole of the asp, and the weaned child shall put his hand on the cockatrice' den. They shall not hurt nor destroy in all my holy mountain: for the earth shall be full of the

knowledge of the LORD, as the waters cover the sea. (Is. 11:4–9 KJV)

"And we know that all things work together for good to them that love God, to them who are the called according to *his* purpose. For whom he did foreknow, he also did predestinate *to be* conformed to the image of his Son, that he might be the firstborn among many brethren" (Rom. 8:28–29 KJV).

For all that there is violence, pain, deceit, betrayal, and despair in this world, it is helpful to remember that there is something better to come for the saints. It behooves all of God's people to review the end of the story, as it were, as laid out at the end of the book of Revelation:

> And I saw an angel come down from heaven, having the key of the bottomless pit and a great chain in his hand. And he laid hold on the dragon, that old serpent, which is the Devil, and Satan, and bound him a thousand years, and cast him into the bottomless pit, and shut him up, and set a seal upon him, that he should deceive the nations no more, till the thousand years should be fulfilled: and after that he must be loosed a little season. And I saw thrones, and they sat upon them, and judgment was given unto them: and *I saw* the souls of them that were beheaded for the witness of Jesus, and for the word of God, and which had not worshipped the beast, neither his image, neither had received *his* mark upon their foreheads, or in their hands; and they lived and reigned with Christ a thousand years. But the rest of the dead lived not again until the thousand years were finished. This is the first resurrection. Blessed and holy *is* he that hath part in the first resurrection: on such the second death hath no power, but they shall be priests of God and of Christ, and shall reign with him a thousand years.
>
> And when the thousand years are expired, Satan shall be loosed out of his prison, and shall go out to deceive the nations which are in the four quarters of the earth, Gog

and Magog, to gather them together to battle: the number of whom *is* as the sand of the sea. And they went up on the breadth of the earth, and compassed the camp of the saints about, and the beloved city: and fire came down from God out of heaven, and devoured them. And the devil that deceived them was cast into the like of fire and brimstone, where the beast and the false prophet *are,* and shall be tormented day and night for ever and ever.

And I saw a great white throne, and him that sat on it, from whose face the earth and the heaven fled away; and there was found no place for them. And I saw the dead, small and great, stand before God; and the books were opened: and another book was opened, which is *the book* of life: and the dead were judged out of those things which were written in the books, according to their works. And the sea gave up the dead which were in it; and death and hell delivered up the dead which were in them: and they were judged every man according to their works. And death and hell were cast into the lake of fire. This is the second death. And whosoever was not found written in the book of life was cast into the lake of fire. (Rev. 20:1–15 KJV)

The first heaven and the first earth will pass away, and there will be a new heaven and a new earth (with no more sea). The holy city, the New Jerusalem, will come down from God out of heaven, and there will be no more tears, death, sorrow, crying, or pain, and the former things will have passed away. The New Jerusalem will have the glory of God, and the light will be like a jasper stone, clear as crystal; the wall will be made from jasper, and the city will incorporate pure gold that is as clear as glass; there will be no temple, as the Lord God Almighty and the Lamb are the temple of the city; there will be no sun or moon because the glory of God and the Lamb will be the light; and there will be no night there, and the nations of the saved will walk in the light of the city (Revelation 21). Jesus is the root and offspring of David, and the bright and morning star (Revelation 22). Praise be to Yeshua, the Messiah and the Rock of Salvation. *Maranatha!*

AFTERWORD: HOW TO SPOT A MORTAL ENEMY

Those who are enthralled with the ways of the world are shocked and amazed that some still believe in the Way of Jesus, indeed the ways of the Way, the Truth, and the Life. I place the turning point in the United States' trajectory at the point when the pot-smoking, sexually promiscuous hippies exploded onto the scene in the early Sixties. That open-minded mob was open to just about anything except Biblical Christianity, and the unrepentant among them have passed on their love of sin to their own children and their children's children.

Strangely enough, my own life has given me a wide-spectrum view of the hippies' doings. Conceived in 1961 and born in 1962, my path has been right alongside the hipsters who, by definition, are "familiar with the latest trends and styles." But one must admit that it's rather strange that a major upheaval in American culture would be spearheaded by those familiar with new trends and styles—that's circular, saying only that the new trends would be spearheaded by those familiar with new trends! My point is that their naming was vacuous;

> If people don't call things what they really are, then whatever ill effects are borne by those things will go unchallenged. This is not an arcane linguistic point, but rather it is to say that much of revolution has to do with re-naming society-changing events, movements, and groups in such a way that normally unacceptable things are slipped in under the cloak of prettified names.

more to the point, they were a mass movement of fornication and rebellion against the Christian bulwark of the society of the time. The empty-name (or essentially unnamed) "hippies" revolutionized America under the cover of nothingness, in much the same way that the Obama supporters got sucked into another empty chant: "hope and change." Hope in what, and change to what? Hope in more entangling alliances with foreign dictatorships (Communist China, Saudi Arabia, etc.), and change through terrorism staged by dark banker-traitors? What are the real meanings of "Pearl Harbor," the "Gulf of Tonkin," and "9-11?"

If people don't call things what they really are, then whatever ill effects are borne by those things will go unchallenged. This is not an arcane linguistic point, but rather it is to say that much of revolution has to do with renaming society-changing events, movements, and groups in such a way that normally unacceptable things are slipped in under the cloak of prettified names. In effect, people are bamboozled by linguistic sleight of hand and rendered almost impotent in the face of enemy onslaughts.

I would view the trend-familiar hippies as self-absorbed, country-loathing youths who were conspicuous for their lack of knowledge. Through them the warning of Hosea 4 shimmers with urgent relevancy:

> Hear the word of the LORD, ye children of Israel: for the LORD hath a controversy with the inhabitants of the land, because *there is* no truth, nor mercy, nor knowledge of God in the land. By swearing, and lying, and killing, and stealing, and committing adultery, they break out, and blood toucheth blood. Therefore shall the land mourn, and every one that dwelleth therein shall languish, with the beasts of the field, and with the fowls of heaven; yea, the fishes of the sea also shall be taken away. ... My people are destroyed for lack of knowledge: because thou hast rejected knowledge, I will also reject thee, that thou shalt be no priest to me: seeing thou hast forgotten the law of thy God, I will also forget thy children. (Hosea 4:1–3, 6 KJV)

It turns out that knowledge is exceedingly important, and the lack of same is very dangerous.

Testing the Spirits

What exactly is the danger of lacking knowledge? How is it that a people could be destroyed for lacking knowledge? A people who ignore God will be given over to their evil devices (Romans 1), and without God's protection they are liable to walk into the jaws of their enemies: "Ephraim ... *is* planted in a pleasant place: but Ephraim shall bring forth his children to the murderer" (Hosea 8:13 KJV). Could there actually be a commune on the horizon that hates the United States and fantasizes about slaughtering our people?

There is one country that stands out for its predatory actions against America as well as its duplicity and coldness towards our people and against our Judeo-Christian heritage: Maoist China. The numbers of recent Chinese immigrants in the United States are shocking, given that their Buddhist-Taoist-Confucian-atheist society is really very strange to the West's tradition of Judeo-Christian principles and institutions. Could Communist China be like a strange woman in our midst (Proverbs 2), seducing our people away from our roots and slyly grabbing our means of production (manufacturing), wealth, and power? If one swallows the Communist trick of renaming things so that what is evil appears good, then China looks very exotic and exciting.

But if one takes the time to analyze its actual traits, then China shows itself to be a mortal enemy that covets America like a bully that cannot share. It comes down to having genuine, godly knowledge about factors touching on US national security. One cannot discern the real face of Communist China unless one knows something about American and Chinese history and is willing to analyze recent and current events through the prism of Bible knowledge.

Richard Nixon, Henry Kissinger, and others delivered Americans into the clutches of Maoist negotiators, playing on the assumption that we have to rehabilitate the Communists by drawing them into the family of nations. Secretaries of State have positively fawned all over Communist China. It's practically a slobber-fest. There was lots of money to be made

> Why not just sway to the strains of Peking Opera, practice mahjong, and watch Chinese movies? Why not giggle over Jackie Chan, gobble up potstickers, and plaster our walls with panda and dragon posters?

by certain transnational tycoons and their sell-out lieutenants in the short term, and there was a chance to pull America sharply to the left; but in the long term, the price of appeasing a mortal enemy is inestimable. So a most strange union began. A strange woman was in our midst (Proverbs 2). She could not have been ushered in were it not for our inept leaders' lack of godly knowledge and our people's spiritual whoredom.

Why not just sway to the strains of Peking Opera, practice mahjong, and study Mao's "poetry"? Why not giggle over Jackie Chan, gobble up potstickers, and plaster our walls with panda and dragon posters? As for me, having grown up in Mount Shasta, Santa Rosa, Davis, and Berkeley (California towns), I witnessed just enough of our fading Judeo-Christian heritage to know that the atheistic, mercenary style of Peking's Communist dictators is a strange match-up indeed (Proverbs 2).

My family used to go to Russ's Chevron on South Mount Shasta Boulevard, back when there was a Kimberly-Clark sawmill in town and logging trucks and lumbermen were everywhere. Russ was a manly, good-natured fellow and there was a sense of kinship. Our people had not yet been divided by the diversity weapon, and we had a cultural center of mass. Foreign gods had not yet invaded en masse, sodomy was still scorned, women wore dresses, and the churches were full. Nowadays, one is just as likely to pull in, talk to someone who barely speaks Engish, and get a full tank of diversity without a smile.

In marriage, we are called on to be equally yoked, and in national affairs, we also should strive for suitable allies and true friendships—not empty homilies that hide disaster. It appears to me that anti-American, anti-Christian globalists burrowed their way into the American halls of power and took advantage of domestic social upheavals, slipping a bad pill of Communist treachery into our drinks when we weren't looking (ie, when we were being entertained by a witch's brew, a.k.a. a piece of Holly Wood).

But how could we have continued to avoid looking at the obvious—the obvious idea that China is America's enemy—for so many decades? We've been taught pro-Asian hype in our schools, propagandized, and duped. The mechanism is the same here in the United States as it was in Hitler's Germany—make a lie big enough and people won't dare to believe that the potential danger could actuate, because the explosion of a previously winked-at danger would prove that the people had been duped.

I see our national security system as being weak—too many agencies and almost no common sense. Government managers are often left-leaning shills, completely beholden to political, ethnic, and sexual diversity and dedicated to the expansion of false gods and false idols. Diversity-educated, lacking in nationalism, and without a strong Biblical foundation, many national security advisors find themselves unable to call an enemy enemy. The motto of Western defense organs should be, "Ever learning, and never able to come to the knowledge of the truth" (2 Tim. 3:7 KJV). Information does not equal knowledge, but rather, "The fear of the LORD is the beginning of knowledge" (Prov. 1:7a KJV).

I worked as an analyst near Baltimore, Maryland, for most of ten years and feel less secure now after having been in close proximity to the center of American policy making. But why even mention this? This is negative information, capable of rankling a person whose habit is to ignore national defense and not in keeping with the emotional highs of football games, hoops, movie-opening galas, and dumb-down pop music. I believe that many Americans, due to their decreasing levels of Bible knowledge, have begun to view history as linear, thinking that we have collectively gone through the tough wars, and our land is safe from here on out.

I have the opposite view. I think that some processes are cyclical—specifically, the cycle of a people from believing in Jesus and blessed; to fat, smug, and spiritually "diverse" (prostituted); and finally, to rampant unbelief and consequent judgment. The Bible is full of these lessons.

I lament that our precious land is under direct and immediate military threat from the Roman Catholic generals (Jesuit secret societies); Russian and Chinese Communists; insidious, occultic banker-traitors; and Islamic killers (Zechariah 6 and Revelation 6). It appears that these four groups have slinked their way to the top of Western governments. We would do well to make plans to protect ourselves from these enemies, keeping in mind that our strength comes from a saving relationship with the Lord Jesus Christ.

Statue in the People's Park of Shenyang, honoring Mao supporters who fought against Chiang Kai-shek's KMT forces in the 1940s. Statues of people violate the Second Commandment; moreover, it's better to be anti-Mao.

If "Protestant" Christians are still "protesting" the errors of the papacy and Catholic-led paganism, then such Protestants must stand up and exert their influence before it is too late. If it's correct that we're more vulnerable now than at any point in our nation's history, then warnings are more needed now than ever. Jefferson had a copy of the Muslim book to figure out who the Barbary pirates were; likewise, Americans should study their enemies. If you love your family, know your enemy (so as to hold him off). If I could turn to Ezekiel 3 to make the point:

> [T]he word of the LORD came unto me, saying, Son of man, I have made thee a watchman unto the house of Israel: therefore hear the word at my mouth, and give them warning from me. When I say unto the wicked, Thou shalt surely die; and thou givest him not warning, nor speakest to warn the wicked from his wicked way, to save his life; the same wicked *man* shall die in his iniquity; but his blood will I require at thine hand. Yet if thou warn the wicked, and he turn not from his wickedness, nor from his wicked way, he shall die in his iniquity; but thou hast delivered thy soul. (Ezek. 3:16b–19 KJV)

When the Lord is speaking judgment against a people, that judgment should be articulated through His watchmen on the wall. It is possible to warn the wicked from his wicked way in order to save his life. By issuing the warning, the warning party has delivered his soul.

I am begging my countrymen (God-fearing Americans) to avoid certain false paths: moral relativism, evolution, uniformitarianism, the New Age, humanistic psychotherapy, interfaithism (or ecumenism), the demonic one-world religion, and the godless one-world bestial government. The American people must stand in the Biblical faith, the faith of our fathers, and oppose the ungodly incursions of the Roman Catholic generals; the Russian, Chinese, and other Communists; the occultic, globalist banker-traitors; the Islamic killers; and all anti-Israel parties. "Woe unto them that call evil good, and good evil; that put darkness for light, and light for darkness; that put bitter for sweet, and sweet for bitter!" (Is. 5:20 KJV).

As a veteran of three Chinese literature programs, I would recommend to concerned Americans the following reading materials about Communist China: the *Communist Manifesto;* Sun Tzu's *The Art of War; Outlaws of the Marsh* (a Ming-dynasty classic about trickery and fighting strategy); and any white papers written by Chinese Communist generals. Skip the wordplay of Chinese diplomats. Try anything written by Chen Yonglin— the political consul at the Chinese consulate in Sydney, Australia, who defected to Australia in 2005, claiming that there were 1,000 Chinese spies (special agents and informants) in Australia; anything by "Han Guangsheng," another defector who reportedly was in charge of Shenyang's public security and labor camps; or anything by Hao Fengjun, a former member of the 6-10 Office which is tasked with eradicating the Falun Gong group.

By playing defense (and being diffident spectators), American Christians have allowed the conversation to be about whether to take down a Christian cross at Ground Zero in Manhattan; if Christians were to be assertive, as they should, the conversation should be about how to go about safely dismantling the Egyptian obelisk that is the so-called "Washington Monument" (more linguistic dumbing down) and other pagan statuary that mock this nation's founding. Remember the lesson of the diligent and faithful King Hezekiah: he rid his land of many false idols and his land was blessed as a result.

The First and Second Commandments should persuade us that religious diversity, pagan statues, and statues of men should all be repudiated with a view towards honoring the God of Israel and preserving the beautiful Judeo-Christian heritage that was America's:

> I am the LORD your God, who brought you out of the land of Egypt, out of the house of slavery. You shall have no other gods before Me. You shall not make for yourself an idol, or any likeness of what is in heaven above or on the earth beneath or in the water under the earth. You shall not worship them or serve them; for I, the LORD your God, am a jealous God, visiting the iniquity of the fathers on the

children, on the third and the fourth generations of those who hate Me, but showing lovingkindness to thousands, to those who love Me and keep My commandments." (Ex. 20:2–6 NASB)

America should be devoid of statuary that are in the likeness of men! Men walk on the earth, and we are commanded by the God of Israel not to make for ourselves idols or likenesses of what is on the earth! Washington walked the earth, as did Lincoln, Jefferson, and Martin Luther King Jr.; therefore we are commanded to have no idols or likenesses of them! Based on the clear words of the Second Commandment, those who make idols or likenesses of men are opening the door to the worship of men!

In my opinion, the most audacious and Communistic of all statues in the nation is that of King. Its sheer size and the ruthlessness of the statue's aspect is akin to Communist statues around the world. Social revolutionaries have taken a need for some ethnic integration and, with the unveiling of the hideous King statue, segued into the wholesale worship of social and religious diversity. Remember, after King, the "diversity people" took down the Lincoln and Washington holidays, minimizing our Judeo-Christian heritage and making way for Communist social-reorganizing in one fell swoop. Whatever King stood for, his stony likeness is now a stamp of victory for the any-god-will-do Trojan horse of humanism and valueless diversity that has brought America to its knees—indeed, a stamp of victory for the embrace that smothers.

American TV, film, radio, and print media should be devoid of blasphemy; therefore there should be a ban on products that take the Lord's name in vain, out of respect for the Third Commandment. The matter of resting from our labors and worshipping on the seventh-day Sabbath should be rediscovered, out of respect for the Fourth Commandment; and, of course, the sacredness of the other six commandments should be taught across the land so that our people can rediscover the spiritual vibrancy that our forefathers, the Pilgrims and the Puritans, knew.

Let us push off (or extract) our enemies and reestablish the pillars of our goodly Judeo-Christian heritage. Let us require that foreign powers treat the brethren and the Jews well as a precondition for "intercourse" (in the old sense of the word) with us. Additionally, let us consult the Amish, Mennonites, and other distinctly American Christian groups on all matters of trade, national security, and faith.

POSTSCRIPT: FAILED DIVERSITY POLICIES

Diversity training has been a net loss for the United States. The government, companies, schools, and other public institutions all practice open-minded mushiness to the point where the tail is wagging the dog. Statistically, most Americans are still at least professing Christians, yet they find themselves shoved around by small groups that often take glee in parading sexual perversion, anti-Christian blasphemy, "intercourse" with dictators and other Communists, and political and military treason in the name of false unity (in conjunction with the very anti-Jewish United Nations). Anyone who has tried to yank a dog by the tail knows that the dog will snap, so why haven't American Christians snapped back at the insipid distorters of American freedom?

When it comes to protecting the Judeo-Christian heritage of the United States of America, the fix has been in for many decades now. The message to false churches and enemy governments is abundantly clear: bring in your Trojan horses and do your worst. The flattering and honey-oozing words of diversity policy have seduced our once-discerning people, and now we pride ourselves in being all things to all people and being easily shaped by globalist banker-traitors and anti-Christian tyrants.

From the godly instruction of Proverbs 2, we know that, as a country, we should avoid the strange woman, the flattering adulteress who left the companion of her youth and forgot the covenant of her God. Most analysts would stop right there, making no tangible conclusions in light of recent political, economic, and military developments, yet how can we avoid the strange woman if we can't identify her? *We must identify her.*

Lest we forget where we came from as a people. This beautiful Amish girl prays to the God of the Bible; she is worth protecting. "Truly I say to you, whoever does not receive the kingdom of God like a child will not enter it *at all*" (Mark 10:15 NASB). America's free-trade appeasement of Communists and diversity-driven spiritual whoredom: are they good for this beautiful girl's future?

Something little known is that China began with men and women who were well acquainted with the God of the Bible. The very orthography, or writing system, of Chinese incorporates clues of very Biblical themes. For instance, the character for boat, *chuan,* is composed of components that mean "eight," "mouth" (actually the measure word *kou,* which comes to connote "person"), and another word for boat, *zhou.* In effect, the word *chuan* for boat means "eight people on a boat"! That's an obvious reference to the Noahic Flood and Noah's family of eight that took mankind from the pre-flood era to the post-flood era on the most famous boat of all time.

Another character, *zao,* meaning "to create," contains components that mean "dust," "mouth" (or "breath"), and "to walk." That's an obvious reference to the creation of Adam, who was created from dust, given breath, and then walked: "Then the LORD God formed man of dust from the ground, and breathed into his nostrils the breath of life; and man became a living being" (Gen. 2:7 NASB).

Those people who were dispersed from the Tower of Babel and went to the area of the Yellow River Valley in present-day China would have carried with them a thorough knowledge of the power of the living God who judged evil mankind with a flood, saved a family of eight to continue the race of men, and judged men again for idolatry at the Tower of Babel, scattering them around the world in various linguistic groups. In effect, American Christians have kindred spirits in the earliest of Chinese as well as the good and decent Chinese brethren who ache presently under Communist oppression and persecution.

According to the October 10, 2011, Congressional-Executive Commission on China, "China's constitution guarantees 'freedom of religious belief,' but the government and Party continued to promote 'theological reconstruction', the process by which the state-controlled church attempts to eliminate elements of the Christian faith that do not conform to Party goals and ideology."

What does that mean for the seventy to one hundred million unregistered Protestants in China? For Chinese House Church Alliance Vice President Shi Enhao, it meant being detained on June 21, 2011 on suspicion of "using superstition to undermine the implementation of the law." Shi was ordered to serve two years of reeducation through labor *(laogai)*. Unregistered Protestants are often put under soft detention *(ruanjin)* (ie, home confinement) and are prevented from accessing their worship sites.

It's probably worth noting that the millions of unregistered Protestants in Communist China presently are about the same number as those killed or otherwise slaughtered in the Great Leap Forward and the Cultural Revolution. Is there a message there? God will have His remnant of believers—the bad men can cut men down, but God will have His Christian soldiers, His angels, and His sovereignty. Praise the God of Enoch and Elijah! Praise the risen Lord Jesus!

The anti-Christian Chinese Communists are rapacious and unscrupulous and should be opposed at every turn. Trading with them, having military-to-military patty-cake visits with them, and teaching tens of thousands of their students our computer arts (so many of them can turn around and stick us in the back with strategic hacking) is a disgrace to America's once godly heritage. Nikita Khrushchev said, "When it comes time for us to hang you, your capitalist will sell us the rope." It looks like the Communists could strike us with computer sabotage using techniques that we taught them and bomb us with quiet subs using technology we sold them.

It is my considered opinion that to the extent that China has for much of its history been a largely Buddhist, Taoist, and Confucian nation, it has in effect been a nation that "left the companion of its youth and forgot the covenant of its God" (a la Prov. 2:17). China's religious diversity is like a plague, and when she touches other countries, she can drag them down. For this reason, I believe America's forging of political and economic ties with Communist China (soon after the horrendous mass slaughters of the Great Leap Forward and the Cultural Revolution) was tantamount to fornicating with an adulteress, spiritually speaking—a mistake of devastating proportions and one that probably was orchestrated by Communist-sympathizing American traitors.

Needless to say, America's flirtation with literal fornication (sex, drugs, and rock-and-roll) in the fifties and sixties formed the background for the spiritual fornication of the Mao-Nixon handshake in the seventies. The result of the Mao-Nixon love-in, according to Prov. 2:16–19a, would be that the flattering adulteress (Mao nation) would sink down to death, going to the dead, and also taking her "lovers" to their deaths. That's a spiritual analysis of a macrorelationship between two giant countries; fortunately, there will be many saved followers of Jesus in both countries who resist the evil forces of false teachings, political oppression, and brutality. Similarly, I believe the Gorbachev-Reagan handshake was horrendous, and that Communists are the avowed enemies of free, Christian people everywhere.

The Martin Luther King, Jr, statue has all the earmarks of a Communist idol; it has the same raw look of impish arrogance that the personality-worship idols have in Communist countries. Upon inspection, the picture gets even uglier. Referring to the statue, Paul Ibbetson, in his article "Through Greed and Communism the Dream Is Lost," noted that "people on the National Mall will now view a Marxian mountain that is too arrogant and more fitting [of] a Communist bloc."

A Marxian mountain in the middle of America's capital—that really captures the nub of the problem because America is not a Communist country, right? If there are still any naysayers, there shouldn't be: the Marxian idol was sculpted out of Chinese granite by a Chinese sculptor who is well known for his sculptures of mass murderer Mao and, wouldn't you know it, King's face was given narrow eyes to make it look Chinese. Just as the Washington Monument honors the false gods Baal and Ashteroth, having nothing to do with Washington, so too the King Marxian mountain has little to do with King's civil rights and everything to do with community organizing, reeducation-through-labor *(laogai)* camps, and unspeakable Communist horror. Mark it down: this Communist horror went up on Obama's watch, consistent with his campaign helper, anarchist Bill Ayers, his many Communist-style czars, and his love of reorganizing communities.

The King Marxian idol is nothing short of a victory stamp for the Communist Party of America, the Communist Party of China, Communist countries around the world, and America's own despicable banker-traitors. It should be sent back to Changsha, Hunan, on the steamer that it came in on—and we should bill the Chinese for troubling us with their infiltration. And to think that we let them lecture us on how to not interfere in another country's internal politics! Isn't anybody minding the store?

The Marxian mountain ruse by the Communist Chinese harkens back to a time when French Jesuit secret-society persons conspired to have a similarly insipid stone goddess delivered to the fledgling United States, calling it the Statue of Liberty. The Jesuit and Communist infiltration-by-statue trick typically involves a wolf in sheep's clothing: therefore, the false and anti-Christian goddess (wolf) is dressed up in wafty notions of liberty (sheep's clothing); the Egyptian phallus fetish (wolf) is wrapped in the august reputation of America's first president (sheep's clothing); and the Chinese Communists' granite-clacking harbinger of war (wolf) is wrapped in the unimpeachable motives of racial justice (sheep's clothing).

What's a little dark statue humor between friends? That's exactly the point: real friends don't give dark, evil gifts. Designed and built by French Freemasons Auguste Bartholdi and Gustave Eiffel, respectively, the Statue of Liberty was originally intended to go to Egypt to mark the opening of the Suez Canal in 1867; that is why the statue is in the likeness of the Egyptian goddess Isis.

The King statue recalls dictator Hu Jintao's strange gifting of President Bush (Jr) with a copy of Sun Tzu's *The Art of War* in 2006, which I believe was another war declaration. The symbolism of *The Art of War* and a huge rock of a "Sino-fied" American seems to say that what is American will soon be Chinese (ie, seized by China). By the way, how is the Chinese Communists' urgent quest for racial justice going in the Uighur town of Urumqi, Xinjiang, or in the Tibetan town of Lhasa or in the many African countries whose resources the Chinese are raping? Americans should not sell their coal to the Chinese, and Albertans should not sell their tar-sands to the Chinese. We should not put our resources up for sale to the enemy. Trade with real allies. (Note to self: Maybe the infiltrators figured that if they called their elaborately crafted conditioning tools the Statue of False-Goddess Treachery, the Sexually Perverted Ashteroth Pole Designed to Stain the New Christian Republic, and the Long-Kill Maoist Hammer from Changsha, then the good people of America might catch on to their evil designs.)

Coal cars waiting for transport in Kentucky. Let us show some appreciation for our Christian founding fathers, fighting men and women, coal miners, and trainmen. Let us trade with real allies, not with Communists or anti-Semitic regimes.

As Christians, we must remember that we are in a spiritual fight against spiritual forces of evil: "Put on the full armor of God, so that you will be able to stand firm against the schemes of the devil. For our struggle is not against flesh and blood, but against the rulers, against the powers, against the world forces of this darkness, against the spiritual *forces* of wickedness in the heavenly *places*" (Eph. 6:11–12 NASB).

Reagan's dictum of "trust but verify" has been much ballyhooed but, in my estimation, it is wrongheaded—the dictum should have been verify and proceed with baby steps in areas that have no bearing on national or economic security, and then if the foreigners have disavowed their anti-Jewish or anti-Western screeds (such as the *Palestinian Charter,* the *Communist Manifesto,* or Stalinist or Maoist writings), engage them in somewhat more substantial areas that still have no bearing on US national or economic security. Trust but verify is a fool's journey into diversity-based muddle-headedness and a subtle rationalization for America's selling out to dictatorships.

In regard to the Statue of Liberty, the Washington Monument, and the King Stone of Hope, Americans have trusted without verifying. Basically, Americans have been brainwashed. Amazingly, the Chinese Communists are so confident that we are incapable of waking up, that they even added a Mountain of Despair to the Stone of Hope. A mountain is much bigger than a stone, so in fact, the Communists are saying, "Enjoy your short-lived hope because we have a mountain of despair, our specialty, that's about to smash you on the head." **Let us act on the warning to the church in Sardis: "Wake up, and strengthen the things that remain, which were about to die; for I have not found your deeds completed in the sight of My God. So remember what you have received and heard; and keep *it,* and repent. Therefore if you do not wake up, I will come like a thief, and you will not know at what hour I will come to you" (Rev. 3:2–3 NASB).** [Bold type mine]

The good news is that Jesus saves, and believers can cling to the Rock of Salvation, Jesus Christ. The Communists' kingdom will not endure forever, but Jesus' kingdom will:

> In the days of those kings the God of heaven will set up a kingdom which will never be destroyed, and *that*

kingdom will not be left for another people; it will crush and put an end to all these kingdoms, but it will itself endure forever. Inasmuch as you saw that a stone was cut out of the mountain without hands and that it crushed the iron, the bronze, the clay, the silver and the gold, the great God has made known to the king what will take place in the future; so the dream is true and its interpretation is trustworthy. (Dan. 2:44–45 NASB) [Author's Note: The great God destroys the statue of the man depicted in Daniel 2—that's the Second Commandment in action.]

What is discernment if we can't even figure out who our friends are and who are enemies are? It's important to use godly knowledge, wisdom, and discretion and not get lured into bad trade deals and the indirect funding of the largest Communist army in the world. That's pretty simple, yet our "diversified" leaders chant empty homilies about how it's not dangerous appeasement but rather some ineffable "bringing the rogue into the family of nations." Balderdash! The US-Communist relationship is appeasement of tyrants on a massive scale; it is spiritual fornication and a slap in the face to the spirit of freedom that engineered the Declaration of Independence and the US Constitution; and it is dragging America down exactly as per the warning of Proverbs 2 (avoid the strange woman). The Chinese Communist tyrants put on Western suits and fooled an unsuspecting world (see *Outlaws of the Marsh,* the Ming-dynasty warfare classic); the occultic banker-traitors have mocked the living God with their blasphemous statues for too long, and plot the ruin of this nation through a series of staged attacks that will lead to prefabricated authoritarian solutions (more and more departments and agencies to "watch and protect" us); the Jesuit secret societies plot against the true brethren; the jihadists kill; and the United Nations are largely united against America and Israel.

America should replace the diversity training program with a Bible-training program for government employees, corporate employees, and students. Therewith, the Bible-centered legal structure that informed the work of the first Supreme Court Justice, John Jay, and which was still in place well into the 1900s, could be given its original preferred place. Then we could interpret laws based on the original meaning of the US

Constitution; sever ties with our enemies; safely dismantle the mass of anti-Christian (pagan) idols that litter our land; reinstill godly instruction in our schools (including homemaking and sex ed, Bible style); take unbiblical, pagan influences (interfaithism) out of our government, military, and schools; strengthen our military; and put all US ports under exclusive US control (including Long Beach).

APPENDIX: ANATOMY OF APPEASEMENT

God is not a respecter of persons, because He is God and His ways are higher than our ways. Therefore, as we go about shaping a government and a society, we should follow God's ways and not the humanistic personality-worship that is the hallmark of Communism and humanism:

> Peter opened *his* mouth, and said, Of a truth I perceive that God is no respecter of persons: But in every nation he that feareth him, and worketh righteousness, is accepted with him. ... How God anointed Jesus of Nazareth with the Holy Ghost and with power: who went about doing good, and healing all that were oppressed of the devil; for God was with him ... whom they slew and hanged on a tree: Him God raised up the third day, and shewed him openly; not to all the people, but unto witnesses chosen before of God, *even* to us, who did eat and drink with him after he rose from the dead. And he commanded us to preach unto the people, and to testify that it is he which was ordained of God *to be* the Judge of quick and dead. To him give all the prophets witness, that through his name whosoever believeth in him shall receive remission of sins. While Peter yet spake these words, the Holy Ghost

fell on all them which heard the word. (Acts 10:34–35, 38, 39b–44 KJV)

If God is not a respecter of persons, then doesn't that imply we should favor rule of law over rule by personality cult? Americans should follow the Lord Jesus Christ who rose from the dead on the third day, not evil-doer Mao Tse-tung. Of a truth, "A man of violence entices his neighbor, and leads him in a way that is not good" (Prov. 16:29 NASB). Just as the beguiling strange woman of Proverbs 2, the horrendously violent Chinese Communists are bad for America.

- January 1, 1979 — The United States commenced normal diplomatic relations with China.
- 1980 — Deng Xiaoping initiated economic reforms.
- After the June 4, 1989, Tian'anmen Square Massacre, Bush Sr sent Brent Scowcroft and Lawrence Eagleburger on secret missions to Peking to reassure the Communists that the United States would maintain ties. (Author's Note: Why all the secrecy for the Scowcroft/Eagleburger missions? Wasn't everything on the up and up? Were mission planners self-conscious about the possibility that the missions may be construed as a betrayal of America's Constitutional heritage, a coddling of abject dictators?)
- 1991 — China joined the Asia-Pacific Economic Cooperation (APEC). Also, Bush Sr met with Premier Li Peng at a United Nations conference.
- October 1, 1992 — Clinton says, "I do believe our nation has a higher purpose than to coddle dictators."
- September/October 1993 — According to the April 13, 1998, *New York Times*, Hughes Electronics CEO Michael Armstrong wrote Clinton letters in the fall of 1993 complaining that sanctions were damaging his company.
- November 12, 1993 — Clinton grants Hughes and Martin-Marietta waivers to launch US satellites from Chinese rockets.
- November 18, 1993 — Clinton permits the sale of an $8 million supercomputer to China.

- November 19, 1993 — Chinese leader Jiang Zemin meets Clinton at an APEC meeting in Seattle. Clinton says, "I think anybody should be reluctant to isolate a country as big as China with the potential China has for good." (Author's Note: Given China's appetite for stability through mass slaughter, maybe a better analysis would be, "I think anybody should be willing to isolate a country as big as China, given the tendency China has for evil." Matt. 15:19 applies to Chinese as well: "For out of the heart come evil thoughts, murders, adulteries, fornications, thefts, false witness, slanders" [NASB]. Trust but verify was wrong, the dictum of an actor; in real life, it should be "Verify, and extend feelers until it can be determined if there is any cause to trust at any level and regarding any sector.")
- January 1994 — The United States resumes financing for the United Nations Population Fund (UNFPA), which funds China's coercive abortion program (population control).
- May 3, 1994 — Clinton says, "I do not seek, nor would it be proper, for the United States or any other nation to tell a great nation like China how to conduct all its internal affairs." (Author's Note: Why should China be accorded "great" status when dishonesty and brutality are two of its favorite calling cards? Why shouldn't Americans demand that all their trade partners have integrity? China is not qualified to lecture anybody about the merits of not interfering in another country's internal affairs. Do American presidents kowtow more when a foreign country has all the earmarks of a dictatorship?)
- June 2, 1994 — Clinton says he will no longer link trade with human rights in evaluating China's Most Favored Nation (MFN) status.
- October 7, 1994 — China conducts an underground nuclear test.
- March 6, 1995 — Johnny Chung receives a $150,000 wire transfer from the Bank of China. Chung admitted to

funneling funds from the Chinese Army to the Democratic Party, according to *The New York Times*.
- March 9, 1995 — Chung brings $50,000 check to Mrs. Clinton's office, made out to the DNC. (Author's Note: Peking must be experiencing some confusion. The Chinese worked to interfere in an American presidential election as a warm-up to their interference in Taiwan's presidential elections a year later. How on earth can Peking lecture anybody on the importance of not interfering in another country's internal affairs?)
- May 15, 1995 — China conducts an underground nuclear test.
- August 17, 1995 — China conducts an underground nuclear test. (Author's Note: Feel the power.)
- August 25, 1995 — Clinton announces that Mrs. Clinton will go to China to attend a UN Conference on Women.
- September 1995 — Clinton pushes for the leasing of the Long Beach Naval Station to COSCO, a Chinese state-owned enterprise (SOE).
- October 9, 1995 — According to the May 17, 1998, *New York Times*, Secretary of State Warren Christopher noted in a classified memo that lifting export restrictions (on commercial satellites) would "raise suspicions that we are trying to evade China sanctions." (Author's Note: Could there be a mole in the soup?)
- May 10, 1996 — Loral-led review commission gave China its report on a rocket explosion, which contained "sensitive aspects of the rocket's guidance and control systems," according to the April 13, 1998, *New York Times*.
- According to "How Boeing Woos Beijing," in the May 26, 1996, *Seattle Times*, US plane maker McDonnell Douglas sold "five axis" tooling technology to China on the agreement it would be sent to a nonmilitary factory in Beijing, but the Chinese broke their pledge and sent the tooling machines to Nanchang, a major center for missile programs. (Author's Note: McDonnell Douglas' selling of vital missile-related

Testing the Spirits

technology to Communist China was misguided. National security should never be compromised for a dollar.)
- June 8, 1996 — China conducts an underground nuclear test.
- 1996 – China conducted military exercises and ballistic missile tests in the Taiwan Strait as a protest over Taiwan's presidential elections.
- March 25, 1997 — Gore signed for Boeing's $685 million sale of jetliners to China and for a $1.3 billion joint venture between General Motors and China's state-owned Shanghai Automotive Industry Corp.
- 1998 — Clinton visited China to reassure Jiang Zemin that the United States opposed Taiwanese independence and Taiwan's membership in international organizations as a state.
- 2000 — Clinton granted China permanent normal trade relations. (Author's Note: China smells our weakness. If a nuclear bomb goes off underground, does it make a sound?)
- April 1–11, 2001 — American EP-3 intelligence plane likely forced down on Hainan Island, China. The 11-day crisis was described by Congressman Tom DeLay as "Communist piracy." Bush Jr sent condolence letter to widow of the Chinese fighter pilot who apparently perished as a result of the mid-air crash. (Author's Note: Shouldn't the US president be sending letters of recognition to the US servicemen, not to the family of one who caused the American plane to make an emergency landing? Why would the US apologize for China's treachery?)
- October 2001 — Bush Jr attended the APEC conference in Shanghai (meeting Jiang Zemin), just weeks after the September 11 attacks against the United States.
- December 11, 2001 — China granted admission to the World Trade Organization (WTO). Taiwan was granted admission to the WTO as Chinese Taipei on Jan. 1, 2002.
- February 2002 — Bush Jr visited China (Jiang).

- October 2002 — Bush Jr received Jiang in Crawford, Texas, during the general time frame of the APEC conference in Mexico.
- June 2003 — Bush Jr met Hu Jintao at G-8 meeting in Evian.
- October 2003 — Bush Jr met Hu prior to APEC meeting in Bangkok, assuring Hu the United States would continue to oppose independence for Taiwan. (Author's Note: If Bush Jr was against independence for Taiwan, was he for independence for America? It's a fair question because the back of the dollar bill is full of independence-slaying technology, but instead of reining in the Federal Reserve, he expanded the Fed's financial reign. I would have thought that the president of an independent nation would feel a kinship with the Taiwanese, relating to their struggle for independence.)
- December 2003 — Bush Jr received Wen Jiabao in Washington.
- November 2005 — Bush Jr visited Hu and Wen in Peking and pushed for the spread of democracy and universal human rights and freedoms. (Author Note: So-called human rights are not the same as the liberties derived from the Bible's Ten Commandments. The right of women to slaughter their babies, as per the pro-abortion UNFPA, is consistent with the abhorrent Molech worship from the Old Testament but inconsistent with the Ten Commandments. The Ten Commandments are higher than the United Nations; the Holy Bible should still be our guide in spite of the gobbledygook coming out of the frightful United Nations.)
- August 2005 — Secretary of State Robert Zoellick visited Peking to initiate a US-China senior dialogue in which the two countries would take turns hosting discussions on global issues.
- December 2005 — Zoellick received Vice Foreign Minister Dai Bingguo as part of a process of "advanc[ing] **security and peace** around the world."

- January 1, 2009 — On the 30th anniversary of US-China diplomatic relations, Bush Jr indicated, "We have worked as global leaders to promote open markets as the best way to foster economic dynamism and development. It is my hope that ... our governments will ... advance the causes of **peace, stability,** and development."

For you yourselves know full well that the day of the Lord will come just like a thief in the night. **While they are saying, 'Peace and safety!' then destruction will come upon them suddenly like labor pains upon a woman with child, and they will not escape.** But you, brethren, are not in darkness, that the day would overtake you like a thief; for you are all sons of light and sons of day. We are not of night nor of darkness; so then let us not sleep as others do, but let us be alert and sober. ... For God has not destined us for wrath, but for obtaining salvation through our Lord Jesus Christ, who died for us, so that whether we are awake or asleep, we will live together with Him. Therefore encourage one another and build up one another. ... Do not quench the Spirit; do not despise prophetic utterances. But examine everything carefully; hold fast to that which is good; abstain from every form of evil. (1 Thess. 5:2–6, 9–11a, 19–21 NASB)

For the mystery of lawlessness is already at work; only he who now restrains *will do so* until he is taken out of the way. **Then that lawless one will be revealed whom the Lord will slay with the breath of His coming;** *that is,* **the one whose coming is in accord with the activity of Satan, with all power and signs and false wonders, and with all the deception of wickedness for those who perish, because they did not receive the love of the truth so as to be saved.** For this reason God will send upon them a deluding influence so that they will believe what is false, in order that they all may be judged who did not believe the truth, but took pleasure in wickedness. … **So then, brethren, stand firm and hold to the traditions which you were taught"** (2 Thess. 2:7–12, 15b NASB). [Bold type mine]

- April 2006 — Hu was received in Washington state, **toured Boeing and Microsoft facilities, and dined at the home of Bill Gates.**

At that time Berodach-baladan a son of Baladan, king of Babylon, sent letters and a present to Hezekiah, for he heard that Hezekiah had been sick. Hezekiah listened to them, and **showed them all his treasure house, the silver and the gold and the spices and the precious oil and the house of his armor and all that was found in his treasuries. There was nothing in his house nor in all his dominion that Hezekiah did not show them.**

Then Isaiah the prophet came to King Hezekiah and said to him, "What did these men say, and from where have they come to you?" And Hezekiah said, "They have come from a far country, from Babylon." He said, "What have they seen in your house?" So Hezekiah answered, "They have seen all that is in my house; there is nothing among my treasuries that I have not shown them."

Then Isaiah said to Hezekiah, 'Hear the word of the Lord. "Behold, the days are coming when all that is in your house, and all that your fathers have laid up in store to this day will be carried to Babylon; nothing shall be left," says the Lord. "Some of your sons who shall issue from you, whom you will beget, will be taken away; and they will become officials in the palace of the king of Babylon." (2 Kings 20:12–18 NASB) [Bold type mine]

- December 2006 — First US-China Strategic Economic Dialogue held in Peking, with the theme of "China's

Development Road and China's Economic Development Strategy." **Cochaired by Treasury Secretary Henry Paulson** and Vice Premier Wu Yi. Regarding the 2008 request for $700 billion in TARP (Troubled Asset Relief Program) funds, Paulson's original plan would have granted the Treasury secretary unlimited spending power, making him above congressional or judicial review. Section 8 of **Paulson's original plan stated, "Decisions by the Secretary pursuant to the authority of this Act are non-reviewable** and committed to agency discretion, **and may not be reviewed by any court of law or any administrative agency."** (Author's Note: In light of Paulson's authoritarian power grab, the question arises: Is America making China more open and harmless or is China pulling America into tyrannical methodologies a la Proverbs 2? Vidkun Quisling, a Norwegian politician who helped the Nazis conquer his own country in hopes of landing a top spot in the newly conquered regime, has become synonymous with traitor. We learn from 2 Timothy 3 that the last days will be perilous, that men will be lovers of their own selves—covetous, unthankful, and traitorous. We are to turn away from such men, not promote them to top offices in the land.)

[Sources: US Embassy, Beijing, China, website; "How China Conquered America," WhiteoutPress.com, originally published in *Human Events*. Note: Bold type is mine.]

ACKNOWLEDGEMENTS

I thank the God of David for granting me grace, mercy, and salvation; an exquisite family; and a sense of the beautiful and the playful. Truly, God's eternal power and Godhead can be plainly seen in what He has made: the 850-pound Siberian tiger tromping through the taiga, silent and majestic; the strident blue jays, swooping down and inquiring if, perchance, there may be some bird food available; the towering Douglas fir forests that dance and whistle in the wind; and the gentle banter of a family over dinner. The God of Moses has protected me, shown me into the company of the brethren when I needed evangelizing and kindness, and kept me going in spite of my frailties. Praise be to the God of Israel! I am as a weak pot; but my potter, Jesus, the King of kings and Lord of lords, is majestic, mighty, and worthy of praise!

My parents have shown me the value of honesty and hard work while encouraging me with affection and good cheer. My older brothers have looked out for me, variously helping me off a raging mountain, putting a blanket over me, offering excellent guidance, and even healing me. I played doubles tennis with one brother and played amidst the corn stalks with my other brother—sweet moments like those give a hint of the brotherhood of the saints.

Teachers who have inspired me include Edward Schafer of UC Berkeley's Oriental languages department; the old Chinese man who cried over the sad stories in *Liaozhai-zhiyi* at Taiwan Normal University (I think he cried over the poignancy of love lost); and Robert Schildgen of the UC Berkeley Extension Publishing Program. (It should be noted that a saving relationship with Yeshua the Messiah is a story of love found.)

Praise be to the Lord Jesus: "Believe on the LORD Jesus Christ, and thou shalt be saved, and thy house" (Acts 16:31b KJV). My parents have been most gracious, seeing that my brothers and I got to the Episcopalian church in Dunsmuir, California, in the mid-1960s, conveying a sense of God and the sacred. They have showed what it is to be a loving couple (a very good present) and have been patient, kind, and decent with their boys, extended family, and family friends. Dad is strong and Mom was beautiful. He watched for enemy aircraft from the central California coast during WWII, guarded the Taiwan Strait (from the Communists) in the 1950s, tended patients at all hours of day and night (the old-fashioned way), flew all kinds of aircraft, and protected his family. She nurtured the family with the civility of Atlanta, the exuberance of San Francisco, and the sunbeams of Seattle; taught elementary school; performed as a brilliant puppeteer; drove an ambulance; nourished a family of mostly men for decades; designed beautiful gardens; and showered a gentle love on immediate as well as extended family. May the Lord God of Israel shower grace and salvation and blessings on all of my family forever!

I still think about Taiwan: the northern-style cuisine by the circle in Tian Mu; the delectable place on Xin-yi Road that makes vegetable fried rice a world-class dish; the Sichuan-style eateries that can make string beans into a main course; and the roadside stands that serve *xian doujiang* (salty tofu-based breakfast in a steaming porridge on cold mornings).

To my brothers and sisters in Christ in Taipei and to the elegant American Baptist missionaries who showed me kindness at Zhong-Yuan Christian University, I miss you and may the peace of the living God be with you. Riding scooters amid the throng of traffic in Taipei, walking in the well-laid parks, and jogging through rice paddies left an impression of an old and vital culture. May the mainland Chinese Christians (in concert with the more open Taiwanese) make a deep impression on the minds and souls of their domination-minded cousins in Peking: men are weak; the God of Israel is great; and it is better to give than to receive.

Thanks also to iStockPhoto of Calgary, Alberta, Canada, for the graphics used in this work: © iStockPhoto.com.

ENDNOTES

Front Matter

John Bunyan, *The Pilgrim's Progress.* (New York: Washington Square Press, 1964), 23.

Chapter 1 — Arguing for Absolute Truth

1. James Perloff, *Tornado in a Junkyard: The Relentless Myth of Darwinism.* (Arlington, Mass.: Refuge Books, 1999), 152.
2. Scott M. Huse, *The Collapse of Evolution.* (Grand Rapids, Mich.: Baker Books, 2000), 54.
3. Ibid.

Chapter 2 — Debunking the Hoax of Evolution

1. John F. Ashton, ed., *In Six Days: Why Fifty Scientists Choose to Believe in Creation.* (Green Forest, Ark.: Master Books, 2000), 10.
2. Michael D. Lemonick and Andrea Dorfman, "One Giant Step for Mankind: Meet Your Newfound Ancestor, a Chimplike Forest Creature That Stood Up and Walked 5.8 Million Years Ago," *TIME.* (2001): 58.
3. Huse, pp. 135–136.
4. Perloff, p. 84.
5. Huse, p. 136.
6. Ibid, p. 139.
7. Perloff, p. 101.

8. Lemonick and Dorfman, pp. 60–61.
9. Ibid, p. 61.
10. Perloff, p. 103.
11. Michael J. Behe, *Darwin's Black Box: The Biochemical Challenge to Evolution.* (New York: Touchstone, 1998), 5.
12. Perloff, p. 249.
13. Ibid, p. 247.
14. Ibid, pp. 133–134.
15. Huse, p. 141.
16. Lemonick and Dorfman, p. 46.
17. Ibid.
18. Ibid, pp. 42, 44.
19. Ibid, p. 47.
20. Henry M. Morris, ed., *When Christians Roamed the Earth: Is the Bible-Believing Church Headed for Extinction?* (Green Forest, Ark: Master Books, 2002), 23–24.
21. Ibid, pp. 122–123.
22. Ashton, p. 263.
23. Huse, p. 19.
24. Perloff, p. 137.
25. Huse, p. 51.
26. Perloff, pp. 112–113.
27. Ibid, p. 113.
28. Ibid.
29. Ibid, p. 115.
30. Ibid, p. 61.
31. Ibid.
32. Ibid, p. 59.
33. Ibid.
34. Ibid, p. 62.
35. Ibid.
36. Ibid, p. 70.
37. Ibid, pp. 70, 74.
38. Ibid, p. 75.
39. Ibid.
40. Ibid, p. 73.

41. Ibid, p. 118.
42. Ibid.
43. Ibid, p. 117.
44. Ibid.
45. Ibid.
46. Ibid, p. 158.
47. Ibid, p. 161.
48. Huse, p. 159.
49. C. S. Lewis. Page 78 of a work that author has since misplaced. Nearly identical passage in C. S. Lewis, *Christian Reflections*. (Glasgow: Fount/Collins, 1985), p. 118.
50. Ashton, p. 153.
51. Ibid, p. 149.
52. Ibid, p. 294.
53. Behe, p. 39.
54. Ibid, p. 68.
55. Ashton, pp. 161–166.
56. Perloff, p. 34.
57. Ashton, p. 144.
58. Huse, p. 28.
59. Ibid, p. 29.
60. Ibid, pp. 33–34.
61. Perloff, p. 26.
62. Ibid.
63. Ibid, p. 27.
64. Ibid, pp. 25–26.
65. Ibid, p. 25.
66. Ibid, p. 49.
67. Ibid.
68. Ashton, pp. 254–255.
69. *The Quest Study Bible,* New International Version. (Grand Rapids, Mich.: Zondervan Publishing House, 1994).
70. Morris, pp. 87–88.
71. Kerri Westenberg, "From Fins to Feet," *National Geographic.* (1999): 116–117.
72. Ibid, p. 119.

73. Ibid.
74. Ibid, p. 126.
75. Ibid.
76. Ibid.
77. Huse, p. 87.
78. Perloff, p. 38.
79. Huse, p. 20.

Chapter Three — America's Social Decline

1. Os Guinness, *Fit Bodies, Fat Minds: Why Evangelicals Don't Think and What To Do About It.* (Grand Rapids, Mich: Baker Books, 1994), 98.
2. Norman Cousins, ed., *'In God We Trust': The Religious Beliefs and Ideas of the American Founding Fathers.* (New York: Harper & Brothers, 1958), 380–381.
3. Ibid, p. 362.
4. Ibid, p. 373.
5. David Barton, *America: To Pray or Not To Pray?* (Aledo, Tex.: WallBuilder Press, 1988), 42.
6. Cousins, p. 347.
7. Ibid, p. 377.
8. Barton, p. 41.
9. Ibid, p. 20.
10. Ibid.
11. Cousins, pp. 378–379.
12. Ibid, pp. 375–376.
13. Ibid, p. 351.
14. Ibid, p. 383.
15. Robert Bork, *Slouching Towards Gomorrah: Modern Liberalism and American Decline.* (New York: Regan Books, 1996), 8–9.
16. Ibid, p. 9.
17. Ibid, pp. 18–19.
18. Ibid, p. 26.
19. Ibid, pp. 30–31.
20. Ibid, pp. 86–87.

21. Ibid, p. 83.
22. Barton, pp. 16, 19.
23. Ibid, p. 19.
24. Tom Wolfe, *The Electric Kool-Aid Acid Test*. (New York: Bantam Books, 1968), 119–123.
25. Ken Hamblin, *Pick a Better Country*. (New York: Touchstone Books, 1996), 90.
26. Ibid, pp. 88–89.
27. Ibid, pp. 82–83.
28. Wardell B. Pomeroy, *Boys and Sex*. (New York: Delacorte Press, 1981). In Barton , p. 24.
29. Barton, p. 29.
30. Bork, p. 95.
31. Guinness, p. 70.
32. Carl Bernstein, "The Idiot Culture," *The New Republic*. (1992): 24–25. In Guinness, p. 70.
33. From an October 1985 speech Koppel gave to the International Radio and Television Society in New York City. In Guinness, p. 80.
34. Neil Postman, *Amusing Ourselves to Death*. (New York: Viking, 1985), 4. In Guinness, p. 76.
35. Bork, p. 267.
36. Ibid, p. 269.
37. Ibid, p. 257.
38. Ibid, pp. 253–255.
39. Robert Hughes, *Culture of Complaint: The Fraying of America*. (New York: Oxford University Press, 1993), 66–67.
40. Pat Buchanan, *The Death of the West: How Dying Populations and Immigrant Invasions Imperil Our Country and Civilization*. (New York: Thomas Dunne Books, 2002), 148.
41. Hughes, p. 117.
42. Ibid, pp. 119–120.
43. Dave Hunt, *Occult Invasion: The Subtle Seduction of the World and Church*. (Eugene, Ore.: Harvest House Publishers, 1998), 138, 141.
44. Hughes, pp. 142–146.

45. Buchanan, p. 220.
46. Ibid, p. 219.

Chapter Four — Wallowing in the Conceits of the New Age

1. Tal Brooke, *When the World Will Be as One: The Coming New World Order in the New Age.* (Eugene, Ore.: Harvest House Publishers, 1989), 156.
2. Henry David Thoreau, *Walden* (New York: New American Library, Signet Classic, 1960), 67. In Brooke, pp. 160–161.
3. Henry David Thoreau, *Walden and Civil Disobedience* (New York: W. W. Norton & Company, 1966), 247.
4. Thoreau, *Walden and Civil Disobedience,* p. 250.
5. Brooke, p. 160.
6. Ibid, p. 161.
7. M. K. Neff, *Personal Memoirs of Helena P. Blavatsky,* p. 244. In Brooke, pp. 173–174.
8. Pierre Teilhard de Chardin, *The Phenomenon of Man* (New York: Harper and Row, 1965), 219. Quoted by Dave Hunt, *Occult Invasion: The Subtle Seduction of the World and Church.* (Eugene, Ore.: Harvest House Publishers, 1998), 18.
9. Marilyn Ferguson, *The Aquarian Conspiracy: Personal and Social Transformation in the 1980s* (Los Angeles: J. P. Tarcher, Inc., 1980), 50.
10. Perloff, pp. 80–81.
11. Hunt, p. 250.
12. Albert Pike, *Morals and Dogma of the Ancient and Accepted Scottish Rite of Freemasonry.* (Supreme Council of the Thirty-Third Degree, 1964), 104–105. In Hunt, p. 251.
13. Manly Palmer Hall, *The Lost Keys of Freemasonry* (Macoy Publishing, 1976), 48. In Hunt, p. 251.
14. Ferguson, p. 61.
15. Alan W. Watts, *Nature, Man, and Woman.* (New York: Vintage Books, 1970), 4.
16. Bhagwan Shree Rajneesh, *Yoga: The Science of the Soul, Volume III.* (Rajneeshpuram, Ore.: Rajneesh Foundation International, 1976), 9.

17. Swami Kriyananda, *The Path: Autobiography of a Western Yogi.* (Nevada City, Calif.: Ananda Publications, 1979), 621.
18. Ibid, p. 67.
19. Marc Allen, *Tantra for the West: A Guide to Personal Freedom.* (Mill Valley, Calif.: Whatever Publishing, 1986), 131.
20. Rajneesh, p. 179.
21. Ibid, pp. 179–180.
22. Shakti Gawain, *Living in the Light: A Guide to Personal and Planetary Transformation.* (Mill Valley, Calif.: Whatever Publishing, 1986), 60.
23. Ibid, p. 59.
24. Rajneesh, p. 22.
25. Alan Watts, *The Essence of Alan Watts.* (Millbrae, Calif.: Celestial Arts, 1977), 122.
26. Ferguson, p. 29.
27. Kriyananda, p. 143.
28. Rajneesh, p. 12.
29. Ibid, p. 24.
30. Gawain, pp. 24–25.
31. Ibid, p. 31.
32. Ibid, p. 33.
33. Ferguson, p. 70.
34. Brooke, p. 233.
35. Rajneesh, p. 79.
36. Gawain, p. 39.
37. Allen, p. 76.
38. Kriyananda, pp. 151–152.
39. Ferguson, p. 82.
40. Ibid, pp. 202, 214–217.
41. Brooke, p. 166.
42. Allen, p. 72.
43. Watts, *The Essence of Alan Watts,* pp. 55–59.
44. Pam Murray, "The Eden Project Part II," *Sedona Journal of Emergence!* (2003, 13, 4): 39.
45. Lee Carroll, "Plain Talk," *Sedona Journal of Emergence!* (2003, 13, 4): 31, 33.

46. Brenda Hill, "Confusion, a Powerful Articulation of Thought," *Sedona Journal of Emergence!* (2003, 13, 4), 65–66.
47. Tom Kenyon, "Truth and Lies in Global Politics and the Push for Higher Evolution," *Sedona Journal of Emergence!* (2003, 13, 4), 78–79.
48. Thoreau, *Walden and Civil Disobedience,* p. 250.
49. Ibid, p. 251.
50. Watts, *The Essence of Alan Watts,* p. 193.
51. Ibid, pp. 145–146.
52. Watts, *Nature, Man, and Woman,* pp. 26–28.
53. Ibid, pp. 84–85.
54. Ibid, p. 37.
55. Rajneesh, pp. 20–21.
56. Ibid, p. 4.
57. Ferguson, p. 368.
58. Gawain, p. 73.
59. Watts, *Nature, Man, and Woman,* p. 81.
60. Brooke, p. 182.
61. Ibid, p. 183.
62. Watts, *Nature, Man, and Woman,* p. 106.
63. Gawain, p. 56.
64. Ibid, p. 41.
65. Rajneesh, p. 67.
66. Ferguson, p. 32.
67. From the essay by Thomas Riedlander, "Two Classic Trips: Jean-Paul Sartre and Adelle Davis". In Charles S. Grob, ed., *Hallucinogens: A Reader* (New York: Jeremy P. Tarcher/Putnam, 2002), 49.
68. From the essay "The Psychedelic Vision at the Turn of the Millennium: A Discussion with Andrew Weil, MD". In Grob, p. 133.
69. Grob, p. 119.
70. Ibid, p. 115.
71. Ibid, p. 75.
72. Ibid.

Chapter Five — Psychological Self-Absorption

1. Sigmund Freud, *Moses and Monotheism*. (New York: Vintage Books, 1955), 110.
2. Ibid, p. 111.
3. Ibid, p. 110.
4. Ibid, p. 157.
5. Ibid, p. 165.
6. Carl G. Jung, ed., *Man and His Symbols*. (New York: Dell, 1969), 43, 89.
7. Ibid, p. 76.
8. Ibid.
9. Alan W. Watts, *Psychotherapy East & West*. (New York: Ballantine Books, 1970), 123.
10. Ibid, p. 124.
11. Ibid, p. 48.
12. Ibid, pp. 118–119.
13. Ibid, p. 126.
14. Ibid, p. 25.
15. Rollo May, *The Cry for Myth*. (New York: W. W. Norton & Company, 1991), 27.
16. Ibid, p. 28.
17. Ibid, p. 34.
18. Ibid, p. 145.
19. Ibid, p. 166.
20. Ibid, p. 254.
21. Rollo May, *Man's Search for Himself: How We Can Find a Center of Strength Within Ourselves To Face and Conquer the Insecurities of This Troubled Age*. (New York: Signet, 1967), 156.
22. Ibid, pp. 182–184.
23. Watts, p. 143.
24. Jack Forem, *Transcendental Meditation: Maharishi Mahesh Yogi and the Science of Creative Intelligence*. (New York: Dutton, 1973), 120–124.
25. Ibid, pp. 224–225, 228.

26. Watts, p. 116.
27. May, *Man's Search for Himself,* pp. 175, 181.
28. Martin L. Rossman, *Guided Imagery for Self-Healing: An Essential Resource for Anyone Seeking Wellness.* (Tiburon: H. J. Kramer, 2000), 88.
29. May, *The Cry for Myth,* p. 163.
30. Jung, p. 85.
31. Ibid, p. 84.
32. Ibid, p. 85.
33. Ibid, p. 91.
34. Rossman, pp. 86–87.
35. Ibid, pp. 94–95.

Chapter Six — The Unholy Pride of Unitarianism

1. Jack Mendelsohn, *Why I Am a Unitarian.* (New York: Thomas Nelson & Sons, 1960), 141.
2. John Sias from interviews with Rev. Steve Edington, *100 Questions Non-Members Ask about Unitarian Universalism* (Transition Publishing, 1994), 13. Cited in Alan W. Gomes, *Unitarian Universalism.* (Grand Rapids, Mich.: Zondervan Publishing House, 1998), 94.
3. Mendelsohn, pp. 30–31.
4. Ibid, pp. 184–185.
5. Ibid, p. 28.
6. Ibid, p. 175.
7. Ibid, p. 150.
8. Ibid, p. 27.
9. Ibid, p. 24.
10. Ibid, p. 89.
11. Ibid, p. 71.
12. Ibid, p. 193.
13. Ibid, pp. 64, 132–135, 193.
14. John A. Buehrens and F. Forrester Church, eds., *Our Chosen Faith: An Introduction to Unitarian Universalism.* (Boston: Beacon, 1989), 134. In Gomes, p. 91.

15. *Karl M. Chworowsky and Christopher Gist Raible, "What* Is a Unitarian Universalist?" in Leo Rosten, ed., *Religions in America.* (New York: Simon and Schuster, 1975), 267–268. In Gomes. p. 91.
16. Mendelsohn, p. 35.
17. William D. Watkins, *The New Absolutes: How They Are Being Imposed on Us, How They Are Eroding Our Moral Landscape.* (Minneapolis: Bethany House Publishers, 1996), 56.
18. Joyce Appleby, "The American Heritage — the Heirs and the Disinherited," in Joyce Appleby, ed., *Liberalism and Republicanism in the Historical Imagination.* (Cambridge, Mass.: Harvard University Press, 1992), 225. In Watkins, p. 58.
19. Mendelsohn, p. 103.
20. Ibid, pp. 17–18.

Chapter Seven — Toward a False One-World Religion

1. Dave Hunt, *A Woman Rides the Beast: The Roman Catholic Church and the Last Days. (Eugene, Ore.: Harvest House Publishers, 1994),* 418.
2. Ibid, p. 417.
3. Ibid, p. 424.
4. Gary H. Kah, *The New World Religion: The Spiritual Roots of Global Government.* (Noblesville, Ind.: Hope International Publishing, 1998), 127.
5. Ibid.
6. Ibid, p. 128.
7. Hunt, pp. 426–427.
8. Ibid, pp. 420–421.
9. Ibid, p. 421.
10. Guillot, "Paranormal playground of cemeteries, scary homes," *The Washington Times* (2003): D1.
11. Michael de Semlyen, *All Roads Lead to Rome? The Ecumenical Movement.* (Bucks, England: Dorchester House Publications, 1993), 14.
12. Ibid, p. 13.

13. Ibid, p. 152.
14. Ibid, p. 33.
15. Ibid, pp. 173–174. Originally this citation appeared in *Romanism and the Reformation* by H. Grattan Guinness, DD: Focus Christian Ministries, Lewes, Sussex.
16. Ibid, pp. 174–175.
17. Ibid, p. 173. Originally this citation appeared in the October/December 1981 edition of *Bible League Quarterly*.
18. Ibid, pp. 170–171.
19. Michael de Semlyen, *All Roads Lead to Rome? The Ecumenical Movement*, p. 172. This material was originally taken from the *Keston College News Service*.
20. Ibid, p. 175. This material was originally quoted in *The Times* on November 9, 1988.
21. Kah, pp. 156–157.
22. Hunt, p. 46.
23. Grant R. Jeffrey, *Apocalypse: The Coming Judgment of the Nations*. (New York: Bantam Books, 1994), 207.
24. Hunt, p. 45.
25. Kah, pp. 207–208.
26. Jeffrey, pp. 207–208.
27. Kah, pp. 141–142.
28. From the testimony of journalist Samantha Smith, who was in attendance at the State of the World Forum, San Francisco, September 27-October 1, 1995. Quoted in Kah, p. 142.
29. Kah, p. 142.
30. From the International Institute for Sustainable Development's *Youth Source Book on Sustainable Development* (Winnipeg, Manitoba, Canada: IISD, 1994), 63. Quoted in Kah, p. 146.
31. From the *Report of the United Nations Conference on Environment and Development* (A/CONF.151/26), Annex III, Closing Statements. Quoted in Kah, p. 147.
32. From Mikhail Gorbachev's speech "The Earth Charter" at the Rio+5 Forum, March 18, 1997. Quoted in Kah, p. 151.

CPSIA information can be obtained at www.ICGtesting.com
Printed in the USA
BVOW040522011012

301699BV00001B/6/P